OFFICIAL MAKERS OF PUBLIC POLICY
CONGRESS AND THE PRESIDENT

LOUIS W. KOENIG
New York University

with an introduction by
JOSEPH S. CLARK

SCOTT, FORESMAN AMERICAN GOVERNMENT SERIES
Joseph C. Palamountain, Jr., Editor

SCOTT, FORESMAN AND COMPANY
Chicago • Atlanta • Dallas • Palo Alto • Fair Lawn, N.J.

The American System of government strikes a balance between unity and diversity. There is a unity to our system, but it is a unity which tolerates—indeed, requires for its vigor and viability—a broad diversity of institutions, processes, and participants. By organizing the analysis of the sprawling complexity of the American system into smaller, coherent, but interlocking units, the Scott, Foresman American Government Series attempts to reflect this pluralistic balance.

This approach, we believe, has several important advantages over the usual one-volume presentation of analytical and descriptive material. By giving the reader more manageable units, and by introducing him to the underlying and unifying strands of those units, it puts him in a better position to comprehend both the whole and its components. It should enable him to avoid the not-uncommon circumstance of viewing the American system as a morass of interminable and unconnected facts and descriptions.

This approach certainly permits us to tap the expertise and experience of distinguished scholars in the fields of their special competence. Each writes about his specialties, and none is forced to deal with subjects remote from his ken or heart for the sake of "completeness." The unity of the series rests on the interlocking of the various volumes and, in the general emphasis on policy and policy-making, on the method of analysis as opposed to simple description. It does not rest on a unity of approach. The authors vary in their values, their accents, and the questions they ask. To have attempted to impose unity in these matters would have been to water down the series, for the diversity of approach reflects the diversity of the system, its participants, and its commentators. But the final value of this series and its ultimate balance between unity and diversity rest, of course, in the use to which it is put by the reader.

The series is most fortunate to include this volume by Louis Koenig, whose many previous studies have uniquely qualified him for this assignment. He presents the beginning student with a clear statement of the fundamentals in an area where they are too often obscured by naïve assumptions or by constitutional doctrines whose domains are smaller than their pretensions. Perhaps the unique contribution of this volume, however, is the wealth of aptly chosen illustrations which give the fundamentals life, significance, and drama. I am sure the reader will find the book a source of excitement as well as of knowledge and wisdom.

Joseph C. Palamountain, Jr., *Editor*

INTRODUCTION

Professor Koenig's exploration of the policy-making process in our national government is both thorough and instructive. His theme is the pluralistic nature of policy-making. Policy appears, he writes, "as a mosaic of many interacting particles."

The closer one is to the policy-making process, the more one is aware of the truth of this observation. What may appear to a citizen to be a sudden and arbitrary action by his government is often seen on closer examination to be the product of long and agonizing study, compromise by many participating groups both public and private, and lengthy consideration by the Congress and the President.

This may seem an obvious point, but it is not well understood. A Senator's mail, for example, reveals an estimate of his powers to affect policy which far transcends his actual constitutional and political position. In a typical day I may be asked to secure a tariff reduction on some commodity, immortalize someone's hero by the creation of a new national holiday, halt the closing of a defense facility, and liberalize the Social Security Act. Whether the action requested requires the passage of legislation or a change in administration policy, my correspondents frequently exhibit a blind faith in my capacity to achieve the desired action if only I am persuaded of its merits. Any suggestion that my agreement with the goal may be accompanied by an inability to achieve it alone is taken for hypocrisy rather than a candid account of the relative powerlessness of a single United States Senator.

It is this defect in civic understanding which Professor Koenig's book should go far to remedy. Much has been written about the power of our institutions of government and their officers. This book reveals the limitations of power by analyzing the anatomy of policy-making. It does so through a series of observations about policy and the process of its formation that are supported by opposite case studies. In the American system of government, Professor Koenig points out, policy "rests on the competitive principle" and is commonly "the product of several or more individuals and of protracted procedures." This comes about not only because of the system of separation of powers but, more important in these times, because policy-making "is essentially a response to change" and therefore has "increasingly become functionally interdependent," as Professor Koenig insists. The variety of interests which must be accommodated in any viable policy and the rapidly changing factors which impinge on that policy necessarily make it so.

All of this, however, raises grave questions about the adequacy of the governmental policy-making machinery. Congress is, or should be, the essential conduit which transforms ideas into law. It is, or should be, the central policy-making institution. Yet it has dangerously ceased to be so.

The significant loss of policy-making functions by the Congress in the field of foreign affairs has long been an accomplished fact. "The transaction of business with foreign nations," Thomas Jefferson once noted, "is executive altogether." The need for speed and secrecy in external affairs accounts for this, and it is largely vain to lament the trend. As the Supreme Court observed in the *Curtiss-Wright* case, in foreign affairs the President must be accorded "a degree of discretion and freedom from statutory restriction which would not be admissible were domestic affairs alone involved."

More disturbing is the more recent trend toward a similar evolution in the field of domestic affairs. Here, too, Congress has ceased to be an equal partner with the President in the policy-making process. The initiative in legislation has increasingly tended to cohere around the presidential office, and Congress has lost much of its role of independent policy-maker.

Part of this growth in presidential power derives from the tradition established by Andrew Jackson that the President is "the tribune of the people" because he is the sole official elected by the whole national electorate. Congress is made up of 535 individuals representing constituencies which differ widely. No matter how much an individual member of Congress may seek to represent the national interest, his constituency will at some points place limits on his ability to do so. President Johnson's governmental career clearly reflects this truism.

Some, at least, of this accretion of power in the White House is due to the increasing complexity of our society and the consequent reliance upon technical expertise which the executive alone can provide. These are largely irreversible developments, the importance of which Professor Koenig makes clear.

But a good deal also is due to what I call congressional lag, by which I mean the failure of Congress to keep pace with the executive. Congress has tended to cling to rules and procedures long obsolete which have reduced its effectiveness and rendered it incapable of competing effectively with the President as a source of policy. Congress' contribution to the policy-making process has too often been a negative imposed by a minority of that body's membership. That minority— what I have elsewhere called the Congressional Establishment— derives its power in turn both from an essentially local, as distinguished from national, power and from those same obsolete rules and procedures.

It is comforting to learn from Professor Koenig that the sources of policy within the executive branch are diverse and conflicting and that the "monolithic power of the Federal Executive," a specter dear to the hearts of conservative critics, is largely mythical. But it would be more comforting if Congress were restored to its proper constitutional place as an effective partner of the President as a maker of public policy.

Happily, there are portents that developments are moving in this direction. Court-ordered reapportionment, unless defeated by the parochialism mentioned above, will make the Congress more representative. Republican gains in the South may in time usher in a genuinely nation-wide two-party system.

Such developments as these are making themselves felt in the Congress. The House of Representatives moved, at the beginning of 1965, to curtail sharply the powers of that Establishment bastion, the Rules Committee. The Senate has, regrettably, been slower to act, but reform sentiment is steadily growing in that body. It is important for our democracy that it do so. It is no doubt true that in the formulation of policy within the executive branch a variety of views must be consulted and a variety of interests conciliated. This does tend to protect minorities from the imposition of harsh policy, which is one of the hallmarks of democracy.

But it is important not only that affected interests be consulted but that the public at large be kept informed while policy is being evolved. This is the role which the representative assembly in a democracy should play. By its very nature, the executive branch cannot perform this function. Congress, and Congress alone, can provide a public forum for the making of policy. Even here much will go on behind the scenes, but much more will take place in public view. Congress alone can make the process of policy formulation truly visible to the public.

I am confident that Professor Koenig's careful study of the President and the Congress will contribute to that public understanding of the policy-making process which is the true shield of the Republic.

Senator Joseph S. Clark

TABLE OF CONTENTS

The Policy-Making Community

Policy-making is the most consequential activity of government. It can produce great works like the Panama Canal and the transcontinental highways; it can brighten the twilight days of citizens with old-age pensions; and it can send men into outer space. On the other hand, policy-making can produce corruption on the scale of the Teapot Dome scandal of the 1920's and such debacles as the abortive 1961 invasion of Cuba. Thus the policy enterprise ranges over a wide spectrum. It embraces what C. P. Snow, the British novelist and scientist, has called "the cardinal choices . . . made by a handful of men: in secret . . . ," choices which "determine in the crudest sense whether we live or die."[1] It embraces also the seemingly simple decision to raise letter-rate postage from four to five cents, with consequences that daily affect millions of citizens.

THE PLURALISM OF POLICY-MAKING

In the United States, as in any other democratic society, policy-making occurs on a pluralistic basis: that is, policy is formulated and influenced by a variety of individuals and organizations, both public and private. Public policy is made by the President and his aides, by agencies of the executive branch, by Congress, and by the courts. In addition, our federal system of government, as established in the Constitution, sanctions a vast policy-making domain for our state and local governments. For example, much public regulation of business and the majority of our policies governing education and health are effected by states and localities.

Basic economic policies in American society are also made by government. By its power to tax, government can commandeer a substantial part of the annual national economic product and devote it to such public purposes as maintaining the nation's military defenses, financing the inspection of food and drugs, and retraining the unemployed to better prepare them for the needs of industrial society. Government's regulation of credit and its spending policies have important consequences for general economic activity; government can countenance or, to a degree, stem the concentration of private economic power.

Policy-making in a pluralistic society, however, is often a matter of private decision. What to produce and how much, what prices to charge, what to buy, how to dispose of profits—all these are essentially private decisions. General Motors decides the style, quantity, and prices of its annual new car models; the Columbia Broadcasting System chooses to acquire the New York Yankees; the homemaker selects commodities in the supermarket; and the student decides what vocation to pursue. These are all essentially private choices and policies.

The division of policy-making between governmental and private spheres is fluid rather than fixed. Government may encroach upon private enterprise by creating a Tennessee Valley Authority, which, among other activities, sells electrical power. Government in the Kennedy-Johnson era may look over the shoulders of the steel industry and the steel union as prices and wages are set; it may press for restraint in the interests of holding back inflation, improving the nation's balance of payments, and increasing foreign trade. At the same time, private economic organizations, as they grow in power and form alliances with one another, can dictate policies of government or use government as a mere tool in vying with one another for aggrandizement.

Similarly, government influences and is influenced by social groups and the workings of the social order—by cultural, scholarly, and scientific activity in the nation and in the world at large. The ultimate impact of Harriet Beecher Stowe's *Uncle Tom's Cabin* upon the institution of slavery rivaled that of the Emancipation Proclamation. The closeness of President Kennedy's relationship to the scientific and intellectual community enlarged its influence upon public policy in the brief span of his administration.

The pluralistic nature of policy-making is fostered by constitutional arrangements that hold government within prescribed bounds and permit private persons and groups to organize, meet, speak, publish, petition, and engage in other activities to influence public policy. The bulk of these safeguards appear in the Bill of Rights, which both specifies an array of rights and freedoms and bars encroachments by the national government upon them. Pluralistic policy-making in an advanced industrial society such as the United States reflects the existence of numerous and powerful private pressure groups; such groups tirelessly seek to achieve at least some of their purposes through public policy, a two-edged sword that can harm their interests as well as help them. The National Association of Manufacturers and the AFL-CIO, for example, find their own or their members' interests at stake when government sets tariff policy, allocates defense contracts, or decides whether to launch an antitrust prosecution.

Private organizations and groups, both in setting their own policies and in influencing the government's, enjoy independence because they possess power. Power is multiform; it can be seen or felt—or both. The union and the business firm can sustain themselves with their own incomes. A labor union can strike or threaten to strike; a business can raise its prices. The intimacy of officials of both such organizations with those of government, and their expenditures of toil, money, and publicity in electoral campaigns, all are assertions of power capable of influencing governmental policy-making.

The pluralism of policy-making—the presence of self-willed units wielding power and influence—makes the public policy process a competitive venture, often in fact a power struggle. A leading Founding Father, James Madison, viewed government as a kind of arena in which opposing interests struggle. "A landed interest, a manufacturing interest, a mercantile interest, a moneyed interest, with many lesser interests," he wrote, "grow up of necessity in civilized nations, and divide them into different classes, actuated by different sentiments and views. The regulation of these various and interfering interests forms the principal task of modern legislation."[2] In Madison's view, the essential problem of government was to establish a system of checks and balances capable of preventing any one interest from attaining dominance within or over the government.

Paradoxically, government in an advanced industrial society may make more policy than government in a simpler society, but it commands less authority. Authority requires the dimension of *distance;* as Robert Michels has written, "Authority can neither arise nor be preserved without the establishment and the maintenance of distance between those who command and those who obey." In American society, however, pressure groups are intimately involved in public policy development. The intimacy between interest groups and public officials is cemented by the necessities of election and re-election: to capture the presidency or a legislative seat requires votes, workers, and money, which interest groups excel at providing. To win election to national offices, therefore, candidates must cast their nets wide to gain support from diverse groups, by pledging themselves to platforms and policies which are responsive to the interests of the groups.

The focus of this book is upon the legislative and executive branches of the national government—the two branches that engage in policy-making on the broadest scale and that are, as the explicitly political organs of government, the most intimately and consequentially involved with pressure groups and their play upon policy. Both the legislative and the executive branches, unlike the third branch—the judiciary—were deliberately fashioned for political involvement when the Constitution was created. Unlike the courts, both the legislature and the President are chosen by popular election. Both follow working procedures (also unlike the courts) that afford pressure groups the fullest access to policy-making processes and personnel. Both are subject to periodic review in regular elections, in which the voters, whether acting as members of the general public or of interest groups—or both—express their pleasure or displeasure with the performance of the political policy-makers. The courts and their handiwork are subject to no such review.

THE DEFINITION OF POLICY

Before proceeding to further examination of our legislative and executive policy-makers, we need to define "policy." Karl Mannheim has described policy as a process that begins where precedent ends.[3] The suggestion that policy is innovative and creative is altogether fitting, although the choice to perpetuate precedent is policy, too. Policy combines elements of *fact* (observable evidence which we can see, hear, touch, taste, or smell) and *value* (judgments of what "ought" to be, statements which are outside the realm of the senses and are metaphysical assertions). Policy aims to transmute value into fact, the judgment of what ought to be into hard reality.

Public policy will be our central concern in this book, although the enormous impact of private policy upon public policy is acknowledged and at times will be viewed. Governmental or public policy is the only kind of policy that is authoritatively applicable to society as a whole. Public policy is expressed in an almost infinite variety of ways: in statute and resolution, in executive order and regulation, in letter and conversation, in gesture and mood. It represents the *official* will but by no means always the *real* will of the political branches that make it. For example, a chief executive may acquiesce with minimum comprehension to the highly technical counsel of specialists who assist him. The legislator may cast his vote after being pushed and prodded by giant pressure groups. Both President and legislator, in making policy choices, are mindful of the approaching election and the state of constituency opinion. Public policy-making in a democracy is inescapably a political act.

THE ENVIRONMENT OF POLICY-MAKING

THE GOVERNMENTAL STRUCTURE

The legislature and the executive make public policy in an environment of jumbled elements and forces. Like other terrestrial creatures, they make adaptive responses to their surroundings. A principal environmental element is the constitutional arrangement of the governmental structure by which policy is made. The Founding Fathers, at the Philadelphia convention of 1787, applied two basic structural concepts in fashioning the legislature and the executive: *separation of powers* and *checks and balances*. Taking their cue from such writings as John Locke's *The Two Treatises of Government* and Montesquieu's *Esprit des Lois (Spirit of the Laws)*, they viewed the concentration of policy power as an invitation to tyranny. They deemed liberty to be best protected if power was distributed among several branches of government; hence three branches were created—the executive, legislative, and judiciary.

Checks and balances, the second formative principle, was also predicated on a distrust of coupling human beings with power. In resorting to checks and balances, or "balanced government," the Founding Fathers were utilizing an idea which harked back at least to Aristotle and Polybius. This old conception had been given a new vogue in the era of the Founding Fathers by Isaac Newton's scientific writings on the balance of nature, which was readily related by metaphor to the problem of government. As John Adams, an articulate champion of balanced government, put it, governments could and should be "erected on the simple principles of nature."[4] James Madison also reflected Newtonian phrasing when he wrote that a natural government must be so constructed "that its several constituent parts may, by their mutual relations, be the means of keeping each other in their proper places."[5] A balanced government, the Founding Fathers believed, would check not only branch against branch, but also interest against interest, class against class, and faction against faction.

The result was a considerable functional overlapping in the Constitution, especially between the legislative and executive branches. Lawmaking was shared between the two-house Congress and the

President, treaty-making and appointments between the President and the Senate, and so on. In its totality, the governmental design admirably fitted John Adams' proposal in his *Defence of the Constitutions* that aristocracy and democracy be so incorporated in the organs of government as to neutralize each other. Each was given its own house of the legislature—the Senate representing aristocracy and the House democracy—with an added check provided by a strong executive equipped with a veto power. Above all, the constitutional arrangement was a strong check on the majority—the most dangerous of all factions, in the eyes of Founding Fathers like Madison and Hamilton. The extent of the political society that the Constitution embraced, and the number and variety of local interests, made the citizens who shared a common majority interest "rendered by their number and local situation, unable to concert and carry into effect their schemes of oppression." The propertied interests, according to Madison, writing in *The Federalist*, No. 10, would enjoy a maximum safety from the most dangerous public policies: "a rage for paper money, for an abolition of debts, for an equal division of property, or for any other improper or wicked project." Thus the safeguards incorporated in the governmental machinery were reinforced by the pluralistic nature of American society.

The handiwork of the Founding Fathers in fashioning checks and balances has endured for more than a century and a half. Neither the rise of political parties (which the Fathers did not anticipate), nor the expanded activity and enlargement of the executive branch, nor the country's prodigious growth and changing situation have blunted the restraining effect of checks and balances upon relations between the branches. Congress, for instance, will, in any typical year, reject substantial parts of the President's legislative program.

THE ORDERS

Legislative and executive policy-making influences and is influenced by a series of orders existing in our pluralistic society. The behavior of public officeholders, of members of interest groups who act through political means, and of the general body politic is influenced first of all by the *cultural order*—expectations, aspirations, values, and behavior standards absorbed from the society in which they have been reared. Americans, for example, optimistically expect problems to be solved and goals won: witness our daring to expect in World War I that the world could be made "safe for democracy" and our haste promptly after World War II to "bring the boys back home," in the conviction that peace was really restored. We are confident of our ability to improvise; we prefer expedients to plans and "know-how" to theory. Our public policies rarely take the form of a "program" in the usual sense of the word; that is, they rarely constitute a coordinated and integrated body of measures reflecting a common goal and philosophy. At best, the New Deal—probably the most elaborate policy enterprise the nation has ever experienced—was a collection of improvisations notable for their inconsistency.

Then there is the *social order*, a great web of ordered relations comprising institutions such as the family and the church and practices such as custom and ceremony. The social order molds man's life-habits and life-attitudes, and it regulates the conduct of its members, particularly the young. Its fundamental institution, the family, regulates behavior and the use of property and satisfies fundamental needs in providing protection, food, shelter, love, and care for young and old. Government is itself a product of the social order, a centralized social agency cloaked with unique authority. But government is also dependent upon the social order—upon the willingness of its members to abide by laws incorporating public policy, and upon its decisions in democratic elections to retain in office those who govern or to cast them out and substitute others.

The *moral order* is a suborder or extension of the social order. Its most formal and centralized institution, the church, formulates and asserts a moral law that is capable of regulating much human conduct. The moral order may shape what is done in the political order. For example, much of the struggle for civil rights in the 1950's and 1960's was conducted on a moral plane, both in the preachings of clergy and in the statements of Presidents and legislators. William Jennings Bryan, thrice a presidential nominee, tended to view public policy issues in moral or religious terms. "The great political questions," he once declared, "are in their final analysis great moral questions . . ."[6]; in his campaigning, Bryan so treated the money question, imperialism, and other issues of his day. Far less sanguine about the usefulness of morality, and therefore of standards of right and wrong to determine the desirability of social legislation, was Supreme Court Justice Oliver Wendell Holmes. To Holmes, the moral system was little more than "a body of imperfect social generalizations expressed in terms of emotion," many of which could not be "confirmed by fact accurately ascertained."[7]

In a pluralistic society with a capitalistic system, the *economic order* is a powerful, wide-ranging source of policy. The economic order engages in considerable self-regulation, thus relieving American public policy-makers of many concerns which engross policy-makers in socialist and totalitarian countries. The economic order can also be viewed as an elaborate network of participants who cooperate and conflict for its product. Participants include owners, managers, the labor force, and the mass of unorganized consumers. At one time or another, government, through its policies, may assist any or all of these in their struggles.

Finally, there is the *political order,* whose principal apparatus, government, is the largest of all human enterprises. No private corporation, church, or cultural organization compares with government in the scale, variety, and number of its tasks. There are not one but many governments in the political order: international organizations such as the United Nations, alliances such as NATO, and hosts of nations around the earth with varying friendliness, neutrality, and hostility toward the United States. An American President or legislator, in determining what he does or says, must consider his probable impact on various observers and audiences, official and unofficial, at home and abroad.

Within the United States, the political order includes the governmental structure and officialdom—legislators, executives, and judiciary, arranged in a federal system with several levels: national, state, and local. It includes also semiofficial bodies such as political parties, as well as pressure groups and private individuals.

Government, which the political order provides, has several kinds of relationships with the other orders. Government provides law and security, both domestically and in international relations. Government is a provider of education, which may build understanding and acceptance of the values on which other orders are based. Government is formally supreme over the other orders. Its supremacy, however, is limited by the Constitution, which establishes in the Bill of Rights an area of inviolable freedom for the private orders. This freedom assures struggle between the several orders to extend their dominion and purposes. Viewed historically, the political order has often dominated the economic order. Particularly in the twentieth century, government has encroached by means of taxation and regulation upon the prerogatives of wealth, and to a degree it has regulated the behavior of labor unions. But government, despite its proven prowess, is subject to pulls and pressures from the other orders. What power government wields and what policies it effects may depend critically upon the other orders. Governmental action may, for all practical purposes, be precluded by their hostility. What government is called upon to do may be simply an outcome of the struggle within one or more of the private orders.

THE IDEALIZED ISSUES

The environment of legislative-executive policy-making is supercharged with an array of overriding idealized issues that go to the heart of man's relations with government. They are issues which to some men seem the master key to a better future—when, in fact, their relevance may be highly limited. They may appeal more to emotion than to reason. Men are willing to fight and die for idealized issues and to stake their election to public office and their entire political futures upon them. Because of their fundamental character and because they are largely abstractions which are meaningful only in concrete, transitory situations, they are issues which can never be conclusively settled once and for all time. Not surprisingly, therefore, a body of idealized issues has long existed in the American political environment; some indeed are as old as the Republic itself. They appeared in one kind of situation in 1800 and reappeared in a wholly new context a century later, seldom failing to raise the tension levels of political discusssion. They sometimes divert attention from the merits of more specific and immediate policy issues and obscure them in clouds of irrelevant emotion. More often, however, they constitute the real core of controversy, and no little part of the secret of their extraordinary lasting power is their attractiveness as guides to men in any age faced with the necessity of making difficult policy choices.

At the forefront of idealized issues is the one of *privatism versus governmentalism*—of the relative merits of governmental action as against private enterprise and self-reliance. This issue produced as much heat in the 1964 presidential campaign as in the Herbert Hoover–F. D. Roosevelt era of the 1930's or a century and more earlier, when John Taylor of Carolina wrote his luminous political tracts of southern Virginia. A contemporary of Jefferson, United States senator, and wielder of a ready pen, Taylor was known as "the philosopher of Jeffersonian democracy." The issue of privatism versus governmentalism was at the forefront of the struggle between Hamilton and Thomas Jefferson and the political parties arrayed behind them—the Federalists and the Antifederalists. Hamilton proposed that the national government transform the simple agricultural society of his day into a mixed economy, with a vast development of commerce, manufacture, and trade. He called upon Congress to create a national currency and a national bank, semipublicly owned, to construct internal improvements and to encourage commerce and trade by tariffs, bounties, and guarantees, and by rewarding invention with patents and copyrights. Jefferson, in contrast, wished to minimize the role of government in the nation's life and to elevate the individual—the free man born with inalienable rights. Jefferson was especially distrustful of a centralized government remote from the people and therefore difficult to make responsive to their will. "Were we directed from Washington when to sow and when to reap," he warned, "we would soon want bread." Jefferson was distrustful of governmental action as a means of helping the poor; like others of quickened social conscience in his day, he thought of it chiefly as a means of helping the rich. National governmental action summoned the image of the Hamiltonian system of interest-bearing debts, taxation, banks, bounties, and tariffs—none of which was a sword for the poor.

In the more modern framework of the early twentieth century,

the eminent sociologist and paleontologist Lester F. Ward was critical
of the laissez-faire school of economics, of the trusts and the growing
concentration of economic power in fewer private hands that "extort
tribute from the rest of mankind." "Government," Ward contended,
"was instituted to protect the weak from the strong," and if brigandage
were to be stopped and the forces of society liberated, government
must be recognized as "the most important among the instruments
which man can use for the building of a better order."[8] In contrast,
President Herbert Hoover, faced with a crumbling private economic
system which left one fourth of the labor force unemployed, never
wavered in his preference for private over governmental economic
action. His book *American Individualism* (1922) attributed the nation's
seeming well-being at that time to "individualism," which Hoover
believed had industrialized the nation and given it the world's highest
living standard. Private competition assured that the public received
the best possible economic leadership and the best products at the
lowest prices. The test of proper governmental action was, "Does it
maintain the initiative of our people?"

The idealized issue of *localism versus nationalism* dominated public
discussion of slavery and abolition and pervaded the civil rights debate
in the 1960's. It, too, played a major part in the struggle between Jefferson and Hamilton. The latter urged national action to speed economic growth. In counsel to President Washington, Hamilton developed
the doctrine of "implied powers" to justify the constitutionality of the
Bank of the United States. This doctrine was articulated in John Marshall's opinion in *McCulloch* v. *Maryland*.[9] Jefferson, on the other hand,
championed states' rights and, therefore, local action; he deemed the
United States of his own day "too large to have all its affairs directed
by a single government."

On several occasions, the issue of localism versus nationalism
has involved the question of the perpetuation of the union itself. The
alien and sedition laws passed in the John Adams administration were
challenged by the Kentucky and Virginia resolutions, the former
drafted by Jefferson. The Alien and Sedition Acts empowered the
President to deport undesirable aliens and made it a crime to criti-
cize the government or its officials. The Federalist Adams administration applied the laws zealously against members of the opposition
party, Jefferson's Democratic-Republicans. The Kentucky and Virginia resolutions provided the basis for the Jeffersonians to challenge
the legitimacy of the alien and sedition laws. The resolutions asserted
that the Constitution was a compact of sovereign states, with each
state retaining "an equal right to judge for itself" the constitutionality of acts of the central government "as well of infractions as of the
mode and measure of redress." Jefferson invited other states to "concur in declaring these acts [Alien and Sedition] void and of no force."

The question of union and states' rights erupted again in the War of 1812. in the Hartford Convention of 1815 threatening New England's secession, and once again in the nullification crisis of 1832, when a special convention in South Carolina passed an ordinance holding the tariff laws of 1828 and 1832 unconstitutional and not binding upon the state. Moves were launched to resist enforcement of the acts and to take South Carolina out of the union. President Andrew Jackson put aside his former states' rights convictions and mastered the crisis, holding that "the duty of the Executive is a plain one. The laws will be executed and the Union preserved by all the constitutional and legal means he is invested with. . . ."

The localism-nationalism issue was articulated and intellectualized in John C. Calhoun's apologia for the institution of slavery. Beholding slavery as essential to the nation's peace and prosperity, he went on to seek the perpetuation of that institution by formulating a theory of concurrent majorities. Under its terms, the central government enjoyed only limited powers which could not be exercised merely by decision of the dominant northern majority, but which required the concurrence of the less populous South. Calhoun's logic swept inevitably into a doctrine of nullification, well articulated by his colleague, Robert Y. Hayne of South Carolina, in his famous Senate debate in 1830 with Daniel Webster. The confrontation centered upon the choice between localism and nationalism. Hayne, advancing his nullification views, contended that the Constitution had not given the national government the power to pass a protective tariff law that would benefit the people of one section—the North—and harm those of another—the South. When the national government passed such a law, it went beyond its powers. The injured states could nullify, or had the right to refuse to obey, a law that the national government had no right to pass. Webster replied that the people of the United States, rather than the states, had created the Constitution and that the Constitution provided for a Supreme Court to decide just what were powers of the nation and of the states. Only thus could there be "Liberty and Union now, one and inseparable."

Abraham Lincoln, faced with the realities of southern secession and the attack on Fort Sumter and with the necessity of rallying northern energies to put down the rebellion, resorted to the idealized plane of localism versus nationalism for an appealing rationale to support his policy needs. The union, Lincoln declared, could not be broken because in legal contemplation it was perpetual; no state, therefore, "upon its own mere notion could lawfully leave it." Soon men were fighting and dying for their ideals of localism and nationalism on the battlefields of the Civil War.

In modern times, discussion of the respective roles of the nation and of the states has cut across the entire sectors of public economic and social policy. The American Liberty League and other opponents of Franklin D. Roosevelt's New Deal incanted the old texts of states' rights and the necessity of state action. President Eisenhower's personal and public positions on a variety of social and economic questions were premised upon the preferability of state to national action. His administration's policy positions on education, public health, natural resources, agriculture, and other areas were governed time and again by his view that "This administration was committed to . . . decentralizing as far as possible to the states."[10]

Political individual versus political group is an idealized issue that has operated on at least two distinct planes, one of which involves the relation of the public officeholder to his party organization. The typical legislative and executive policy-maker tends toward conformity with party needs and policy. Thus Abraham Lincoln as a political careerist was no maverick, but was, in his prepresidential positions on policy questions, a steadfast party regular. On the bank issue, on internal improvements, on the Mexican War, and on the tariff, he was an unswerving, orthodox Whig.

A far less common tradition—but nevertheless a strong one—is that of the maverick. The party organization, not surprisingly, does not suffer him gladly. Thomas Jefferson as President and party leader was a stickler for party orthodoxy who could not bear the flights of independence of his colleague Congressman John Randolph. Randolph, who in Jefferson's initial presidential years was House floor leader, was displeased with the administration's handling of the Yazoo land frauds and its request for a secret appropriation to purchase Florida. He disclosed his sentiments with stinging words on the House floor. Jefferson soon made known that "Mr. Randolph's late conduct is very astonishing and has given me much uneasiness." The party organization proceeded to punish the maverick. Randolph was deposed as floor leader; John W. Eppes, Jefferson's son-in-law, took up residence in Randolph's district and eventually captured his seat. In the twentieth century, the maverick tradition has been maintained by senators like George Norris, Estes Kefauver, and Wayne Morris, each of whom, in maintaining his political independence, offended sectors of his party organization—which invariably included its leader, the President.

On a second plane, the issue of individual and group has centered on the relation of majority rule on public policy questions to minority opinion and to the solitary, private individual. Abel P. Upshur, state judge and delegate to the Virginia convention of 1829–1830, and later Secretary of State in the Tyler administration, found no right in the majority to "restrain, to abridge, and consequently to destroy all the rights of the lesser member." Upshur believed that the right of the individual and his minority group to dissent was sanctioned by the state of nature.[11]

John Calhoun, defender of the imperiled southern system and the minority section of the country in which it held sway, contended that governments based upon mere numerical majorities were inevitably unstable. Only governments which represented the entire community, and therefore both majority and minority interests, with each accorded a weight to offset the other, could be stable.[12] Henry David Thoreau in a later day objected in his writings and by the example of his withdrawal to Walden Pond to the submersion of the individual in the state, to the tendency of citizens to resign their consciences to legislators. "Why has every man a conscience then?" asked Thoreau. "I think we should be men first, and subjects afterward." Legislators, for their part, reflected the majority who ruled not "because they are most likely to be in the right . . . but because they are physically the strongest."[13]

In our American political experience we have been torn between fear and faith in the *strong executive* and the *strong legislature*. Although the Founding Fathers were impressed with the need for a strong chief executive and painstakingly provided for one, they were wary of executive excesses. Hence checks and balances and separation of powers were established, and Convention debate made frequent references to the monarchical evil. The British King George III had left a lingering image of tyranny among the general public; it was he, above all, who inspired harsh comment in the Convention. In the subsequent experience of the presidency, every strong incumbent of the office has stirred up critics who cry of the danger of executive power. It was fear of executive power that led to the adoption in 1951 of the Twenty-Second Amendment, which limited the President to two terms, and to the lengthy campaign in the 1950's for the Bricker Amendment, which proposed to cut back drastically the President's powers in foreign affairs.

Our fear of the strong legislature has been neither so pointed nor so enduring as our fear of the strong executive. The Founding Fathers were driven in no small degree to provide for a strong executive by the general chaos produced by the strong legislatures holding sway in most states at the time of the Convention. At various junctures in our subsequent experience under the Constitution, however, friends of executive power have been distressed by the apparent strength of Congress. Time and again, Congress has demonstrated, to the discomfort of the executive, that its great strength rests in its ability to assume and maintain a general do-nothing position. It is a great bulwark of negativism, against which the best efforts of not a few skillful and popular Presidents have proven little availing. In the early 1960's for example, particularly in the Kennedy era, when Congress was holding back legislation in major policy areas such as education, medical care for the aged, housing, and mass transportation, a considerable outcry developed in liberal commentary against a negative and powerful Congress and for the "reform" of its houses. To these critics, Congress was the bastion of conservative opinion, manipulated by an alliance of southern Democrats and rural and small-town Republicans. Despite campaign promises, a President—whether Republican or Democrat, Eisenhower or Kennedy—faced the prospect of losing his key social and economic proposals in Congress. Liberals lamented the strength and success of Congress in casting its negative vote. The reforms proposed were designed to realign Congress into greater harmony with the policy positions of the President and of the national consensus which they reflected.[14] In 1965, concrete achievements resulted when the powers of the House Rules Committee, long an obstacle to the President's programs, were curbed in two important respects. Its ability to bottle up a bill and to prevent a bill from going to a conference committee—composed of senators and congressmen, appointed to iron out differences over a bill between their houses—was sharply reduced.

Outstanding among the early advocates of the strong executive is Alexander Hamilton, whose views are best articulated in *The Federalist,* No. 70. In Hamilton's opinion, "energy" stood first among all the qualities requisite for good government, and energy was to be found principally in the executive branch. As Secretary of the Treasury and trusted counselor of President Washington, as author of the Great Reports setting forth a program of vast executive action, Hamilton established the executive as a strong leader in public policy-making; the executive, he believed, should call attention to problems and pose solutions, and, in addition, should use energetically and interpret broadly powers delegated by Congress.

The Washington-Hamilton pattern of the strong executive was followed and elaborated upon by later "strong" Presidents such as Jackson, Lincoln, and the Roosevelts. The strengthening of the administrative role of the President on the model of the strong business executive has been the subject of study and proposals by such bodies as the Brownlow committee of 1937 (President's Committee on Administrative Management) and the first Hoover Commission of 1949 (Commission on Organization of the Executive Branch of the Government). Chiefly by strengthening the President's staff, budgetary, and personnel policy resources, both studies hoped to enhance the presidency's policy-making and administrative activity.

Those who have faith in, and desire, a strong Congress, have at various times numbered those who favor and those who oppose a strong executive—that is, those whose political views are conservative, and those who are liberal. Conservatives admire a strong Congress whose negativism can safeguard the status quo of society against changes proposed by a liberal chief executive. Present-day liberals, on the other hand, anxious to make Congress a positive organ of government whose work is relevant to the needs of twentieth-century society, look toward a Congress that can readily pass major laws. Such a strong Congress will harmonize with a strong executive, since both presumably will reflect a national popular majority. The possibility of a harmony of strength has been perceived before. Alexander Hamilton and Theodore Roosevelt, both advocates of a strong executive, were also champions of a strong Congress. To Hamilton, the legislature was strong if it grappled with problems in which the nation and the executive were interested and if it interpreted its mandate generously and enacted sweeping laws. In the 1960's, most resolute champions of a strong Congress are Hamiltonian in their view of a properly functioning legislature. Vice-president Hubert Humphrey and Senators Clifford Case and Joseph Clark, the most active exponents of congressional reform, seem bent upon securing a kind of legislature whose views on national and international questions approximate those of the chief executive. These views, in turn, are expected to reflect those of a national popular majority.

THE GOALS OF POLICY-MAKERS

Among the livelier elements in the political environment are the goals which drive the legislator and executive into action. These goals, whether entertained by a legislator, President, or bureaucrat, are of at least three main types: personal goals, policy goals, and organizational goals. Not all goals fall neatly into a single basket; they may be of two or even all three types.

Like other human beings, policy-makers ordinarily have career goals; they hope to climb the ladder to more prestigious and influential administrative or political positions. Such goals, understandably, are seldom publicly acknowledged, and indeed they may be denied or dealt with coyly. Nevertheless, they may be inferred from overt conduct. Many members of the House of Representatives are likely not to regard that body as the apex of their political career but to aspire to a Senate seat or to a governorship. The political career of John F. Kennedy led by conscious choice and straightline promotion from the House to the Senate, then to an unsuccessful bid for the vice-presidency, and finally to the presidency itself. Lyndon B. Johnson traversed the same course with a stop-off at the vice-presidency.

The career ascent may combine political positions with politico-administrative positions, in the manner of Theodore Roosevelt's incumbency as New York City Police Commissioner and United States Civil Service Commissioner as well as Governor of New York and Vice-President of the United States. The member of the executive bureaucracy faces a career line established with elaborate precision in the hierarchical arrangement of the civil service classification system. The drive to climb the career ladder may determine whether the policy-maker faces or dodges a policy issue, and it may shape the substance of his position if he does choose to face it.

Policy-makers also may—or may not—entertain policy goals. During World War II, Senator Arthur Vandenberg became convinced that the United States must steadily assert constructive leadership in world affairs. Vandenberg abandoned his resolute prewar devotion to isolationism and became a leading exponent of internationalism. He was a principal delegate to the San Francisco Conference, which created the United Nations Organization; he was also a leader in guiding the Charter of the United Nations through the Senate, the author of a Senate resolution clearing the way for United States membership in the North Atlantic Treaty Organization, and a regular delegate to the foreign ministers conferences of the 1940's. The reasons for Vandenberg's about-face from isolationism to internationalism are to be found in his exposure, through service on the Senate Foreign Relations Committee, to world affairs—to what impressed him as the operative realities of the postwar world—and in the pressures of a long-building fatal illness, which nourished his ambition to leave behind a legacy of constructive policy-making.

An office seeker's policy goals may be little more than an annex of his career goals. Apart from his own native political talents, nothing can propel an office seeker upward in his career faster than his timely espousal of an issue in which great numbers of voters are interested or can be made interested. William Jennings Bryan's meteoric rise to the Democratic presidential nomination in 1896 at the age of 36, and to it twice thereafter, was owed in no little degree to his ability to seize and exploit popular issues. In the presidential campaign of 1892, the Populists demonstrated that of all the planks in their platform the silver plank had the widest appeal. Bryan quickly took up the silver issue in his quest for the presidential nomination in 1896. He swept the Democratic convention of that year off its feet with his impassioned "crown of thorns" speech on the silver question, which he hoisted to a place of supreme priority when he declared, "When we have restored the money of the Constitution all other reforms will be possible; but . . . until this is done there is no other reform that can be accomplished." It does Bryan no injustice to say that he had at best only a limited grasp of the complexities of the silver issue. "I don't know anything about free silver," he declared in his congressional campaign of 1892. "The people of Nebraska are for free silver and I am for free silver. I will look up the arguments later."[15]

Office seekers are often nimble in dropping issues that do not catch fire with the electorate; then, within the limits of the electoral timetable, they scramble to discover others that will. After 1896, with the silver issue on the wane but with his appetite for the presidency unslackened, Bryan seized upon a new and likely issue in the wake of the Spanish-American War—anti-imperialism. He first stressed Philippine independence as the rallying cry for the approaching 1900 elections. As the pre-election months passed, Bryan found anti-imperialism a sterile issue and turned desperately to others—anti-trust and free silver. The nation's general prosperity, however, made the electorate apathetic to these issues as well.

In the quest for legislative office, basic shifts in the attitudes and needs of the constituency make comparable shifts in the policy of the positions of the officeholder or office seeker a matter of survival. Early in his congressional career, John C. Calhoun presented a perfect image of the dedicated nationalist. As leader of the "War Hawks" he, more than anyone else, induced Congress and the President to go to war in 1812. Following the war, Calhoun persisted as a nationalist, urging the widest use of national powers. He championed a protective tariff, a national bank, a strong army and navy, and a system of roads and canals to bind the nation together. He warned that "the extent of our country exposes us to the greatest of all calamities next to the loss of liberty—disunion."

But in the next twelve years, Calhoun the ardent nationalist became no less the ardent champion of states' rights. Coincidental with his about-face were basic shifts in his home state of South Carolina. With the cotton economy spreading, South Carolina became predominantly a staple-growing state. Its planters, working their fast-depleting lands and being hard presssed to compete with the freshly tilled interior, found the exactions of the protective tariff unbearable. Fiery local statesmen made it impossible for a politician to survive unless he identified himself strongly with the needs and interests of his state and section. Calhoun read the handwriting on the political wall and became an ardent champion of states' rights. He attacked the tariff act of 1828 as unconstitutional, contending that a state could declare it null and void and refuse to obey it.

For at least a part of this twelve-year period of devotion to states' rights policy, Calhoun pursued another goal—a career goal—which posed the need for an altogether different strategy on issues. He aspired to the presidency and, like anyone seized with that ambition, had to extend his strength beyond his state and region and develop intersectional support. In pursuit of his strategy he built an alliance with the fast-rising western politician Andrew Jackson and his supporters. Calhoun hoped that Jackson, a planter and fellow Republican of Jeffersonian vintage, would take up policies acceptable to the South and would some day hand over the presidency to the South Carolinan. Calhoun proposed to cement an alliance between the great agrarian sections, the South and the West, against the East. He carried out his plan to the point where, in both 1824 and 1828, he was Jackson's vice-presidential running mate and for a brief time a leading contender to succeed Jackson.

It is possible—and indeed not uncommon—for office seekers to climb the political ladder to the most influential policy-making offices without demonstrating in any clear and reliable way what their policy goals really are. This remarkable phenomenon of projecting a blurred image in situations of heavy policy responsibility is known even in the presidency itself. For all the strength, issues, and activity of his presidency, Andrew Jackson's personal policy convictions remain an almost impenetrable enigma. Historians are still in dispute over the substance of his policy views. A man of action, Jackson never formulated the implications of the democratic movement on which his name has been impressed. Historian Charles M. Wiltsie has observed, "Those who have succeeded in giving Jackson either a consistent policy or an intelligible political philosophy have been able to do so . . . only on the basis of incomplete analysis or misinterpretation of essential facts."[16]

A political careerist may spend years in responsible posts and leave behind a slate utterly bare of policy achievements. In no public act or private comment does he betray commitment to any ideal or goal other than the sheer satisfaction of holding high office. Such a man seems to have been James G. Blaine, the vastly popular "plumed knight," a man of unusual intellectual talent for a politician, twenty years a congressman and senator, thrice a Speaker of the House of Representatives, twice a Secretary of State, once a presidential nominee, and twice more a serious contender for the nomination. With such a record, it is not surprising that he was charming and highly effective both in personal relations and in public address. Yet he left behind him, as Richard Hofstadter has noted, "not a single constructive achievement, hardly even a constructive suggestion; his chief contribution to American politics was to lower its tone."[17]

Political officeholders and members of the bureaucracy reflect in their goal selection the cultural values of society. In American society, the dominance and prestige of free enterprise have tended to derogate civil servants, often exposing them to the charge that they have "never met a payroll." In response to this ill esteem, civil servants often seek to build their morale by emphasizing their growth in and mastery of professional competence. This stress upon professionalism tends to divert loyalty away from higher personal authority, such as the supervisor or bureau chief, and to concentrate it upon impersonal functions.

The organizational goals which may shape policy concern the survival, growth, and prestige of the office and institution of which the policy-maker is an incumbent. Many a President has shown a ready disposition to defend the powers and prerogatives of his office against encroachment from Congress and the judiciary. Individual legislators, out of concern over the doubted efficiency of their respective houses in making policy, may undertake to effect reforms in congressional organization and working procedures. These legislators were sufficient in number to bring about the Legislative Reorganization Act of 1946—the first and only concentrated self-examination in which Congress has engaged throughout its history.

Policy-makers, of course, cannot limit their concern to their own goals alone. American society, like any other society, entertains goals that shape the behavior of official policy-makers. Above all, society aims to survive; it expects its policy-makers to provide security against external danger and to protect its members and groups from bodily harm and destruction. Society wishes normally to retain the existing order in all of its cultural, moral, economic, and political parts. Legislative and executive policy-makers face society's expectation that they will maintain policies of the past and follow precedent and established procedure. But society may also desire change in public policy. If depression attacks with the severity it did in the 1930's, society may not only expect but insist upon innovation. Franklin D. Roosevelt and the Congress of his day were handed a mandate to reform the existing economic order.

Private groups and organizations entertain goals with which policy-makers must reckon. Pressure groups, whether economic, nationality-oriented, racial, or otherwise, promote purposes that can be assisted and advanced by official policy-makers. The labor union that wants higher levels of employment, the farmer who wants a higher price for his produce, the nationality leader who wants a higher immigration quota for his people, the temperance leader who wants to save his fellow citizens from the depredations of King Alcohol—these and scores of other causes, whether to advance some principle, to gain some advantage, or to hold what has already been won, concern the pressure groups in their demands upon policy-makers. What pressure groups want is often the spark and substance of policy.

Still other groups and organizations abound in the political environment whose goals of survival, growth, and prestige influence policy-making. The political party normally cherishes victory and its rewards of spoils and pork barrel. Such appetites stimulate the party's candidates to take those sides on policy questions that are most likely to appeal to a majority of voters. And a presidential administration is normally eager to leave a full page of accomplishment upon the record book of history.

THE DYNAMICS OF CHANGE

Since policy-making is essentially a response to change, policy-makers are forever wrestling with change in the circumstances of their constituency, in the nation, and in the world. In American experience such changes have been prodigious. The country has grown from a simple agricultural economy sustaining three million inhabitants concentrated in a narrow coastal area, to nearly two hundred million occupying an area of supercontinental proportions and engaged in a mixed economy whose output and standard of living are unparalleled. The most radical changes in our domestic society—and, therefore, in public policy—have stemmed from the enormous shift of population from farm to city. In the past half century, the ratio of urban to rural dwellers has reversed, from 40 to 60 in 1900 to 64 to 36 in 1950. The 1960 Census disclosed an urban majority of 70 per cent, although there had been a population shift from the central city to the surrounding suburbs.

The urban dweller tends to need and demand more governmental services than does his country cousin, whether in services such as education, health, and welfare relief or in regulation of housing and conditions of employment. Population shifts have so concentrated political concern upon the urban area that John Kennedy in his quest for the presidency in 1960 focused to an unprecedented degree upon the urban voter; he made a lengthy list of pledges to launch major policy initiatives such as medical care for the aged, civil rights protection, mass transportation facilities, aid to education, urban renewal, and higher levels of employment.

Equally jarring to the processes of policy-making has been the American nation's emergence from long isolation to the forefront of world affairs. The era since World War II has seemed to outdistance all others in the convulsive changes and challenges it has thrown upon the nation: the advent of nuclear weaponry with its awesome capabilities for destruction, imperiling the entire human race; the rise of formidable and resourceful Communist competitors; the stirrings of peoples everywhere, both at home and abroad, for political rights and economic opportunities; and the new scientific revolution, which is only beginning to unfold, with its phenomenon of automation and its threatening implications for human employment. To the American policy-maker of the 1960's, his nineteenth-century counterpart must seem to have resided in a lazy green valley of modest change.

Change also occurs in the relative roles and influences of the executive and legislative branches in policy-making. In the nineteenth century, the United States' absorption in its domestic development and its removal from foreign affairs permitted Congress a general ascendance. The nation's subsequent deepening involvement in foreign affairs, in two world wars, and in an enduring race with its Communist rivals has served to expand the policy role of the executive. Any close view of the two branches in this latter-day period, however, would disclose that the tug of war for policy influence shifts from issue to issue and from President to President. Franklin Roosevelt was in firm ascendance in 1933–1934, but considerably less so in 1937–1938. Against his successors, Congress has taken liberties that it never took with him, in tampering with nominations dispatched to Capitol Hill, in launching investigations, in attaching riders to legislation, and in rejecting policy projects. All these affronts and setbacks Roosevelt's successors have suffered on a scale unknown in his day.

Although their impact upon policy-making may fluctuate between the branches, joint and cooperative policy enterprises have been increasing perceptibly. Rarely in the past decade has Congress passed important legislation without endorsement from the presidential administration. Social and economic policy, as well as defense and foreign policy, increasingly turns upon complementary policy-making between the branches. Civil rights is dealt with both by legislation and by presidential initiatives involving exercise of independent power or prerogative. Congress set basic tariff policy in the Trade Expansion Act of 1962 but delegated to the President a discretion of unprecedented scope to raise or lower rates by 50 per cent. In foreign affairs, our joining of NATO, our undertaking of aid to Greece and Turkey, and the initiation of the Marshall Plan were all the policy products of interbranch cooperation. Opposing this tendency, however, is the persistent tendency to conflict between the branches, with Congress prone to represent local views and conservative policy preferences, and the presidential administration national and international viewpoints and a liberal policy orientation.

A trend which persists unslackened and will surely deepen is the blending of foreign and domestic affairs. What we can do in foreign affairs depends increasingly upon what we have done and are doing in domestic affairs, upon our economic growth, upon the quality of our population in health, in education, and in access to services and opportunities betokened by the phrase "civil rights." Our policy-making has increasingly become functionally interdependent. Nikolai Lenin long ago perceived the heightened effectiveness gained from treating diplomatic, economic, military, propagandistic, and psychological policy as parts of a common mosaic. Our policy-making apparatus, highly fragmented as it is in our pluralistic political society, makes the kind of integration Lenin recommended difficult; but we have, as we shall see, made strides toward achieving it.

CHAPTER TWO

Congress

Far more than any other legislative body of the major nations of the world, the Congress of the United States makes policy. While foreign parliaments faithfully enact policy formulations of the executive, Congress is everlastingly assertive in revising and rejecting— as well as in accepting—the President's legislative proposals.

Like any other political organ involved in meaningful activity, Congress comes in for its share of criticism. Today, as regularly in the past, critics lament the low estate into which Congress has fallen in public esteem. The snail's pace of its work and its failure to legislate on urgent social questions give it an air of irresponsibility and vex its critics. The caricature of the legislator, with his string tie, half-gallon hat, and addiction to bombast—the "Senator Claghorn" of an earlier decade—still lingers in the public image. The excesses of Joe McCarthy, Huey Long, and "Pitchfork" Ben Tillman are not forgotten. But Congress, particularly the Senate, was also the locale of the acts of heroism described in John F. Kennedy's *Profiles in Courage.* Despite its defects, Congress is the most accessible and most responsive source to which the citizen can turn when he is faced with the oppressions or complexities of government and society. To the average citizen the governmental bureaucracy is labyrinthine and impersonal, the courts slow and expensive.

THE SETTING OF CONGRESS

Congress stands in an old and rich legislative tradition in the American and the Anglo-Saxon governmental experience. The legislature has played a vital part in freeing man from executive tyranny and in converting democratic ideals into realities. England is the mother of parliaments, and the American colonial legislature derived root and branch from an evolution of centuries of British parliamentary practice. Parliament, by hard-won gains, came in time to legislate by bill, to levy taxes, and generally to counterbalance the power of kings. The lower houses of the American colonial legislatures also built strength by developing controls over purse strings and administration; they adhered to the principle of representation, since their members identified with the geographic districts from which they were elected. During the Revolution, state legislatures possessed broad powers and were typically the dominant organ of government; this trend was encouraged by popular mistrust of executive power, symbolized by King George III and the colonial governors. Under the Articles of Confederation, the country's central government was entrusted to its Congress, which possessed not only legislative power but also the executive and judicial powers vested in the central government. There was no separate and identifiable executive endowed with policy-making power.

Although American legislatures became rather discredited during the Revolution and in the era of the Articles of Confederation, the Founding Fathers, in framing the Constitution, provided after hard debate for a strong legislature. The make-up of Congress, the subject of an intensive struggle between the large and small states, was finally resolved by compromise. The small states were mollified by the equal representation which the Senate afforded all states, regardless of population. To satisfy the large states, representation in the House was based on population. In theory, the Senate represented the states and the House the people.

The House of Representatives was from the beginning set up very much as it is today. The Senate, however, has changed. Until 1913, when the Seventeenth Amendment was adopted, Senators were elected not by the people but by the state legislatures. Members chosen by the state legislatures often tended to be conservative; for a time, beginning in the late nineteenth century, the Senate was known as a "rich man's club."

Since most public policies of any importance require laws,

money, and authorization of administrative personnel, Congress has steadily played a major, and often a dominant, role in national affairs. Those issues that have rent American society most severely have had their natural and principal forum in Congress; like any legislature, Congress systematically provides for the representation and expression of diverse opinion—a feature not found to such a degree in the executive branch. The repeated conflicts over the tariff have been aired in Congress, as have the questions of monetary bimetallism, the slave issue, and civil rights.

Congress has clearly been the dominant governmental organ over long stretches of national history. Legislators like Henry Clay, Daniel Webster, and John C. Calhoun, in their influence upon public policy of their day, outshone all Presidents but one or two. The long era between Abraham Lincoln and Theodore Roosevelt was, with little exception, one in which Congress' hand in public policy was the strongest.

THE STRUCTURE OF CONGRESS

The Senate and House each has its own distinct individuality. Each house's view of the nature of policy-making is idiosyncratic. Senatorial treatment of policy-making reflects a keen consciousness of the mixture of fact and value. Senators speak of making "judgments" on policy questions. As President, John Kennedy persisted in speaking of making judgments—a way of thinking he took with him from the Senate. In the Senate, there is no "debate" in the ordinary sense but a succession of "colloquies" in which senators express their judgments upon an issue. Judgments are often touched off by obviously leading or loaded questions asked by cooperative colleagues. In contrast, the style of discussion in the House stresses far more the making of flat assertions.

The nature of constituencies and the terms of office also impart individuality to House and Senate policy-making. The senator hails from a constituency that is larger and more diverse than that of his House colleague; in the upper chamber, this circumstance tends to elevate the ability to effect compromises to a high and venerated art. The House member, in contrast, represents a small district that tends to homogeneity. Compare, for instance, a congressman from a Philadelphia district and another from the vast forested reaches of western Pennsylvania with a senator of the state who must represent both extremes of diversity.

The House's short term of two years means that by the time major legislation reaches the floor, the coming electoral campaign is seldom much more than a year off. The representative votes on policy issues with the approaching election well in mind. Except in the two years prior to an election, the senator is enabled, by grace of his six-year term, to be "statesmanlike"—even to the point of voting against the evident will of his constituency on selected issues.

The houses also have important similarities. In each house the bulk of important policy-making occurs in the standing committees. An altogether apt and valuable cliché of Capitol Hill is that the committees do the "real" work of Congress. The houses rarely consider legislation that has not been studied by a committee. The committees consider policy not in the round or in a vacuum but in concrete terms as it appears in bills referred to them. Bills, as vehicles by which policy is proposed, place a premium upon detailed technical knowledge of existing statutes, court decisions, and administrative rulings. The policy issues before Congress seldom are completely new; they evolve from years of discussion, study, and legislative action. Most likely the committee chairman, who normally holds his place by seniority, has a mastery of background information and technical detail which is superior to that of any junior member. The policy interests of most legislators tend to cluster in the several policy areas covered by the committees on which they serve. Upon the floors of their respective houses, the views and recommendations of committee members—particularly the chairmen—carry great weight, owing to their specialized knowledge and to each house's dependence upon and regard for committee work.

Committees both develop policy and suppress it. Woodrow Wilson once aptly called committee rooms "dim dungeons of silence," for only a small percentage of bills referred to committees ever. emerges from them. Committees are highly autonomous; the intervention of party leaders of the House and Senate in their affairs tends to be minimal. Intervention seldom occurs in minor legislation. For major bills, party leaders expect to be informed of the progress of legislation within committees and of the difficulties encountered. They are more likely to exert themselves in behalf of speeding up the consideration of a bill in committee than in an attempt to alter its substance. They are not apt to ask committee members of their party to vote against either their consciences or the apparent desires of their constituents. If the committee chairman is a reliable party man, these duties most likely will fall to him. If he is not, a good party man on the committee, preferably the member ranking next to the chairman in seniority, may take on the party chores, aided by the party leadership.

Committees are highly individualistic in character; they differ substantially in prestige and autonomy, among other factors. In the

Senate, committees like Foreign Relations, Finance, Armed Services, and Judiciary are "prestige" committees, to whose memberships legislators ordinarily aspire. At the nether end of the pole are Rules and Administration, Post Office and Civil Service, and District of Columbia, which have little, if anything, to do with major public policy. Senators, as Donald Matthews well demonstrates, are not attracted to committees simply because of their policy-making potential; they often prefer committees of especial importance to their constituents. Thus the Committee on Interior and Insular Affairs may be composed overwhelmingly of senators from the public land states of the far West, and the Agriculture committee of senators from the Great Plains and the South. A senator's previous skills and experience also shape his preferences. Lawyers tend to prefer Foreign Relations most and Finance least; with businessmen, the choices are reversed.[1]

Committees differ greatly in operating style. "The character changes," one congressman has said, "with different chairmen and with different Congresses."[2] Committees derive their individuality from their freedom to set their own procedures, to move at their own pace, to hire their own staffs, and to display a sturdy streak of independence against the urgings of the party leadership of their house and of the presidential administration. Committees may differ strongly in mood and method. Some rely heavily on staff, pressure groups, and the executive branch; others are overtly inhospitable to such influences. Some committees are strongly partisan; others are decidedly not and are likely to report measures to the floor with complete or near unanimity.

Important committee work transpires in closed rather than open sessions. In closed sessions, committee decisions are made, bills revised, and testimony, which in the public interest must be kept secret, is taken. In recent years, from 30 to 40 per cent of committee meetings have occurred in "executive" or closed sessions.

With few exceptions, standing committees function with subcommittees, which also vary widely. Subcommittees are set up by subject matter; sometimes their titles are too general to be a guide to their jurisdiction. All, nevertheless, may permit their chairmen broad discretion. The dependence of committees upon substantial numbers of subcommittees is a consequence of the 1946 Reorganization Act, which reduced the 81 existing standing committees to 34—19 in the House and 15 in the Senate. The sharp decrease in the number of standing committees and the necessary enlargement of their jurisdiction made the expanded use of subcommittees inevitable. The number of subcommittees has risen steadily: more than 250 now exist in Congress, most of them in the House. Subcommittees permit recognition of less senior members and give play to the special concerns of individual members. Occasionally, a subcommittee may become so powerful that it exceeds the influence of the parent committee. The professional calibre of committee staffs was upgraded by the 1946 Legislative Reorganization Act. In 1963, nearly 500 persons were employed by House committees, most of them for special and select investigating committees rather than for standing committees.

CONGRESSIONAL RULES

Outstanding in its power is the House Rules Committee, whose decisions do much to determine the kind of consideration given a bill on the floor. Most important bills reported out of legislative committees, such as Agriculture, Foreign Affairs, and the like, reach the House floor by dint of a "rule" which the Rules Committee submits to the House. The rule allocates time for debate on the bill and may stipulate the number and kinds of amendments, if any, that can be offered. Prior to 1965, the Rules Committee's refusal to grant a rule almost invariably precluded floor consideration of a bill. The prohibition of amendments may in effect preclude the compromises which are necessary to build up support for the bill. In 1965, the Rules Committee's powers were limited in two important particulars. The Speaker was empowered to recognize the chairman or another member of a legislative committee to bring a measure before the House for consideration if it had been before the Rules Committee for 21 days without having been granted a rule—either through inaction or by rejection of a request for a rule. Prior to 1965, also, the Rules Committee had virtually a life-or-death power over a bill in deciding whether to adopt a rule permitting a bill to "go to conference"—that is, to a conference committee composed of members of both houses, appointed to iron out differences between the houses over a bill. If the Rules Committee refused to report out a rule, the bill could go to conference only by a very difficult procedure. Under changes adopted in 1965, the Speaker can recognize a member to offer a motion by which the bill can go to conference by majority vote.

The Rules Committee tends to cooperate with the legislative committees and the House leadership; seldom is a rule granted for a measure opposed by the leadership. Prior to 1965, however, bills which the leadership favored occasionally were not reported out or were given an unfavorable rule, such as one which bars amendments. From 1937 to 1965, social and economic legislation of progressive or liberal emphasis frequently encountered rough sledding in the Rules Committee, whose membership was dominated by southern Democrats and conservative Republicans.

As the Rules Committee illustrates, the House of Representatives is "rules centered." Its large size and its preference for action on legislation, as opposed to debate, have brought the House to function by what is truly a maze of rules. When Asher C. Hinds, long the House parliamentarian, published his five massive volumes of House precedents, he compiled a total of 7346 different technicalities of House procedure.

Despite its regard for action, the House in its rules shows special deference to its standing committees. If a committee other than the Rules Committee refuses to report out a bill to the floor for consideration, the bill can be pried loose only by a "discharge petition" signed by a majority of the House's members, a procedure that is infrequently used and seldom successful.

In contrast, the Senate, taking pride in its capacity for deliberation, has rules which are far less elaborate and constraining than those of the House. The central distinction between the rules of the two houses, as far as floor debate is concerned, is that the House permits a simple majority to end debate. The Senate, in contrast, puts no such limit on debate. The virtually laissez-faire conditions of debate are suggested by the fact that the Senate is the home of the "filibuster," a device enabling a minority to prevent the passage of a bill by talking continuously to keep it from coming to a vote. The filibuster is a favorite weapon of senators with strong ideological predispositions. After World War I, progressives, led by Robert La Follette, used the filibuster to arouse public opinion. In more recent decades the filibuster has been the chief weapon of southern Democrats to forestall civil rights legislation.

If the Senate chooses (as it rarely does) to limit debate, it can adopt a "cloture" (or "closure") rule, which requires a vote of two thirds of the senators present and voting to terminate debate. The Civil Rights Act of 1964 was the beneficiary of a successful imposition of cloture to bring to an end a record-breaking filibuster. The Senate's reluctance to invoke cloture is explained by William S. White's observation that "to grant to one's opponent in high political discussion and maneuver each and all the rights that one demands for himself—this is, uniquely in this country certainly, and perhaps in all the world, a Senate rule."[3]

Other differences between House and Senate reflect the Founding Fathers' desire to give maximum effect to checks and balances. Each legislative house, they believed, should be the natural rival and opponent of the other and therefore capable of checking any tyrannical tendency of the other as well as of the President. The Founding Fathers envisaged the Senate as the more mature body of the two, owing to the presumed attractiveness of its longer term to better qualified and more experienced candidates. The sagacious Senate was expected to check the youthful, impetuous House. The Fathers provided contrasting duties and qualifications for the houses—also in the interest of checks and balances. Senators were required to be thirty years old and citizens of the United States for at least nine years. Representatives needed to be but twenty-five years old. Senators were to be the ambassadors of their states, elected by the state legislatures. Members of the House were to represent the people and were to be elected directly by them. The Senate was to serve as an executive council to the President, advising him on treaties and administrative appointments. The House of Representatives was empowered to impeach the President, with the Senate making judgment. A two-year term for the House was intended to intensify that body's responsiveness to the people. A six-year Senate term was expected to make the second chamber impregnable to popular whim and in this respect a check on the House.

INTERHOUSE RELATIONS

The Founding Fathers left it to the two houses to develop means to work out differences in legislation adopted by each. At the first session of the First Congress, the House and Senate agreed to resolve their differences on legislation through specially created conference committees. These committees, which have been a permanent device, negotiate compromises on disputed bills. If conference committees fail to resolve all differences or if the houses reject their handiwork, the entire bill fails to be enacted. Strictly speaking, conference committees are limited to matters in dispute and are not empowered to delete sections of a bill approved by both houses or to add others that have not been included in either version of the bill. In fact, however, such irregularities are often indulged in by the committees and are seldom challenged. Conference committees have achieved great importance, since the decisions they reach are, with rare exceptions, enacted into law.

The House and Senate act together in other ways, such as in joint hearings by standing committees—for example, the House and Senate Armed Services Committees and the Senate and House Committees on Foreign Affairs conducted joint hearings on President Harry S Truman's removal of General Douglas MacArthur from his Korean command. The houses also occasionally work through joint committees, such as the Joint Committee on Atomic Energy and the Joint Economic Committee.

Policy-making endeavor, dependent upon interhouse cooperation, is also affected by the attitudes of members of one house toward the other. Fear of Senate domination tends to make the House leadership averse to increased use of joint committees; it also prompts House members of conference committees to fight hard for compromises that will not be considered concessions to the Senate. House members, according to Charles Clapp's researches, tend to consider themselves more representative of the people and responsive to their views than are senators, with their longer terms and larger constituencies. House members regard themselves superior in committee work; they also believe the House possesses craftsmen and specialists in policy areas which the Senate cannot match. The Senate is deemed excessively "clubbish" and too prone to support a senator's special projects, regardless of merit. Although the Senate captures the lion's share of publicity, it is in the House, its members believe, that the most thorough work is done.[4] Senators, in contrast, think of their chamber as superior to the House, a judgment conveyed in their habit of referring to the Senate as "the upper chamber" and the House as "the lower chamber." Senators take pride in their freedom of debate and take a poor view of the restrictions the House has imposed upon itself in that regard. Senators are conscious of the traditions of their chamber, the imposing array of distinguished public figures who have served there, and the importance of the senator as such—his place in the public eye, his capacity for influence, his status as ambassador in his state. In all these particulars, the House and its members, in the senator's view, compare unfavorably.

Legislative policy-making is affected by other idiosyncrasies of the individual houses. As was mentioned previously, the senator, favored with a longer term, often may feel he can afford to vote without regard to local opinion in the belief that his deed will be forgotten by the next election. The short-termed representative is constantly campaigning for re-election, and he tends to vote accordingly. The individual representative is apt to be lost in the great body of his colleagues. Senators, who are far fewer in number, are the object of greater publicity and deference. Not a few of them from time to time have deemed themselves better qualified than the President to guide the nation's affairs. The Senate, in the eyes of most House members, is a place to which to be "promoted." In 1961, forty-three senators—including the majority and minority leaders—had previously served as representatives. This phenomenon promotes understanding and cooperation between the houses.

The basis of representation is altogether different in the two houses. The Senate, founded upon the states, accords to the 128,643 residents of Alaska the same representation as to the 16,782,304 residents of New York. The House of Representatives, intended by the framers to represent the people, does so in a qualified sense. The Constitution requires that representation in the House be apportioned among the states "according to their respective numbers." In addition, the Constitution specifies that House seats be reapportioned every ten years. The reapportionment is based upon the national census, taken every decade. Congress by law has limited House members to 435 and has empowered the President to submit a reapportionment plan which automatically goes into effect unless Congress enacts a different plan within sixty days. The state legislatures determine what the boundaries of each congressional district shall be and whether any of its House seats shall be subject to election at large. Since one or both houses of the state legislature have historically been weighted in behalf of rural interests, congressional districts, too, tend to overrepresent the rural population and underrepresent urban and suburban dwellers. Because rural dwellers tend toward conservatism on social and economic legislation not directly beneficial to them, the House has been a formidable obstacle to such legislation from the Franklin D. Roosevelt era onward.

In 1964, the United States Supreme Court in *Wesberry* v. *Sanders*[5] struck a heavy blow at rural overrepresentation in the House by ruling that the districts must reflect the principle that "as nearly as is practicable one man's vote in a congressional election is to be worth as much as another's." Congressional districts, accordingly, must be set up along lines reflecting this principle. Acknowledging that congressional districts cannot be drawn with mathematical precision, the Court nevertheless ruled that the Constitution's "plain objective" of making "equal representation for equal numbers of people" must no longer be ignored. The *Wesberry* decision opens the way for the House to reflect in the future the impact of population shifts from rural to urban and suburban areas and presumably the preference of the latter areas for social and economic legislation. While this preference seems generally clear for urban areas, it is at best dubious for suburban areas. More than forty states are expected to be affected by the *Wesberry* ruling, and in many states a revision of congressional districts is well in progress.

Each legislator and each legislative committee employs a staff. The typical office force of a representative comprises an administrative assistant, a legislative assistant, a professional secretary, and several clerk-stenographers. A senator's staff allowance is even more generous. Staff competence varies considerably, but an able staff assistant, in addition to running errands for constituents, can help considerably in policy-making, in research, and in writing speeches. The 1946 Reorganization Act empowered each committee to employ up to four professional aides. Although here, too, quality is uneven, a strong trend has set in toward professional staff careers on Capitol Hill. Other staffs exist for Congress at large, most notably the Legislative Reference Service and the Office of Legislative Counsel. The first, a research unit of the Library of Congress, supplies digests of bills, data, and abstracts of pertinent literature for individual legislators and committees. The Office of Legislative Counsel similarly drafts bills for them and endeavors to make certain that whatever the congressman or committee wants will be fully reflected in the technical language of the bill.

The most powerful element in congressional policy-making is not an individual or group on Capitol Hill but rather the eminence at the other end of Pennsylvania Avenue: the President, his aides, and the executive branch. The President is surpassed by no one as legislative leader. His State of the Union and other messages provide the major legislative agenda. One half of the bills introduced in Congress originate in the executive branch and routinely require the stamp of approval of the President's staff agency, the Bureau of the Budget, to show that they are in accord with his program. Rarely can a major law be enacted without approval of the presidential administration. The President, indeed, sets the agenda of Congress. On the other hand, not all of his agenda will be enacted, and much that is will undergo substantial revision. Organization and leadership inside Congress are so diffused that some external leadership is indispensable if Congress is really to legislate on a scale fitting for the twentieth century. As the only nationally elected official, the President has a national mandate, and his campaign for election in modern times ordinarily stands upon an elaborate platform of promises and policies, most of which require legislation.

THE FUNCTIONS OF CONGRESS

The principal function of Congress is to represent the people in making policy. This function is not explicitly stated in the Constitution but has been steadily operative in practice. To "represent" means different things to different legislators at different times. Legislators ordinarily take the view that in their policy actions they should give the people what they want—that they should "mirror" the opinion of the constituents. Less frequently, legislators, such as many of those portrayed in John Kennedy's *Profiles in Courage*, may choose to defy known popular opinion on policy questions and to support what they consider the nation's best interests. The "people" of a senator's state or a representative's district are highly variable rather than homogeneous. Some are well informed and interested; others are ignorant and apathetic. Sometimes there is a discernible majority opinion; at other times there is not, and the legislator consequently has a freer choice of action.

Congress is charged by the Constitution with the legislative function of lawmaking. Section 8, Article 1 sets forth the "enumerated powers," or eighteen fields of public policy in which Congress is empowered to make laws. These range from declaring war to regulating commerce. The scope of these specific powers is expanded by the blanket "necessary and proper" clause: "To make all laws which

shall be necessary and proper for carrying into execution the fore-
going powers. . . ."

A major activity of Congress is to supervise administration. This
function is not expressly provided for in the Constitution but is implicit in the power of the purse and in the provisions regarding
impeachment, appointments, and treaties. Congressional exercise of
the function—which in itself is an assertion of policy—includes investigation of the activity and inactivity of executive departments and
agencies. (The first such investigation was that of General Arthur
St. Clair's defeat by western Indians in 1792.) Policy takes on meaning
as it is administered, and the investigatory power enables Congress
to be a continuing and influential participant in that decisive stage.
Woodrow Wilson perceived a further by-product of the investigative
power: the "informing" function, whereby Congress apprises and
leads public opinion concerning public problems.

Congress has further functions that bear directly or indirectly
upon policy-making. These include the origination of amendments
to the Constitution, which are themselves substantial innovations of
policy or the fountain of further policies. For example, the income-
tax amendment (Sixteenth Amendment) constitutes the permanent
inception not only of that tax but also of the vast forest of tax and
economic policies that have evolved over the decades.

The Senate also serves as an executive council in providing the
President with its advice and consent on appointments and treaties.
In passing on appointments, the Senate—particularly in the committee hearing stage—may review not only the appointee's qualifications
but his views on policy as well.

When the Electoral College fails to choose a President, the House
of Representatives does so. The Senate acts similarly in the case of
the Vice-President.

Both houses are involved in the impeachment of public officers,
the House levying the charges and the Senate sitting as a court of
judgment. The Senate has functioned in this capacity twelve times,
and its decisions have brought the removal of four judges and the
acquittal of President Andrew Johnson in 1868 and Secretary of War
William W. Belknap in 1876. The existence of the impeachment
power has also prompted the resignation of many officers whose conduct could not bear scrutiny.

Congress makes laws governing the line of succession to the presidency after the vice-presidency; the last such law, passed in 1947, established a sequence that proceeds from the Speaker of the House to the president pro tempore of the Senate and the heads of executive departments.

Finally, the Constitution empowers each house to make its own
rules—a function which, as we shall see, has enormous effect upon
the kinds of policies that are made or are prevented from being made.

THE LEGISLATOR

Policy mirrors the individual legislator. His background, outlook, and political commitments shape—if they do not dominate—his views on issues. Although each legislator operates as an individual center of power in the legislative process, a composite picture of the legislator and his colleagues contributes to an understanding of the human make-up of the houses.

When the 89th Congress convened in 1965, the average age of senators was 57.7 years and of representatives 50.6 years. The oldest senator was Carl Hayden (D., Ariz.) who was 87 and the youngest Edward M. Kennedy (D., Mass.), 32. The youngest representative was Jed J. Johnson, Jr. (D., Okla.), 25, and the oldest Barratt O'Hara (D., Ill.), 82. More legislators (465) cited politics and civil service as their occupations than any other. Among private occupational groups the most numerous were lawyers (305), followed by businessmen and bankers (147). Only one labor union official, three physicians, and two ordained ministers were to be found in Congress. The largest religious groups were Roman Catholic (107), Methodist (88), Episcopal (69), Presbyterian (69), and Baptist (51).

The senator, according to the researches of Donald R. Matthews,[6] is apt to be a "small-town boy" of middle- or upper-class background. Only rarely do the sons of unskilled urban workers become senators. Senators compare favorably with the rest of the population in education. In 1950, according to Matthews, almost 85 per cent of the senators had attended college, although this level of education had been achieved by only 14 per cent of the general population.

Law, a most strongly represented occupation in both the Senate and the House, imparts a discipline and calls for skills highly relevant to the legislative process. By dint of his professional practice, the lawyer becomes a mediator of forces and a specialist in human relations— abilities well suited to the realities of legislative policy-making.

The qualities making for the "good" senator are much affected by the smaller size of the chamber and its trappings of a club. The latter involve such elements as a keen sense of tradition and of propriety, with stress upon tolerance of fellow members, and a feeling of exclusiveness founded upon a view that admission to the Senate is an acme of political success. William S. White finds that senators have a sensitivity to the necessity of compromise, a willingness to abide dissent, and a gift "if not for friendship at least for amicable association with other minds and with the interests of others."[7]

Representatives view their employment in less flattering terms than do senators. The representative is likely to feel that the senator receives greater attention in the press and enjoys superior staff resources and the security and prestige of a six-year term. House members may complain of the limitations on their power. "There is no sense of power resulting from membership in the House, at least until you get to be chairman," a member has said. "If anything, there is a sense of frustration at times."[8]

Not all those who have been elected to the House were enthusiastic about making their initial race. Some entered politics and came to the House primarily to advance their private professional careers rather than to launch a congressional career. To members with such purposes, ideological and policy consideration may be altogether incidental. The representative has less of a sense of job security than does the senator. His shorter term and smaller constituency make the representative feel more dependent upon particular groups back home; his future seems more precarious, since it is dependent upon frequent exercises of will and whim by seemingly ill-informed voters. The House member is more likely than the senator to view his seat as a way to some other, better political position. House members may strongly desire to become senators or governors of their home states. Political statistics since World War II may encourage senators to train their ambition upon the presidency and vice-presidency.

Distinguished achievement in one house is no guarantee of a successful career in the other. A legislator may achieve a position of great leadership in the House but subside to a modest role in a subsequent Senate career. James G. Blaine, the egregious "plumed knight," for six years Speaker of the House and its acknowledged master, entered the Senate for a term of service which is now all but forgotten. Blaine's contrasting fortunes seem to have sprung from several causes: he lacked the seniority in the Senate which he had enjoyed in the House; his temperament was less suited to the more formal and sedate procedures of the Senate; and he fared better in the running fire and interruptions of House debate than in the set speech of the Senate.

The senator's national party committee and the Senate campaign committee rarely can exert effective pressure against any senator. Although the senator naturally welcomes campaign help from these organizations, he knows they are unlikely to withdraw it even if he chooses to take an independent position on policy issues. Like the representative, the senator has distinctive political necessities created by his constituency which shape his views on particular policy questions. In 1961, Senator Joseph S. Clark (D., Pa.), facing the prospect of a tough 1962 primary fight with either Philadelphia Congressman William Green or Governor David Lawrence, both of whom were Catholics, was an enthusiastic supporter for aid to parochial schools, which enrolled over 20 per cent of all Pennsylvania pupils. The senator's position was therefore in conflict with that of his national party leader, President Kennedy.

In their conduct relating to policy questions and to the folkways of their houses, legislators may differ in their tendencies to conformity and nonconformity. Senate folkways encourage members to become "compromisers" and "bargainers," and to use their powers with caution and restraint. Behavioral norms encourage courtesy and regard for colleagues and serve to soften the potential personal antagonisms lurking in policy debate. Despite differences over issues, adversaries can maintain a personal relationship of mutual respect. There are, by legislative standards, several kinds of nonconformity, some more tolerable than others and all bearing consequences for policy-making. Senator Joseph McCarthy, in his loyalty investigations, violated both the written and unwritten rules of decorum, for which the Senate ultimately censured him. President Truman, speaking of two outstanding Senate mavericks in modern times—George Norris and Robert La Follette—once remarked, "You always have to have a gadfly in an organization, and this is what these men were."

Although the personality and purposes of the maverick are a coat of many colors, several qualities are commonplace among the breed. Like his hero-model La Follette, present-day Senator Wayne Morse is prone to fight half measures and demand full measures or nothing. Both legislators were convinced that half measures are evils which tend to quiet public clamor for full-scale action and therefore postpone—sometimes indefinitely—its realization.[9] From 1921 to 1933, nonconformist Senator George Norris kept alive, by tireless advocacy, the idea of federal public power projects, which in the 1930's eventuated in the TVA and the Bonneville and Grand Coulee dams. The Twentieth ("Lame Duck") Amendment, which Norris also sponsored, required ten years of public education before its adoption in 1933.

Displays of independence may involve more than a single legislator. In 1963, a substantial pattern of independent assertion developed among the younger and more newly arrived congressmen. The objects of their concern were the seniority leaders (such as committee chairmen) and the party leaders (such as the majority leader), who were older in years and substantially different in outlook on military, social, and economic policy. Several episodes occurring at the outset of the 88th Congress in 1963 suggest the nature and method of this restive independence. The House Armed Services Committee and its patriarchal chairman, Carl Vinson of Georgia, proposed to confer upon the Defense Department a huge appropriation for the RS-70 bomber. The department did not want the appropriation. Five dissidents on the committee—all young Democrats—fought the chairman on the floor, where they forced a roll-call vote—which, although unsuccessful, revealed that an impressive number of members shared their views. The usual voice vote would not have provided this information so specifically. In another move, young Republicans in the

House, restive under what they deemed to be an image of negativism built up by the older party leaders, managed, by their concerted strength, to insert one of their members, Gerald Ford of Michigan, into the leadership group. (In 1965, Ford replaced Charles Halleck as House Republican leader.) In the Senate, Joseph Clark (D., Pa.), chafing under the conservatism of his party's leadership, launched into a three-day speech, a critique of the Senate "club," remarkable for its candor.

The legislator can also be viewed as a political human endowed with an ideology and with lesser political preferences that influence his views on policy questions. Oscar Underwood, House Democratic leader in the Wilson era, was a Jeffersonian in outlook—opposed to concentration of power in the central government, convinced of the wisdom of state sovereignty and local self-government, and a dedicated foe of "unnecessary" governmental interference with individual rights. Jefferson's caveat, "Our country is too large to have all its affairs directed by a single government," shaped Underwood's responses to policy questions.[10]

A specific policy situation or crisis may bring into focus a legislator's random, semiformed political beliefs. Senator Brien McMahon of Connecticut, who at most seems to have had diffused convictions concerning the relative roles of civil and military authority in public affairs, experienced a sharpening of his beliefs in the development of legislation in 1946 to deal with the newly mastered phenomenon of atomic energy. McMahon, who quickly came to attach high importance to civil authority, resisted the strong initial efforts to establish military control over the administration of atomic energy; he toiled and fought—for a time with little assistance—for the principle of civilian control. His tenacity led eventually to the establishment of the Atomic Energy Commission, an organ of civilian control, in lieu of vesting the function in the military.

A rare legislator may possess the gift of vision and indeed the courage to renounce a general policy premise with which he was thoroughly identified and to take up the opposite premise, which he had previously spurned and castigated. Arthur H. Vandenberg was such a man. Once the nation's leading isolationist, he became its leading internationalist. A draftsman of the neutrality act of 1937 and the principal isolationist candidate for the Republican presidential nomination in 1940, Vandenberg's views were shattered by the attack on Pearl Harbor. "That day ended isolationism for any realist," he wrote. Gradually but steadily he assumed an internationalist position.

Some legislators, faced with policy choices, may hold to principles that are rejected by their constituents. Such legislators may risk electoral defeat and even political extinction. Oscar Underwood, who represented a great industrial constituency centered in Birmingham, Alabama, dared to oppose the protective tariff. He opposed, he wrote, "as a matter of principle . . . the deliberate use of the taxing power of the Government to benefit one citizen at the cost of other citizens." Underwood, to his own good fortune, was spared rejection at the polls by his constituents.

Legislators, too, have pet animadversions which influence, if not determine, their policy positions. Underwood could not bear bureaucracy. "It is an inevitable defect that bureaucracies will care more for routine than for results; or, as Burke puts it, 'that they will think the substance of business not to be much more important than the forms of it.' " Any such manifestations of bureaucracy in testimony of executive branch witnesses before the congressman's committees were quick to rouse his ire. Arthur Vandenberg could not abide those he deemed extremists. These, in his view in 1943, comprised both believers in "total isolation" and those "who would cheerfully give America away."[11]

The legislator also may nurture various kinds of political ambitions. The prizes of ambition may be outside his own house: election to the Senate, the governorship, or the presidency. His own congressional house also presents the challenge of a career ladder of power and influence that is his for the climbing. His movement upward may depend not simply upon his own talents but upon such imponderables as securing the sponsorship of influential colleagues and plain luck. Nicholas Longworth's first solid advance in his distinguished House career occurred when Congressman Charles H. Grosvenor retired as Ohio member of the Ways and Means Committee. Longworth, a Cincinnatian, succeeded to the vacancy; in the work of that important committee, Longworth quickly displayed talent and drew attention. The eye of Tom Connally of Texas in his early House years was drawn to two popular members of the Interstate and Foreign Commerce Committee—Sam Rayburn and Alben Barkley. "Although Barkley stood a notch above Sam in committee seniority," Connally has written, "we Democrats considered them rivals on the committee. Each was looking for promotions in committee influence, but the odds were stacked against Barkley because William C. Adamson, the ranking Democrat there, installed Rayburn as his favorite and pushed him ahead."[12]

A legislator, including one in a high leadership position, may subordinate his policy views and activities in the interest of maintaining sound personal relations with his colleagues. Toward his fellow Republican leader, Robert A. Taft, Vandenberg "always guarded a cordial . . . relationship with the greatest care, and scrupulously refrained from invading what he regarded as Taft's area of major responsibility for domestic problems."[13]

The individual legislator's impact upon policy may be radically affected not simply by the play of his own talents but also by developments in the political environment—over which his control is limited. The 1946 congressional elections, which resulted in Republican majorities in both houses for the first time in sixteen years, gave Senator Vandenberg, a leading Republican policy spokesman, great new opportunities for influence. Republican victory brought him three new positions. First, he became chairman of the Senate Foreign Relations Committee, with primary responsibility for that body's foreign policy legislation. Second, through his contributions to foreign policy, he became the Republican party's recognized spokesman in Congress on that subject. Third, as president pro tempore of the Senate—another gift of victory—he was in intimate touch with its work. His knowledge of its parliamentary situation and current moods proved invaluable in winning prompt action on foreign policy. President Harry S Truman, who succeeded to the office upon Franklin Roosevelt's death, welcomed, in the great challenge so suddenly thrust upon him, all useful support—including a policy-making partnership with Vandenberg, Republican leader in foreign affairs.

In 1948, the elections restored the Democrats to control of Congress and drastically reduced Vandenberg's influence. He was cast out of his positions as Senate president pro tempore and as Foreign Relations Committee chairman. General George C. Marshall, the Secretary of State with whom he had worked closely, now chose to resign, and Vandenberg faced an uncertain personal rapport—and therefore uncertain influence—with a new Secretary of State. Electoral defeat caused Republicans to be discontented with their legislative leadership, including Vandenberg. President Truman had now won the office in his own right by an extraordinary surprise victory, and, by every indication, meant to wield a strong hand.

THE LEGISLATOR'S EXTERNAL RELATIONS

Constituents. The position a legislator assumes on policy questions is influenced and sometimes shaped by his relations with groups and institutions outside Congress. His most permanent and vital relation is with his constituency. Many a legislator follows the view Tom Connally entertained as congressman and senator that his position on policy questions should assert the interests of his state or district. The Texas Democrat steadily pushed measures vital to the welfare of the "folks back home," for which they often showed their encouragement with great quantities of letters. Such displays of constituent will brought Connally to push the Cattle Relief Act in 1933 to prevent the collapse of the cattle industry in a crisis of falling prices and rising costs. He steered the Export Debenture Act of 1933 through Congress in the interest of Texas' biggest crop, cotton. Substantially a commodity for foreign markets, exports of cotton were boosted by the act, which permitted 30 per cent of the tariff duties, collected on goods imported into the United States, to be used by the Secretary of Agriculture to pay bounties to American exporters of agricultural products. Similarly, beleaguered by anguished pleas from the Texas oil industry, which in the 1930's was experiencing expanding production and declining prices, Connally steered through legislation to "save" the industry.

Although in most of these cases Connally's way was lighted by the pleas of his constituents, public sentiment is not always so obvious, and legislators differ in their means of divining and evaluating it. Most senators believe that their mail provides the best single indication of constituent attitudes.[14] Legislators can easily spot and will thoroughly discount "inspired" or "pressure" mail. Even at best, however, mail is but a slender indication of constituent sentiment. Only a few people write their representatives, and they are far from a fair sample of the constituency. Legislators increasingly resort to polls and questionnaires. Although they offer few surprises, polls nevertheless provide confirming evidence of views legislators had already sensed by other means.

Rather than be the mere recipient of constituent opinion, the legislator may seek to influence and shape it. Many legislators attach high importance to this educational function, regarding themselves as something more than mere agents of their constituency.

One of the most effective means a legislator has both to woo his district and to educate it is a newsletter. Fully 90 per cent of the representatives and senators use this method, although the form of the newsletter differs widely.[15] Most legislators seem to deem it unwise as a steady practice to present detailed information about legislation or about their stands on virtually all issues. Legislators frequently resort to radio and television to reach their constituents. The House and Senate provide their members recording facilities at cost. Programs often include statements of the legislator's viewpoint on current issues. Legislators are alert to the uses of the news release, and some are expert in the public relations techniques involved: timing their statements properly and providing newsworthy material in readily usable form.

Legislators are also errand boys for their constituents; in fact, doing things for one's constituents becomes, for many legislators, a task of such magnitude that it seriously competes with their primary function, which is to legislate. Many congressmen are literally inundated with constituents' demands for personal services; they are asked to perform tasks ranging from making hotel and plane reservations to matching draperies and replacing china. The burden of constituent errands multiplies with the growing size of the congressional district (which once averaged 300,000 but in the mid-twentieth century stands as 400,000).

Pressure groups. The legislator can view his constituency as comprising, at least partially, a conglomeration of organized pressure groups. Most bills, especially major bills, are backed by one array of interest groups and opposed by another. Groups may enter into coalition. For instance, when the Eisenhower administration moved to authorize private construction of the Hell's Canyon dam, Senator Wayne Morse (D., Ore.) in a countermove introduced legislation urged by the previous Truman administration for federal construction and operation. A formidable line-up of opposing pressure groups was generated by the legislation. Backing Morse was a quickly formed National Hells Canyon Association, a combination of fifty-six organizations including the Grange, Farmers' Union, AFL-CIO, and local power groups. In the showdown, the Idaho Power Company was aided by other private electric utility companies plus lobbyists for the natural gas and oil industries. Legislative affairs are so cumbrous and involved that the legislator can "cooperate" with pressure groups without most of his constituents knowing it. There are, of course, times when the legislator must vote on policy questions; certain pressure groups may have so much power in his state that to defy them would have serious electoral consequences.

Senators are better situated to deal with group interests and their lobbyists than are representatives. Their longer terms and their larger, more heterogeneous constituencies enable senators to play off pressure groups against one another more easily.

On election day, the legislator must reckon with constituents and pressure groups. Election is a compulsory route up the legislative career ladder. To the political good fortune of the House member, the attrition rate of the nineteenth century has sharply declined in the twentieth. Earlier, as many as two out of three House members were defeated in some elections. In the 1950's and 1960's, only 100 of 435 congressional districts can be deemed marginal.

Frequent elections and the possibility of defeat encourage the representative to coordinate his lawmaking activities with the bread-and-butter job of courting constituents' votes. "Over the years," writes Joe Martin, for more than half a century a congressman from Massachusetts, "I established a reputation as a fighter for New England, and the voters have kept reelecting me because I have given them service."[16]

The President. The legislator is subject to pressures—varying in force and effectiveness—from the President. Modern Presidents, from Theodore Roosevelt onward, have presented to Congress a detailed program of legislation; they court the support not only of legislators of their own party but of opposition party members as well. The President may resort to personal exhortation in conversations with legislative leaders and members. He may brandish the wand of patronage as a source of punishment and reward for the legislator's opposition or support. In the Franklin D. Roosevelt era, the Senate Democratic leader, Joe Robinson of Arkansas, personally opposed several legislative measures of the President; nevertheless, he supported the measures in response to Roosevelt's oral promise to appoint him to the Supreme Court when a vacancy occurred. Robinson, however, died before he could be appointed.

The President may make his appointments to executive posts in a manner which advances his legislative purposes. A factor in F.D.R.'s appointment of Senator Claude Swanson of Virginia as Secretary of the Navy was his intention to make room in the Senate for another Virginian, the then-Governor Harry F. Byrd. The President may manipulate more or less discreetly behind the scenes, as Roosevelt did, to bring about the election of Alben Barkley as Democratic Senate Leader and the appointment of Carter Glass and James F. Byrnes to the Senate Foreign Relations Committee. In elections a President may attempt—as Roosevelt did unsuccessfully in 1938—to "purge" senators and congressmen who have substantial records of opposition to his program.

But the President's relations with the individual legislator of his own or the opposition party may also involve extensive cooperation. The Senate's approval of the United Nations Charter, of the NATO alliance, and of the 1963 test ban treaty are models of cooperation between the President and leaders and members of the opposition party. In the later part of his administration, when the opposition Democratic party controlled both houses of Congress, President Hoover vetoed a Democratic bill that provided employment through a vast program of public works; but Hoover finally compromised with his opponents and agreed to permit such a program, provided the federal government made loans (rather than grants, as the Democrats had originally urged) to the states for the projects.

The legislator has many contacts with members of the executive branch, including department heads, bureau chiefs, and liaison officers. The latter are legion in some departments. In 1958, for example, the Air Force alone had a legislative liaison staff of 138 headed by a major general. In one ten-day period in the same year, the Interior Department received 553 letters and an estimated 200 telephone calls from congressmen.[17] The great preponderance of this interchange involves "errands" for and concerns of constituents, but much of it is requests for information and counsel, indispensable to the legislator as he weighs and decides upon highly technical legislation.

THE LEGISLATOR AS POLICY-MAKER

In appraising the influence of individual legislators in specific occasions of policy-making, one may divide the members of Congress into the major categories of "leaders" and "others." Because of the diffused organization of Congress and the considerable independence of its members, "leadership" is a concept that must be used cautiously. Congress has no unified leadership; those in leadership positions lack many of the means of authority and power associated with leaders of other organizations. Further, since congressional policy-making takes a lengthy, convoluted course, there may be many leaderships, and leadership may shift, leaving the question "who's in charge?" one that cannot always be easily answered.

For convenience, several types of leadership may be identified. One is the elected party leadership, such as the Speaker of the House, who is chosen initially by the conference or caucus of his party and elected by the whole House. In the Senate, the president pro tempore is selected by the same procedure. Each party in both houses elects its floor leader. A second kind of leadership is the seniority leadership: the chairmen and ranking minority members of the standing committees, who rise to those places by surviving in their respective houses through repeated and unbroken re-election. Third, there are policy-making leaders, whose influence is based upon personality, personal confidence, or expertise. Each party in each house has a committee which ostensibly plays a role of leadership. The Legislative Reorganization Act of 1946 established Senate Democratic and Republican Policy committees. In the House, both parties have steering committees, although since 1949 the Republicans have termed theirs the House Republican Policy Committee. All these committees have played at most a minor and sporadic part in both party and policy leadership, a circumstance indicative of the extreme decentralization of power in Congress.

The Speaker of the House. Leadership in policy-making by elected party leaders tends far more to facilitation than to initiative. Of these leaders, the most powerful is the House Speaker. He interprets and applies the rules of the House, quashes dilatory tactics, recognizes members who request the floor, refers bills to committees, and appoints the members of select and conference committees. House rules and precedents allow the Speaker wide discretion in interpreting the rules, and his interpretations are rarely overturned by a majority of the House, which is empowered to do so. In the more than thirty years during the Speakerships of John Nance Garner, Henry Rainey, Joseph Byrns, William Bankhead, Sam Rayburn, Joseph Martin, and John McCormack, the House has never overruled a Speaker's decision.

The Speaker in effect is empowered to guide the affairs of the House as he sees fit, within the limits of fairness.

The Speaker is endowed with other attributes, all radiating potential influence. He is chosen on something of a national basis by the whole body of representatives of all the people. In case of vacancies in the presidency and vice-presidency, he succeeds to the presidency. He is a leader of his party in the House and is normally its chief contact with the President when they are of the same party. Often spoken of as the second most powerful official in Washington, the Speaker is prone to assert his independence and a constitutional equality with the President. Sam Rayburn, the longest-tenured Speaker, who served in the House during the administration of eight Presidents and who was a Speaker during four administrations, denied ever serving "under" a President. "I haven't served under anybody," Rayburn put it, "I have served *with* eight Presidents."[18] Symbolic of the House's deference to the Speaker are the emoluments of his office: a salary of $43,000 compared with $30,000 paid individual congressmen. In addition, he enjoys a special expense allowance, a spacious office, a private hideaway, and a private dining room.

The Speaker's powers, although impressive, have diminished since 1910—the year of the "revolt" against Speaker "Uncle Joe" Cannon. In his hands and in those of his predecessor, Thomas Reed, the Speaker had come to exercise nearly absolute powers. He appointed all members of committees, including the chairmen. He could arbitrarily refuse floor recognition to those who did not fit into his purposes. He chaired the Rules Committee and selected its other members; thus he was assured of a majority for any action he wished taken. The increasingly authoritarian character of Speaker Cannon's rule sparked the revolt of 1910, led by George Norris; as a result, the Speaker was deprived of his power to name the personnel of all standing committees, and he was also denied membership on the Rules Committee. In 1965, in the face of long-building resentment of the capacity of the Rules Committee to block the progress of legislation, the Speakers' powers were strengthened. After a bill has been with the committee twenty-one days, the Speaker can, through his power of recognition, have the bill brought to the floor. Likewise, he can recognize a motion which, if supported by a House majority, can dispatch a bill to conference committee, a step that previously depended largely on the Rules Committee.

Speakers are less identified with policies as innovators and protagonists than as facilitators. "Uncle Joe" Cannon, for all his power, is not remembered as the instigator or champion of any major policy. His predecessor, Thomas Reed, at the peak of his career as Speaker, was spurned by the House on three of his major policies: he opposed war with Spain, annexation of Hawaii, and purchase of the Philippine Islands, but the House approved all three. Sam Rayburn is remembered more for his general effectiveness than for any major role in specific policy accomplishments.

In facilitating the development of policy, his true métier, the Speaker may excel as a conciliator—as a builder of consensus between disputant legislative groups. He can move legislation ahead and get things done, thanks no little to his prestige, his power and his compliant organization of lieutenants. During much of Rayburn's tenure, a group known as his protégés thrived in the House. These included Francis Walter of Pennsylvania, an able parliamentarian; Wilbur Mills of Arkansas, who rose to the chairmanship of the Ways and Means Committee; and various of Rayburn's fellow Texans. On many policy matters Rayburn preferred to work through his protégés rather than through the party caucus and steering committees.

Since major policy rarely advances in either house of Congress without bipartisan support, the Speaker is more than an insulated party potentate. He is its emissary in building good will and accommodation with the opposition party. Nicholas Longworth, Republican Speaker of the 1920's, regularly rode to work with opposition party leader John Nance Garner. Joe Martin, who served alternately as Speaker and floor leader during the Eisenhower administration, has written, "For me to have spent the first six years of the Eisenhower Administration brawling in the House with Rayburn and Representative John W. McCormack of Massachusetts, the Democratic floor leader, would not have advanced the interests of the Republican party one iota."[19]

The Senate has no leadership figure even remotely comparable in power and influence to the Speaker. The Vice-President, whom the Constitution designates as president of the Senate, has few and shadowy powers in that capacity. The president pro tempore of the Senate, elected to preside in the Vice-President's absence, is ordinarily an honorific office.

The Floor Leader. In both houses, each party, meeting in caucus or conference, chooses a floor leader. According to Champ Clark of Missouri, who served eminently in that capacity, the floor leader "must possess tact, patience, firmness, ability, courage, quickness of thought, and knowledge of the rules and practices of the House."[20] Other floor leaders, in discussing their post, have stressed mastery of the fine art of persuasion. "I have never asked a member to vote against his conscience," John McCormack has said, in describing an outer limit of the role. "If he mentions his conscience—that's all. I don't press him any further."[21] Joe Martin utilized what he termed "persuasion and conciliation"; Martin depended on long-established friendships and built bridges to the rival Democratic party. Toward the views and political necessities of his fellow House Republicans, he was understanding, even when votes were badly needed. "Unless it was absolutely necessary," he explained, "I never asked a man to side with me if his vote would hurt him in his district. Whenever I could spare a man this kind of embarrassment I did so and saved him for another time when I might need him more urgently."[22] Martin's consideration for his own party members and his concern for building cooperation and good will with the opposition party eventually displeased the White House staff and presumably the President. The Eisenhower administration, Sherman Adams has written, deemed Martin's leadership "lackadaisical." Martin was eventually overthrown and replaced by Charles Halleck, a self-styled "gut-fighter." This overthrow was accomplished by the latter's aggressive talents and covert administration support. Although Halleck as floor leader drove his fellow Republicans harder than Martin had, he, too, perceived the limits of his power and the necessity of moderation. "You can't push them too hard," he has said. "You've got to know when to let up."[23] Halleck, however much his style differed from Martin's, was also overthrown. In 1965, Halleck was replaced as Republican leader by Gerald Ford of Michigan.

The Party Whip. In both houses, each party has a "whip" and one or more assistant whips. Whips prod party members to appear on the floor for important votes and to vote "correctly." The chief whip has in late years become a party strategist and sometimes substitutes for the floor leader as the party's spokesman. He invests no little time in sounding out party sentiment for the Speaker and the floor leader on important pending legislation.

Committee Chairmen. The seniority leadership consists primarily of the chairmen of the standing committees, whom Woodrow Wilson in his classic *Congressional Government,* written well before the start of his public career, regarded as the principal source of governmental policy-making. (Wilson was speaking of a time when he thought Congress completely dominated the executive.) The committee chairman has persisted as a figure of imposing power. Most committees meet only at the chairman's call, enabling him to kill bills simply by not calling meetings or by scheduling them at times when a quorum cannot be obtained. He appoints his committee's staff and (usually in consultation with the ranking minority member and other members) the chairmen of subcommittees. He manages or names the floor manager for all bills reported from the committee to the floor. He can impede or hasten any bill to passage. He largely controls the timing of a bill's consideration, and timing can determine a bill's fate. With typically a thousand bills referred to a minor committee each year, the chairman's selection of the order in which they are considered by his committee does much to determine their chances of becoming law. Most bills referred to committee are not considered at all and thus die there. The committee chairman has other leverages. He can create a sense of indebtedness among committee colleagues by assigning them a subcommittee of their own and the right to staff it. He can grant special consideration to a committee member's request—one which otherwise would not be acted upon at all.

Committee chairmen, with rare exceptions, are chosen by the principle of seniority. The committee member with the longest unbroken tenure in the given house of Congress becomes the chairman. Since seniority rewards continuous re-election, congressmen from one-party states or one-party districts—the former primarily in the South and the latter in rural and small-town areas—dominate the chairmanships. In Democratic Congresses, Southerners overwhelmingly control the chairmanships, although a significant minority of safe Democratic districts lie in the big cities. Senators and congressmen from closely divided metropolitan areas where party overturn is frequent are penalized by the seniority system. Its chief attraction is that it is automatic and impersonal and avoids the maneuvering and bargaining likely to befall any alternative system.

Illustrative of the more powerful committee chairmen is Carl Vinson, Democrat of Georgia, veteran of twenty-six terms in the House and for many years chairman of the House Naval and Armed Services Committees. Presidents and Secretaries of the Navy and of Defense came and went, but Vinson endured, until his retirement from Congress in 1964. Vinson created consternation in 1961, when for a time he seemed to oppose a major part of President Kennedy's military program. Eventually, after the President's own hard effort to persuade him, the congressman came around, and the fact that he voted for the legislation induced many Southerners and other colleagues who respected his judgment to do so, too. His control over military installations and their location, expansion, and reduction provided him enormous influence among his colleagues. Once when it was suggested that he might well become Secretary of Defense, he replied, "I'd rather run the Pentagon from up here."

Occupying a special place among the committees of Congress is the House Rules Committee, which has no counterpart in the Senate. The House interposes a barrier to a bill, which the Senate does not: before final House debate, a "rule" or special resolution must be obtained from the Rules Committee, providing for consideration of the bill and arranging the conditions of debate. The Rules Committee normally holds hearings on the question of granting a rule, with the chairman, the ranking member of the committee (the minority party member with the longest committee tenure), and the bill's sponsor appearing. The Rules Committee can decline to grant a rule or can inordinately delay granting it. The rules it grants give the committee a broad range of options with significant policy implications. It can provide for only an hour of debate or for days of it; it can specify the day or days when debate may take place; its rule may waive points of order or forbid amendments that are unacceptable to the sponsoring committee chairman. Consistently since the 1930's, the Rules Committee has been a stronghold of conservative opinion. In the Eisenhower era, the committee throttled or gravely harmed such policy matters as public school aid, federal aid to depressed areas, an omnibus housing bill, and the $1.25 minimum wage.

With the Kennedy administration's strong encouragement, Speaker Rayburn brought the House to enlarge the Rules Committee. But even this failed to induce favorable committee action on the administration's broad-scaled 1961 education bill and other measures. In 1964, President Johnson was concerned that the committee, after it had refused to clear for House consideration an administration bill to ease federal regulation of railroad and water carrier rates, might also block the administration's antipoverty bill and its special program of relief and economic development of the Appalachian region. Johnson called in its Democratic members for what was described as a "pep talk"; among those who did not attend was the chairman, Howard W. Smith of Virginia.

Certain members of the House and Senate are in fact leaders even though they occupy none of the elected or seniority leadership positions. They may be members of an informal circle of leaders, the chairmen of major subcommittees, or specialists in important subjects of legislation. "When a man has demonstrated ability," a congressman has explained, "regardless of his formal position of power, by the force of his personality, knowledge, and effective talent he becomes an informal locus of power. He is the true leader who automatically wins followers, regardless of position. In every social structure you are going to find people to whom, for certain purposes, people will automatically turn regardless of their formal status in that group."[24]

Congressional Blocs. Legislators may be leaders or members of various groups, or blocs, of colleagues with particular policy orientations. Some of these groups are *ad hoc*, organized only for a specific policy enterprise; others are more enduring and vary in scope. A special group, for example, sprang up in the Senate in 1937 to combat President Roosevelt's court-packing plan. A steering committee was organized that included Senators Josiah W. Bailey of North Carolina,

Harry Byrd of Virginia, Edward R. Burke of Nebraska, Walter F. George of Georgia, Bennett Clark of Missouri, Millard Tydings of Maryland, Frederick Van Nuys of Indiana, David I. Walsh of Massachusetts, Peter G. Gerry of Rhode Island, Burton K. Wheeler of Montana, and Tom Connally of Texas. Senator Henry Ashurst, the Judiciary Committee chairman, Connally has written, "did not join us openly, but we believed he was with us in spirit."

In the lengthy, consuming fight over the court-packing plan, the group took on the trappings of organization. It met secretly every day in a Capitol hideaway to adjust strategy in light of shifting events. A major strategy was to delay the congressional decision as long as possible. Because of Roosevelt's popularity, the country was expected to favor the court plan, at least initially. The more the struggle was prolonged, however, the more the plan was expected to decline in popularity. A key tactic in the strategy of delay was the protracted hearings of the Senate Judiciary Committee, expertly led by Ashurst, which dawdled away six months in hearings and deliberations on the court bill.

The group lobbied fellow senators intensively in a quest for votes, with Gerry serving as whip to keep records of how each senator stood on the issue and what efforts were in progress to win over opponents. Information about waverers was funneled to Gerry; each waverer was thereupon pursued by bloc members in the Senate chamber, the cloakroom, the Senate Office Building, or at social gatherings. This task was eased when a Senate officer, who ostensibly was working for the administration's forces, informed Wheeler nightly by telephone who on their own side was weakening and who seemed to be weakening among the court plan foes. Wheeler took on the task of winning support outside Congress and served as floor leader. "One of my main problems," he has written, "was trying to keep people on our side from making statements that would play into Roosevelt's hands."[25]

The most formidable blocs are usually those coupled with some economic commodity important to the welfare of one or more sections of the country. From the late nineteenth century through the administration of Franklin Roosevelt, one of the most formidable associations was the "silver bloc" of western senators and representatives. As a member of Congress, William Jennings Bryan speeded his meteoric political rise by his eloquent leadership of that bloc. Another of the most powerful blocs is the farm bloc, which reached peak strength in the 1920's and 1930's and which works to assure federal assistance to key farm crops of the South and Middle West. The farm bloc has a bipartisan cast, joining the votes of southern Democrats and midwestern Republicans. Heavy migration to city areas seems to have eroded its effectiveness in the 1960's.

The most enduring and pervasive sectional bloc is the "southern bloc." Since the inception of Congress, southern legislators have maintained remarkable cohesion and have demonstrated skill in asserting the interests of their sections. More perhaps than the country's other sections, the South has dispatched, as James G. Blaine, the Speaker from Maine once put it, its "best and most talented" men. Southern legislators have excelled in securing their aims both as an independent bloc and in forming alliances for specific purposes with other groups. Their official alliance in the Democratic party with northern and western Democrats, plus the favorable working of the seniority rule, have enabled the Southerners to count heavily in committee chairmanships and processes. The alliance of Southerners with conservative Republicans has checkmated proposals for progressive social and economic legislation since 1937. Southerners are also the mainstay of the farm bloc, as evidenced by the fact that of the six major crops supported by massive federal aid, four—cotton, tobacco, rice, and peanuts—are southern crops.

Ideological blocs are also identifiable in the two houses. One is the conservative coalition, a combination of southern Democrats and conservative Republicans. Some legislators contend that the coalition rests chiefly upon the natural voting inclinations of many members of Congress and possesses little formal organization or group character. Other legislators believe that, in the House at least, close cooperation and consultation prevail between acknowledged leaders of the group, as they did between Democratic Representative Howard W. Smith, Rules Committee chairman, and Charles Halleck during his tenure as Republican leader. The coalition has emerged most readily and emphatically on labor legislation, spending issues, loyalty-security questions, and, as a Republican member has put it, on the "extension of the hand of the federal government."[26]

Several forms of a "liberal" coalition also exist. One, a bipartisan combination of liberal Republicans and liberal Democrats in each house, is far looser in organization than the conservative coalition. Its members usually come from the northern and western urban industrial states and districts; they find common cause on social and economic issues, such as Kennedy's 1961 general program of aid to education and his minimum wage and depressed areas bills.

Each major party has its own liberal bloc. In the House, a specially organized Democratic Study Group comprises the majority of younger, junior-tenured, nonsouthern Democrats. The Study Group originated with House liberals who were convinced that the House Democratic leadership was inadequately responsive to the liberal planks of the party platform. To speed liberal measures, the Study Group organized itself with officers, an executive committee, and whips. Critics of the Study Group consider it excessively sectional in its membership, excluding southern Democrats who are "wrong" on civil rights but "right" from a liberal standpoint on other social and economic questions. In neither house is there a Republican liberal bloc comparable in organization to the Democratic Study Group. One House Republican termed liberals of his party more a "splinter" than a "bloc"—small in numbers and at most only loosely cohesive. "The liberal Republicans are not as clear-cut a group as some other groups here," a congressman has said. "I think Republicans are a little more inclined to divide their vote than Democrats. We don't buy all the liberal program or all the conservative program."[27]

Within the blocs are subblocs, and within the groups are subgroups. The farm bloc divides into wheat and cotton subblocs that often tend to be separate and remote from each other. The peanut subbloc further subdivides into the runner, the southwest Spanish, and the Virginias. Similarly, the wheat subbloc is split according to classes of wheat. Cotton legislators divide between the old cotton South, "the Texas group" (composed of a part of Texas and other cotton states), and "the California group." Texas itself splits; the central part of the state identifies with the old South, and the remainder follows "the Texas group."

Further legislative groupings are more informal and are based upon personal, regional, ideological, or nationality considerations. In 1947, a group of young, predominantly western, Republican congressmen, including Richard Nixon, formed the Marching and Chowder Club, originally sixteen members who met weekly in a colleague's office in the late afternoon for drinks and discussion of issues. Congressman J. W. Fulbright of Arkansas invited such colleagues as Mike Mansfield of Montana, Walter Judd of Minnesota, and Christian Herter of Massachusetts—all interested and well informed in foreign affairs—for discussions of that subject. Congressmen of Polish, Italian, or other national extraction may meet monthly to discuss a foreign aid bill and other pending measures relevant to their national backgrounds. Some state delegations—especially the larger ones like New York, Ohio, and Pennsylvania—may combine on a bipartisan basis on measures of general interest to their states. Some city organizations have wielded an almost tyrannical sway over their House members. In the days of the late William Green, Democratic congressman and political boss of Philadelphia, House Democrats of that city tended to vote as a group. "On party matters," Green once explained, "we are usually agreed ninety-eight or ninety-nine percent of the time. We usually talk it over before the vote."[28]

Individual Self-Assertion. In a genuine sense, each member of Congress, whether senator or representative, is his own leader. There is no leadership or mechanism of pressure or discipline in either house to compel members to do what they do not want to do.

The individual legislator has various means of and opportunities for self-assertion, or at least for the assertion of views that are not held or advocated by the established leaderships. He can have impact as a member of a standing committee or committees. Critics of President Kennedy's legislative leadership contend that he overrelied upon the power of committee chairmen and undervalued the independence and potency of committee members. The Johnson administration could not pry loose its program of health care for the aged from the House Ways and Means Committee during the greater part of 1964 —not simply because it was opposed by Chairman Wilbur Mills of Arkansas but essentially because all ten Republicans on the committee and three of its fifteen Democrats, including Mills, opposed the principle of financing health services through the Social Security tax system.

Various inducements exist in committee processes for the individual member's self-assertion. The committees, with their high degree of autonomy, are the centers of legislative decision, where private deliberations are far more important than anything transpiring on the floor or in open hearings. In the secrecy of committee executive sessions, the member enjoys considerable freedom to advance his personal views. Thirty to 40 per cent of committee meetings are in executive session, where partisan influences are often subordinated. Not a little of the reputation a legislator has among his colleagues is made in committee work. Reputations do not grow in a soil of bland acquiescence. The most extreme form of independence is the member's open challenge of leadership. In 1963, Representative Otis G. Pike, Democrat of Suffolk County, Long Island, a member of the Armed Services Committee, opposed a bill sponsored by committee chairman Vinson; the bill would have made it a court-martial offense for servicemen to follow a Defense Department directive aimed at eliminating segregation near military bases. In a letter to constituents, Pike promised to fight the Vinson bill hard, whatever the consequences. "There are times," wrote Pike, "when a Congressman is badly torn between his desire to live in peace, comfort and affection with his Congressional colleagues and his desire to do what he deems to be his duty to his country and his conscience."[29]

The individual committee member may propose amendments to a bill, as Senator Albert Gore (D., Tenn.) did in 1961 when he cut from the Kennedy administration's housing bill its no-down-payment, forty-year mortgage plan. Picking up a crucial handful of normally liberal Democratic votes, Gore, with the further aid of conservative votes, won by a close roll-call count.

The individual member may exert initiative by assisting, rather than opposing, party or seniority leaderships. The assertive yet co-operative member can become a "strong committeeman," one who pursues his committee duties diligently and skillfully, masters the subjects which come before it, develops expertise, and earns the respect of the chairman and his fellow members. In time, his colleagues may deem him a "specialist" in a given field, one whose judgment they are prone to follow in their votes; at the very least they will seek his advice. The respected specialist often may not be well known to the public. "In spite of the great reputations," Joe Martin has written, "I soon discovered, as new members probably still do, that whenever a particular subject came up, there was always one or perhaps two members who were expert on it and could address themselves to it more intelligently than anyone else. And very often these were members that one had never heard of until he came to Congress."[30]

The individual member can seek to influence legislation in floor debate, although his opportunities for influence there are slim. Most legislators have already made up their minds, and in both houses their audience is apt to be pitifully small and frequently inattentive. House debate is so restricted by the rules that it is almost unknown in modern times for a member to be allowed to address the House for an hour on even the gravest matter. More valuable in both houses than the oratorical gift is facility at private persuasion, at inducing other legislators to come around to one's view of policy questions. Claude A. Swanson, senator from Virginia in the 1920's and 1930's, was, his colleague Burton K. Wheeler of Montana noted, "no orator and he seldom spoke on the floor, but he was one of the best men to have on your side in a fight. Privately, he could persuade more reluctant Senators to go along on a vote than anyone else."[31]

The self-assertive legislator can engage in various parliamentary moves and maneuvers. He can introduce bills; but unless he is in a position of influence, they will die in committee, unnoticed and unmourned. Their chief value may be their contribution to a record which he hopes will impress his constituents. His far more significant contribution to policy may be one of strengthening the bills of colleagues, of building majorities, and of arranging compromises. With small chance of success, he can support a discharge petition to extract a bill becalmed in committee, to bring it forth for floor action. He can launch initiatives against bills, most of which will be unavailing unless he can command majority support. He can move to strike out the enacting clause of a bill and move to recommit the bill to the committee from which it came. The first maneuver, if successful, destroys the bill; the second commits it to indefinite exile. Unless such motions enjoy majority support, they serve only for harrass-ment. The member, whether in cooperation with or in defiance of the leadership, may influence policy by his vote: he may cast or withhold it, and he may employ it, in alliance with others, to exact changes and compromises in developing legislation.

THE FOCI OF POLICY-MAKING

Like the other branches of government, Congress has its own special means and forms for establishing policy. Its most authoritative policy-making process is lawmaking, and the vehicle of lawmaking is the bill. Any member of the House or Senate can introduce a bill merely by sending it to the clerk's desk. This simple act, however, may follow considerable research and drafting. Each Congress in the 1960's typically has had about 14,000 bills introduced, with somewhat less than 1000 enacted. All bills not enacted are wiped off the records at the close of a Congress.

Bills are referred to standing committees, where they are considered in detail and are the subject of public hearings at which the testimony of interested persons is heard. The committee reaches a decision on a bill and embodies it in a report. The committee, most likely, amends the bill, and its report may be extensive. Bills approved by committee are highly likely to be passed by the house concerned. Committee rejection of a bill makes its passage very unlikely. Hearings and reports of committees on major legislation are published. Minority reports also may be filed.

After they are reported out by committee, bills are debated on the floor of the House and Senate. House debates occur chiefly in the Committee of the Whole, whose procedures are free of many of the restrictions of usual House procedure. Debate on a bill is guided by managers, and time is divided between those speaking for and those speaking against the bill. Time for debate is more closely regulated in the House than in the Senate, where the filibuster, or debate for unlimited time, is possible unless it is stopped, as it rarely is, by cloture, invoked by two thirds of the Senate's entire membership. Most procedural scheduling actions occur by unanimous consent.

The vote employed by the House or Senate to indicate approval or rejection of a bill proceeds by several means. The most frequent is the voice vote. If this is indecisive, a "division," or standing vote, follows. Voting with tellers requires the members to file past a given point to be counted for or against the bill. A roll-call vote records each member's vote. All but the last procedure provide no record which the private citizen can examine to learn how his congressman or senator voted.

At the floor stage in both the House and Senate, amendments can be added to bills, although in some instances they may be precluded or restricted. Amendment may sometimes take the form of a "rider," whereby a bill of subsidiary or even unrelated interest is amended onto an appropriation bill. For instance, the United States asserted a quasi-protectorate over Cuba by the Platt Amendment, a rider to an Army appropriation bill of 1901.

If both houses pass identical versions of the bill, it is enrolled, signed, and sent to the President. If the versions differ, the bill is sent to conference committee, composed of three or more members from each house, who attempt to thrash out the differences. Conference committees usually have broad discretion, which they sometimes use to rewrite bills arbitrarily. Not without reason, conference committees have been called the third house of the legislature.

Conference committee proceedings are secret, but the debates of the two houses are printed in the *Congressional Record.* This record, together with committee hearings and reports, is relied upon by the courts and often by executive officials to assay legislative intent and views relevant to the laws. Once enacted and signed by the President, measures become laws and are found in the statutes at large of the United States for the particular session. Statutes are codified from time to time in *The Code of the Laws of the United States,* or the *United States Code.*

CRITICISMS OF CONGRESS

In the 1960's, political writers of a liberal bent have been increasingly critical of Congress' slow pace, its tendency toward negativism, and its meager output of major laws dealing with the urgent social and economic problems of the times.[32] Senator Joseph S. Clark of Pennsylvania has written, "I have no hesitation in stating my deep conviction that the legislatures of America, local, state, and national, are presently the greatest menace in our country to the successful operation of the democratic process." In 1963, congressional slowness and negativism reached a point where there was almost a complete shutdown of President Kennedy's legislative program. As that year ended, the civil rights bill, which Kennedy had presented at mid-year with the most emphatic urgency, was stuck in the House. His tax bill, to which he had accorded an equally high priority, was becalmed in the Senate Finance Committee. A dozen appropriation bills remained unenacted a full six months after the fiscal year for which they were intended had elapsed. Since President Johnson's advent to office, the tax bill, the civil rights bill, and others that Kennedy was denied have been enacted, and others are making progress. In addition, Johnson has proposed much other domestic legislation to further his "Great Society." Yet, for all the scope of his requests, he refrained in 1965 from urging an all-out education program of federal aid for teachers' salaries and school construction, for fear of fatal obstruction at critical points in the legislation's progress through Congress.

Critics of Congress attribute the shutdown that Kennedy faced in 1963, and less serious rebuffs that other Presidents suffer, in no small measure to the committee system and to seniority rule, which vest power in a group of elder statesmen who are unrepresentative of dominant public and congressional opinion. The patriarchs of the "Establishment," as Senator Clark calls it, are Senator Richard Russell of Georgia and Representative Howard Smith of Virginia. Its membership, which is heavily southern and rural, believes in white supremacy, shows more devotion to property than to human rights, supports the military generously, calls for belligerence in foreign affairs, and stoutly resists congressional reform. The base of the Establishment's power is the standing committee; thanks to the seniority principle, nine of the Senate's sixteen committees were chaired by Southerners in 1963. A comparable sectional lopsidedness exists in the House.

To transform Congress from its negative tendencies into a governmental organ capable of responding to its ponderous twentieth-century tasks, several changes are proposed in congressional organization and procedure to enable a majority to act when it wishes. While conceding that the seniority principle is a convenient way of eliminating internal politics in the selection of committee chairmen, critics contend that there are feasible substitutes. One proposal, for example, would have the chairmen of all standing committees chosen at the beginning of each Congress by secret ballot of the committee members of the majority party. In most cases, Senator Clark predicts, the senior senator or representative would be chosen. The practice, however, would permit the defeat of a senior member bent on a course of recalcitrance. Senator Clark also calls for a curbing of the arbitrary powers of committee chairmen by enacting by rule a "Committee Bill of Rights." The rule would prescribe the practice already followed in some committees, enabling a majority of committee members to convene meetings, fix the agenda, call up bills for consideration, regulate the conduct of hearings, and terminate debate within committee after a reasonable time.

Critics look for help from the extensive reapportionment of state legislatures initiated by Supreme Court decisions. Congressional apportionment presumably would also be improved. A likely effect would be the conversion of the "safe" one-party congressional district, bastion of the Establishment's power, into a competitive party district. Party competition prompts congressional candidates to focus more on national, and therefore presidential, issues.

Although the long history of Congress presents only a brief and minor chapter of self-reform on a large scale, notably the Legislative

Reorganization Act of 1946, favorable auguries are not to be over-looked. Legislative majorities have from time to time rebelled against minority tyranny. Woodrow Wilson's New Freedom program of social and economic reforms occurred by dint of such a revolt. "Uncle Joe" Cannon had his wings clipped. The trend suggested by the elections of 1960 and 1962 suggests that the Establishment is markedly weaker than in 1958, and with the increasing migration from farm to city and growing party competition in congressional elections, the trend against it will continue.

A reformed and re-energized Congress would have many uses. It would be better able not only to support the executive but also to check it, to question it, to counsel it, and to redirect it. Hopefully, Congress would play its part in the dialogue, and often dialectical relationship, with the executive more positively than it has in the past.

CHAPTER THREE

The President

The presidency can be viewed as America's foremost political invention—one sometimes copied by newer nations but not always successfully. When the Founding Fathers created the office, they had no precise model to follow. The several experiences with executive power in the preconstitutional period were, on the whole, repugnant. The earliest American political executive, the colonial governor, came to be widely regarded as the enemy of liberty; the reigning British monarch, George III, symbolized tyranny. The Articles of Confederation, reflecting the general aversion to executive authority, made no provision for a separate executive officer nor even for any substantial executive power. The states, reflecting this same mood, provided in their constitutions for only a weak executive; his term was short, he was ineligible for re-election, and he shared important powers with the legislature. New York and Massachusetts, which established strong governors, were exceptions.

The common irresponsibility of state legislatures in the post-revolutionary period and the ineffectiveness of existing government—both under the Confederation and in the states—in maintaining public order prompted the Founding Fathers to create a strong executive. In their act of invention, they borrowed from the strong governorship in New York and, to lesser degree, in Massachusetts. The Fathers also reflected the doctrines of John Locke, Montesquieu, and Sir William Blackstone concerning separation of powers, by creating the executive, the legislature, and the judiciary as individual and self-sustaining branches. Divided governmental power was viewed as a bulwark against tyranny. The Fathers also heeded Montesquieu's counsel of interaction by enabling each branch to exert "checks and balances" against the others, permitting a kind of equilibrium that assured that power would be used with moderation. Illustrative of the principle of checks and balances is the fact that the laws Congress makes are subject both to the President's veto and to judicial review. The President, in turn, is subject to congressional overriding of his veto, to impeachment, to Senate approval of his treaties and appointments, and to judicial review.

Despite a certain dependence upon Congress and the judiciary, the presidency emerged from the Constitutional Convention with strong powers. The executive power was vested in the President; he was made commander in chief of the armed forces, and he was given power to appoint and to make treaties—although he shared these latter functions with the Senate. He was empowered to receive ambassadors and ministers and to grant reprieves and pardons, and he was directed to "take care that the laws be faithfully executed. . . ." He could recommend legislation to Congress, and he could veto it; he could call either or both houses into special session, and he could adjourn them if they disagreed over the time of such a step. The Fathers were encouraged to vest generous power in the chief executive by the confident expectation that the venerated George Washington would become the first President and would serve as long as his strength permitted.

But the Founding Fathers also created a strong Congress. In a sense, the subsequent historical experience can be viewed as a struggle between the two branches for dominance over policy. The pendulum swung first toward one branch, then toward the other. The eras of Washington, Jefferson, Jackson, Lincoln, Theodore Roosevelt, Wilson, and Franklin Roosevelt were periods of clear presidential ascendancy, when the President both used the powers granted him directly by the Constitution and exercised leadership in the enactment of legislation.

George Washington viewed his office as largely autonomous in foreign affairs.[1] On his own authority he accorded diplomatic recognition to republican France, issued a proclamation of neutrality in the Franco-British war, received and dismissed the French minister Edmond Genêt, negotiated Jay's Treaty with Britain, refused to lay diplomatic correspondence before the House of Representatives, and employed executive agents in diplomatic intercourse. Washington was a leader in legislation, powerfully aided by his skillful Secretary of the Treasury, Alexander Hamilton, whose reports on the public credit, manufacture, a bank of the United States, and other subjects provided the substance of legislation.

Presidents who have left a powerful imprint upon the office have added new dimensions or given unprecedented emphasis to its established parts.[2] Jefferson emerged as a powerful party leader who controlled legislation. Jackson thrived as party leader, and employed presidential prerogative in the nullification crisis arising from South Carolina's declaration that the tariff laws were unconstitutional and not binding. In his successful veto of legislation to renew the charter of the second Bank of the United States, Jackson utilized the presidency as a popular office against a powerful private economic organization. During the Civil War, Lincoln produced the novel doctrine of presidential "war power," a conjunction of the commander-in-chief and faithful-execution clauses which claimed unlimited executive authority to conduct the war. Theodore Roosevelt took initiatives that brought the nation to the forefront of world affairs. Wilson extended the nation's involvements as a world war-leader and world peacemaker. Wilson and the Roosevelts pioneered in their use of the presidency as a vehicle of social and economic reform. The second Roosevelt, facing the Great Depression, established in his New Deal an unprecedented series of economic and social policies, of which the Tennessee Valley Authority, the Social Security system, and the regulation of securities and the stock exchanges are representative. His successors, from Truman to Johnson, have all launched important policy initiatives in foreign and military affairs and in grappling with sensitive and complex problems of the economy and of social justice.

Despite the presidency's growth and importance, the nation has also witnessed substantial intervals of congressional assertiveness. The periods between Jefferson and Jackson, between Jackson and Lincoln, between Lincoln and Theodore Roosevelt, between Roosevelt and Wilson, and between Wilson and Franklin Roosevelt were periods of congressional ascendancy. Since Franklin Roosevelt's time, the presidency has declined in its relative position of power and now shares dominion with Congress over policy. Truman, for example, successfully undertook policy initiatives with the Marshall Plan, NATO, Point Four, and aid to Greece and Turkey, but he suffered reversals on civil rights, housing, medical care, and a dozen other key domestic proposals.

Despite the fluctuations of its fortunes, the presidency is the most powerful and prestigious office in the American polity. In times of crisis, American society automatically turns to the President for policy initiatives and solutions. The presidency is beheld by American society as its first line of defense against external enemies, internal disorder, economic malaise, and social injustice.

Because of its colonial and revolutionary experiences, however, the American polity has also nourished a hardy distrust of executive power. To the American Whig of the 1840's, the Liberty Leaguer of the 1930's, and the Goldwater conservative of the 1960's, the presidency is an office of excessive power that verges on—if it does not already exercise—tyranny. Those who abhor government as an organ of economic regulation and as a provider of social services revile the President as the prime mover of the "welfare state," the champion of the ill-deserving masses, and the enemy of hard-working, propertied, self-respecting citizens.

The presidency enjoys a lofty place in American culture. The office has provided the nation with many of its principal folk heroes, all the more striking in a society that stresses private success. In popular myth, if not altogether in fact, the presidency has remained an egalitarian office, within the legitimate grasp of every American youth, regardless of the circumstances of his birth. One's beginnings in a log cabin or on the farm are considered a boon rather than a bar to the office. A presidency may both set and reflect the tone of society. The whiskey scandals of the Grant administration and the Teapot Dome Scandal in Harding's time reflected general ethical letdowns in those eras. President Kennedy's attention to the arts was an innovative act that rejected society's tendency to subordinate such pursuits to materialistic activity and gain.

THE MAN AND THE OFFICE

The presidency is a composite of the man, the prevailing circumstances, and the institution. The man in actuality is rather different from his place in the folklore. Despite the legendary career "from log cabin to White House," only a few Presidents have emerged from the very poor. Most Presidents derive from the upper-middle class; a few, like Washington, Franklin Roosevelt, and Kennedy, have been notably wealthy. Most Presidents have been college graduates, and a majority have had legal training. With few exceptions, Presidents bring to the office prior political experience; indeed most, by far, can be characterized as professional politicians. None has been the open and professed representative of a major special interest, such as business or labor. All Presidents have been Protestant with the exception of Kennedy, a Roman Catholic.

Presidents usually come from large or pivotal states. Of the thirty-six presidential candidates offered by the major parties from 1868 to 1964, twenty-one hailed from one of three states: New York,

Ohio, or Illinois. "Safe" and small states fare badly in presidential selection, and Lyndon Johnson is the first Southerner to hold the presidency since Zachary Taylor's election in 1848.

"What the Presidency is at any particular moment," Edward Corwin has written, "depends in important measure on who is President."[3] Any presidency is stamped primarily with the personality of its incumbent—particularly with his "style," his articulateness, gestures, and values. The office affords him unlimited power to make proposals for action, and he is under formidable influences and pressures to use this power. He is elected by and responsive to a national constituency embracing the great interest groups of labor, agriculture, and business, which are skilled and experienced at stirring up governmental action responsive to their needs. He, far better than anyone else, can capture the nation's attention—and advocate policies—through the communications media. He is in command of the executive branch, with its unrivaled financial resources and specialized manpower. The play of the President's personality is enhanced by the fact that his power to command is limited. Typically, he has only the power to persuade, to seek consensus among economic, nationality, and racial groups and among competing sections of the country. He can command few of the groups he deals with—Congress, pressure groups, the general public, and foreign nations. Even most of those who theoretically are subject to his command—executive agencies and even the military services—are usually managed most effectively if they, too, are persuaded. "The principal power that the President has," Truman once observed, "is to bring people in and try to persuade them to do what they ought to do without persuasion. That's what I spent my time doing. That's what the powers of the President amount to."[4]

The presidency is also an institution. Beyond the man—the transitory incumbent—is the office, the institution: its legal resources, practices, precedents, and protocol; the staff and bureaucratic skills, physical plant and financial resources made available to it; and the place of the office in society and in the culture. The institution serves both to keep the man responsible and to help him. Practice and precedent add authority to the office and serve to convert the achievements and advances of a "strong" President into an enduring legacy for his less gifted successors.

Like any institution, the presidency undergoes growth and change. The electoral college, after brief importance, became perfunctory, its members serving as the automata of their parties in selecting the President. Since the 1930's, a substantial presidential staff has arisen. The White House Staff and the Budget Bureau have expanded, an Executive Office of the President has been created, and among the agencies it encompasses are the National Security Council, the Council of Economic Advisers, and the Office of Emergency Planning. Some 1200 persons comprise these agencies—a sizeable presidential bureaucracy. In addition to providing policy-making aides to the chief executive, the institutionalized presidency, in its growth, has increased the number of more or less stated occasions on which the President is expected to come forward with proposals of program and policy. The principal of these are the budget and its accompanying message and the economic report, which, with the State of the Union message, constitute a trinity of messages presented each January to Congress and incorporate a comprehensive statement of the President's judgment of the nation's needs for new legislation. He also issues messages on more specific problems.

Presidential policy has several foci. It is invoked by the discovery or the rise of a problem or by the escalation of a problem into a crisis. A common thread of difficulty, complexity, or urgency seems to run through presidential policy-making. "There are no easy matters that will come to you as President," Eisenhower counseled the incoming President Kennedy. "If they are easy, they will be settled at a lower level."[5]

The President promulgates policies in a variety of forms and forums. Favorite vehicles for high policy are his messages and speeches. Monroe set forth major elements of the famous doctrine bearing his name in a message to Congress. Truman's important Point Four program was first broached in his 1949 inaugural address. A President's more formal legal acts or policies are incorporated in executive orders and proclamations. Washington's proclamation of neutrality, in addition to stating policy on the subject, set forth the duty of the citizen to obey and provided the basis of legal penalties. The President can also make policy by less formal means: in conversations, telephone calls, interoffice memoranda, and letters. Kennedy's settlement of the 1962 Cuban missile crisis with Krushchev emerged from an exchange of cabled messages.

The President enjoys greater flexibility in framing and promulgating policy than do the legislature and the judiciary. Congress is limited by the form of the statute and resolution, and the courts are limited even more by the set procedure and format of cases and rulings. The President, relative to the other branches, has maximum freedom of choice in deciding when, whether, and how to act.

SELECTING THE PRESIDENT

The President who is finally selected through a convoluted process of many phases is himself a "policy personality," a bundle of attitudes and prejudices on public questions obtained from upbringing, schooling, private career, previous associations, political indebtedness and the present pressures that weigh upon him.[6]

The person selected stands upon an elaborate foundation of support that is distributed across the nation. Since the presidency, with the vice-presidency, is our only national elective office, the candidate who seriously aspires to it must cast his appeal wide and demonstrate a concern for the problems and interests of a broad swath of society. Thomas Jefferson, the first master-politician to win the presidency, took over Patrick Henry's old Antifederalist followers in Virginia and reached out to southern small farmers and planters resentful of Alexander Hamilton's financial program. Jefferson also appealed to frontier settlers of Ohio, Tennessee, Kentucky, and western New York, who harbored similar feelings, to the farmer suspicious of his British creditor, and to the urban mechanic and laborer in North and South.

As this sampling of Jefferson's support suggests, the presidential aspirant may progress from a firm base of local strength to recognition as a spokesman of the interests and ideals of a section; then, by building interpersonal, group, and sectional understanding, he may emerge with truly national support. Eisenhower, on the other hand, represents the reverse of this process; he began with national recognition, which led to local support across the nation.

The selection of the President advances through a series of stages that include the preconvention period, the convention, the postconvention campaign, and the actual election. In all but the last stage, diverse pressures play upon the presidential aspirant; some encourage or almost force him to take stands on policy issues, while others prompt him to evade them.

In the preconvention period, the aspirant may be encouraged toward explicitness on issues by clear and solid public discontent. But the presidential aspirant whose likely support includes groups and sections with conflicting policy aims may choose to avoid or straddle policy questions. Andrew Jackson, his eye fixed on the presidency in the approaching election of 1828, had a large but scattered following whose views on issues clashed. Inland farmers who supported him wanted better transportation facilities at federal expense, while his supporters in New York—a state relatively rich in transportation—preferred no such federal action. Pennsylvania manufacturers looked confidently to him for a rising tariff, while southern cotton planters, another legion of his supporters, stoutly opposed that course. In the dilemma of pressing issues and divided supporters, Jackson chose to maintain a discreet silence, a decision facilitated by his resignation from the United States Senate and his withdrawal to his Tennessee home, the Hermitage. Meanwhile, his supporters in Congress disposed of the day's questions by voting the sentiment of their states and districts.

As he comes closer to serious contention for the nomination, an aspirant may feel compelled to engage in the difficult art of reversing policy positions he has previously taken. Franklin Roosevelt, facing a hard fight for the Democratic nomination in 1932 (a fight made all the more difficult by the rule then in force that the vote of two thirds of the delegates was necessary for the nomination), was gravely embarrassed by his earlier views on the League of Nations. In 1920, as Democratic candidate for the vice-presidency, Roosevelt had strongly advocated United States membership in the League. In 1932, when his presidential nomination was not assured until after a long struggle at the convention, Roosevelt faced a grievous dilemma on the League. If he opposed it, he would offend the "Wilsonians," a group of devoted associates of the late Democratic President. If he supported the League, he invited the wrath of William Randolph Hearst, the isolationist newspaper czar, who was already attacking Roosevelt for his earlier pro-League position. Hearst was important not only for his nation-wide newspaper chain; he was also the dominant figure in California politics, and the California delegation was a decisive factor in the convention's outcome. Roosevelt concluded that it would be politically more advantageous to avoid offending Hearst than to avoid offending the Wilsonians, for he could anticipate a residue of good will among the Wilsonians that might survive a momentary policy rebuff. He therefore issued a statement opposing membership in the League, holding that the League of 1932 was altogether different from the League of 1920. Hearst stopped his attacks; the Wilsonians were stricken with doubts, which Roosevelt sought to allay in soothing private talks with key members of the group. The ultimate support of California and Texas won Roosevelt the nomination. Hearst and his California spokesmen eventually accepted Roosevelt for fear that "someone worse," possibly a dark horse like Newton Baker, might capture the nomination. Texas came over to Roosevelt when Speaker John Nance Garner of that state (whom Hearst had been championing), becoming anxious that an ugly convention deadlock might damage public confidence and cost the Democrats the election, released his delegates. Garner was then nominated for the vice-presidency.

What the candidate really stands for may be well known or little known—even to himself—at convention time. Choosing the nominee is often a kind of blank-check policy decision whose specifics are to be filled in by the concrete situations, problems, and issues of his administration, if he is elected. Of the several types of backgrounds from which presidential nominees commonly emerge, some are more likely than others to provide revelations of their policy preferences. A favorite presidential nominee of both major parties is the military hero: of the thirty men who have been elected President, twelve have been military veterans. The military life, as the prepresidential careers of Generals William Henry Harrison and Zachary Taylor demonstrate, provides an admirable protective shield against the pressures necessitating a stand on public questions. Another frequent source of presidential recruitment, civilian public offices—especially United States senators and state governors—provide in their everyday affairs the necessity for decisions upon policy. But even here the available evidence may be an imperfect guide. Lyndon Johnson as senator opposed the poll tax amendment, designed to abolish a tax upon voting that had long served to disenfranchise many Negroes. As presidential candidate, however, Johnson urged vigorous enforcement of civil rights laws on all fronts, and as President he championed far-reaching civil rights legislation.

The vice-presidential nomination may be affected only obliquely by the man's policy questions. The usual basis of selection is the ideal of the geographically balanced ticket. The Democratic party is traditionally devoted to a North-South alignment, while the Republicans join East and West. Not uncommonly, the presidential nomination may be settled by a "deal" over the vice-presidency; for example, Franklin Roosevelt's nomination in 1932 was clinched by the agreement to make John Nance Garner of Texas the vice-presidential candidate, a concession that brought the big Texas and pro-Garner California delegations over to Roosevelt's support. The "deal," as it turned out, had important policy implications. Although Garner as Vice-President at first supported the New Deal program, he became distressed by its strongly liberal tendencies and engaged in both covert and overt opposition to it, with substantial impact.

The national party convention's most explicit encounter with policy occurs in platform-making. The platform draftsman, to be sure, is subject to pressures and indulges in techniques to avoid a definite stand on policy issues. Platforms are given to "straddling" issues, to a vocabulary of "weasel" words, and to exceedingly general positions that appeal to a great swath of interest groups whose individual objectives may be antagonistic. The first Republican platform, in 1856, was a mixture of basic principles and shrewdly constructed planks to broaden the appeal of the essentially sectional party. In accord with the antislavery principles on which it was founded, the party made "Bleeding Kansas," where the pro and antislavery forces were locked in bitter struggle, its number-one issue. To pick up support outside its northwestern sectional base, the platform called for a Pacific railroad (pleasing to California) and a large-scale program of rivers and harbors improvement (pleasing to all sections). When it finally emerges from the disparate pressures and influences, the platform may be a tissue of contradictions. The Republicans in their 1964 platform, for example, called for a $5-billion budget reduction while advocating a markedly more aggressive foreign policy—one of the surest conceivable ways to increase government expenditures.

In the postconvention campaign, the presidential nominee may assume positions on certain policy questions as part of a basic strategy to win over substantial sectors of the electorate. In 1960, Kennedy's campaign strategy focused upon nine large industrial states—New York, California, Pennsylvania, Ohio, Illinois, Michigan, Texas, Massachusetts, and New Jersey—casting 237 of the 269 electoral votes required to elect a President. In his campaign speeches, Kennedy stressed policies and programs aimed at the needs and interests of the urban voter—a civil rights law, federal medical care for the aged under the Social Security system, full employment, large-scale aid to public school education, expanded urban renewal, and the like. The pattern of his subsequent electoral victory matched the pattern of his campaign.

The apparatus of the election itself—the popular vote and the subsequent electoral college vote—influences the selection of presidential nominees and their approaches to policy issues. Under prescribed constitutional procedure, an electoral college is established in each state. The number of electors and electoral votes a state has equals the total number of its representatives and senators. With rare exception, electors cast their votes according to the "general-ticket" principle: the presidential nominee who captures at least a plurality of the popular votes of a state receives all of its electoral votes. In effect, the general-ticket system, a "winner-take-all" method, grossly favors the large states by permitting them to keep their large bloc of electoral votes intact and hand them over in their entirety to a single presidential candidate. (Proposals to change the present system would apportion a state's electoral votes between the winning and losing presidential candidates.) The electoral-vote/general-ticket system prods the parties into seeking out their presidential candidates from large states like New York, California, and Ohio and concentrating their campaign efforts on such states, while neglecting other states that are smaller or "safe." The general-ticket system also magnifies the pressures and bargaining power of interest groups and minority parties in large, doubtful states. Effectively organized nationality, racial, religious, and economic groups, which are capable of concentrating their votes upon a presidential candidate, can more insistently extract his commitment to their policy aspirations when they are located, as they tend to be, in the large industrial states.

POLICY-MAKING ROLES

The President plays a variety of policy-making roles, some of which are explicitly provided for in the Constitution and others of which are incontrovertibly implied.[7] The Constitution designates the President as commander in chief of the armed forces; it also gives him the power to be director of foreign policy, legislative leader, and administrative chief. Although the framers of the Constitution did not anticipate the advent of political parties, the chief executive they provided for soon became, in the person of Thomas Jefferson, the leader of his party. Even later, the President became a popular leader who rallied the public behind his program. Although Washington was mindful of, and to a degree cultivated, his popularity, Andrew Jackson became the first tribune of the people. The increasing complexity of the economy and the awakening of social conscience have thrust upon the twentieth-century President, particularly at mid-century, two roles that were exercised only sporadically by his nineteenth-century predecessors: he is the chief administrator of the economy, responsible more than anyone else for its health and productivity; he is also a source of social justice for individuals and groups whose rights and interests are trampled on or withheld by society and who look to him for surcease, since they fare less well in Congress, which tends to have a more conservative orientation than does the President.

In the course of a typical day's work, the President's roles are by no means neatly compartmentalized but tend to blur; seldom does he concentrate upon one role to the exclusion of all others. Yet they differ according to the priority he gives them, and they therefore compete for his attention. In June 1963, the civils rights situation, to which President Kennedy accorded an uppermost priority, had become critical to the point where Negro civil rights leaders were urging him to abandon a projected trip to Western Europe. But the President, anxious to strengthen the Western alliance, chose to make his trip, and civil rights, for a time at least, descended on the priority list.

DIRECTOR OF FOREIGN POLICY

The Constitution goes far toward making the President a chief diplomat. Several Presidents have candidly expressed satisfaction with their foreign-affairs powers. Thomas Jefferson termed the conduct of foreign affairs "executive altogether," and Harry Truman once flatly asserted, "I make foreign policy." Although Congress, mindful of its powers in a constitutional system of separation of powers and checks and balances, would disagree, both Presidents boasted of significant accomplishments in foreign affairs in their respective administrations —Jefferson the Louisiana Purchase and the Embargo, and Truman the "Truman Doctrine," the European Recovery Program, the North Atlantic Treaty, and the Point Four Program.

In actuality, many of the President's foreign-affairs powers are shared with Congress, particularly the Senate. The President makes treaties, with the advice and consent of the Senate, "provided two thirds of the Senators present concur." The Senate can reject a treaty outright or impose conditions or reservations which may or may not be acceptable to the President. When the test-ban treaty was under Senate review, President Kennedy dispatched a letter to the chamber carrying "unqualified and unequivocal assurances" that the treaty would not deter him from maintaining a vigorous weapons program. Kennedy gave other assurances, including one that the treaty would never be altered by executive action but only by treaty procedure. The President's pledge headed off threatened Senate reservations.

The President may shun the treaty procedure and resort to executive agreements, which entail no Senate review. The President can make executive agreements with other nations by exercising his independent authority or "prerogative," such as his power as commander in chief and as possessor, under the Constitution, of the executive power. Statutes and treaties also may authorize executive agreements. President Roosevelt's exchange of United States destroyers for British bases in World War II was an executive agreement based upon the commander-in-chief power, the executive-power clause, and a statute authorizing the transfer of "obsolescent" military material.

The President, according to the Constitution, nominates, and, with the Senate's advice and consent, appoints ambassadors and ministers. The Constitution empowers the President to receive the diplomatic representatives of other nations; this power enables him to recognize new governments. By implication, he can demand the recall of foreign diplomats, as Washington did Citizen Genêt, the representative of revolutionary France. Although the Constitution empowers Congress to declare war, presidential war-making is a longstanding adjunct of foreign policy, embracing Jefferson's dispatching of naval frigates to tame the Tripolitan pirates of Kennedy's 1962 imposition of a naval blockade around Cuba. But presidential war-making, as the Korean conflict demonstrates, can be hazardous politically. In time, the American people tired of the Korean venture; in the 1952 elections they rejected the continuation of a Democratic presidential administration. The victor, Dwight D. Eisenhower, when faced in his subsequent administration with crises in Formosa and the Middle East that might assume the proportions of the Korean conflict, moved to couple Congress in his policy determinations concerning those troubled areas and thereby hoped to share with the legislative branch any subsequent political liabilities that might materialize. The resolutions that Congress passed authorized the President to use the armed forces "as he deems necessary for the specific purpose of securing and protecting Formosa and the Pescadores against armed attack." Congress passed a comparable resolution for the Middle East.

For the President, playing an effective role in foreign policy depends not little upon his ability to induce foreign leaders—whether friend, foe, or neutral—to accept his policies. The President is the formulator and negotiator of major foreign-policy objectives: to keep other nations out of the Communist orbit, to build a structure of nuclear interdependence among our allies, and to persist in negotiations with the Communist world as a preferable alternative to armed conflict. President Kennedy's foreign visitors in his first year could be counted by the score. He also corresponded with a wide circle of foreign leaders on major problems. The summit conference, at which the President confers with allied or Communist leaders, or both, has become a standard presidential experience: Roosevelt at Yalta, Truman at Potsdam, Eisenhower at Geneva, Kennedy at Vienna.

Since World War II, the President has had to superintend a series of alliances encircling the globe, from NATO in the west to SEATO in the east. The President is often the chief sponsor and promoter of major shifts in alliance policy. Truman pushed West Germany's rearmament and inclusion in the NATO system. Kennedy and Johnson championed a NATO missile fleet manned by crews of various nationalities.

The President's policy concerns with affairs of an ally may reach the point where he moves to effect change in its government. President Kennedy in 1963 was faced with a badly deteriorating war in South Vietnam and the threat which that situation posed to his own domestic political welfare in the United States. To halt the trend of events in South Vietnam, Kennedy sought to encourage the removal of Ngo Dinh Nhu, whose influence over his brother-in-law, President Ngo Dinh Diem, appeared related to South Vietnam's faltering military performance. In a public statement, Kennedy attributed South Vietnam's failings to its government's loss of touch with the people and suggested the desirability of "changes in policy and perhaps with personnel." President Diem's regime was subsequently overthrown, he and his brother-in-law were murdered, and the "changes" of "personnel" proceeded.

COMMANDER IN CHIEF

The President's constitutional power and responsibility as commander in chief thrust him into a variety of major policy-making capacities. He may be the principal architect of military campaigns. Lincoln, for example, selected points of attack in the Civil War, and Franklin Roosevelt conceived the North African invasion and chose its landing points in World War II. The nuclear age has securely established the President as the nation's principal field commander. He alone under law decides when to use nuclear weapons. The dread possibility of nuclear conflict has thrust upon him the making of many decisions that in a simpler military age fell upon local commanders. Thus Kennedy in the 1962 Cuban crisis, after the imposition of a blockade, was kept apprised of the whereabouts of approaching Communist vessels and personally gave the order to board them.

As commander in chief, the President can also terminate hostilities by arranging an armistice and entering into agreements with the nation's allies to set the framework of the postwar order. Woodrow Wilson thus incorporated his Fourteen Points into the armistice for World War I. Franklin Roosevelt arranged through his personal efforts and those of his field commanders the demarcation of occupation zones, including those for Berlin—which in actuality established areas of continuing hegemony for the Communist and allied powers after World War II.

As commander in chief, the President appoints and removes field commanders. Such acts may be fraught with policy consequences. President Truman dramatically removed General Douglas MacArthur from his command in the Korean War. In a series of public statements, MacArthur had attacked the established administration policy of restricted war and urged instead broadened military action against Red China, including a blockade, air bombardment, and, ultimately, invasion. The General also advocated the use of Chinese Nationalist forces, which the administration was determined to avoid. At stake in these policy differences were the authority of the President and civil supremacy over the military in policy-making. "In view of the specific responsibilities imposed upon me by the Constitution of the United States and the added responsibility to the United Nations," Truman said in announcing MacArthur's removal, "I have decided that I must make a change of command in the Far East. . . . It is fundamental . . . that military commanders must be governed by the policies and directives issued to them in the manner provided by our laws and the Constitution."[8]

As commander in chief, the President may make policy of the utmost consequence for domestic society—for individual freedom, for the functioning of our governmental processes, and for property rights. The most drastic of these assertions occurred in the Civil War, particularly in the war's first weeks, when Congress was not in session. Lincoln, acting as commander in chief, and solely on his own authority, added twenty-three thousand men to the Regular Army and eighteen thousand to the Navy; called forty thousand volunteers for three years' service; summoned the state militias into a ninety-day volunteer force; paid $2 million from the Treasury's unappropriated funds for purposes unauthorized by Congress; closed the Post Office to "treasonable correspondence"; imposed a blockade on southern ports; suspended the writ of habeas corpus in certain parts of the country; and caused the arrest and military detention of persons engaging in or contemplating "treasonable practices."

In World War II, under the commander in chief's authority,

some 112,000 persons of Japanese ancestry—of whom 70,000 were United States citizens—were removed from the West Coast to "relocation centers" in the interior. The commander in chief also may seize property. Six months before Pearl Harbor, President Roosevelt, while the nation was still officially at peace, seized the strike-bound North American Aviation plant at Inglewood, California. Roosevelt based his seizure upon the "duty constitutionally and inherently resting upon the President to exert his civil and military as well as his moral authority to keep the defensive efforts of the United States a going concern" and "to obtain supplies for which Congress has appropriated money, and which it has directed the President to obtain." Other seizures, both before and during our belligerent status, followed. In the Korean conflict, however, President Truman's seizure of most of the nation's steel mills was declared unconstitutional by the Supreme Court.[9]

Labor, too, has felt the force of the commander in chief power. President Roosevelt in World War II created a War Manpower Commission, with responsibilities for both the Selective Service System and the manpower needs of war-production industries. The WMC quickly adopted a "work or fight" policy, which forced all workers engaged in "non-essential" enterprise to choose between induction into the armed forces and transfer to war-production jobs.

REGULATOR OF THE ECONOMY

In peace as well as in war, the President is head of the economic administration of the country. He administers numerous laws promoting, regulating, and planning economic affairs. The Employment Act of 1946, a kind of codification of his responsibilities, bids him to lay before Congress each January an economic report on levels and trends of production, employment, and purchasing power and to recommend policies to stimulate them. As the defeats of Martin Van Buren and Herbert Hoover for re-election in periods of economic distress testify, the nation's economic well-being is vital to the President's political well-being.

Presidents from both parties normally aspire to build business confidence. The Kennedy administration in 1962 concentrated on balancing the budget and securing passage of the Foreign Trade Expansion Act. The administration's top economic priority for 1963 was the reduction of corporate and personal income taxes—all with a view to stimulating general economic activity.

The contemporary President is also preoccupied with containing inflation by inducing industry to hold the line on prices and labor on wages. In 1962, Kennedy succeeded in bringing the steel union to hold its demands at minimum levels, which, according to calculations by administration economists, would not have necessitated a price rise. When United States Steel and other major companies nevertheless proceeded to raise their prices, the President and his aides brought a variety of pressures to bear on them. In a nationally televised news conference, the President questioned the patriotism of the "tiny handful of steel executives—whose pursuit of power and profit exceed their sense of public responsibility." The Justice Department and the Federal Trade Commission scrutinized the price action for possible violation of the antitrust laws. Key administration officials made telephone calls to contacts in steel companies that had not raised prices, gently suggesting the wisdom of continuing such a course. Major military purchases were shifted from the price-raising companies to the abstainers. The offending companies soon rescinded the price increases. Nearly a year later, however, steel companies again raised prices, this time without administration opposition.[10]

Modern Democratic and Republican Presidents tend to respond differently to labor. The contrast is strikingly apparent in presidential actions on labor legislation. The Republican Eisenhower twice vetoed legislation providing federal aid to depressed areas with severe unemployment. When the AFL-CIO proposed amendments to the Fair Labor Standards Act, raising the minimum wage from $1.00 to $1.25 an hour, Eisenhower recommended an increase of only ten to fifteen cents an hour. The Democratic Kennedy pushed through legislation for depressed areas, which Eisenhower had vetoed, and the $1.25 minimum wage, which Eisenhower had resisted.

PROTECTOR OF CIVIL RIGHTS

The modern President is also a dispenser of social justice. Nineteenth-century Presidents were sporadic in their attentions to individuals and minorities who suffered at the hands of superior and arbitrary social and economic power; the actions of their twentieth-century counterparts, however, are more numerous and more forceful. One issue of social justice that no President since World War II has been able to escape is that of Negro civil rights. A prime mover of the issue was Roosevelt, who, in his New Deal policies, was attentive to the plight and needs of the Negro. The National Recovery Act of his administration tended to set a common wage standard for Negro and white wage earners in the South. Relief funds, housing projects, and federal education grants were similarly equitable. Roosevelt's successor, Truman, sought (but failed) to perpetuate the Fair Employment Practices Commission established in World War II. Truman also created a Commission on Civil Rights, whose report, *To Secure These Rights*, was a blueprint for future action. Negro civil rights first assumed crisis proportions for the presidency in the national repercussions of the Little Rock school episode of the Eisenhower era. The Civil Rights Acts of 1957 and 1960, during the Eisenhower administration, were the first laws passed on the subject since the immediate post-Civil War era. Kennedy, faced with growing street demonstrations in 1963, became the first President to place himself at the head of the Negro civil rights movement.

Kennedy asserted his civil rights policies principally through executive action rather than through legislation. The executive tools Kennedy and his aides relied upon were numerous and were wielded with diligence and enterprise. The Justice Department stepped up litigation to bolster Negro rights especially in the fields of voting and education. On occasions of violence or threatened violence—notably, the admission of James Meredith to the University of Mississippi and the Birmingham riots in mid-summer 1963—Kennedy resorted to what amounted to a presidential constabulary, consisting of the Regular Army, the federalized National Guard, and United States marshals.

Presidents have employed the government contract, with its anti-discrimination provisos, to advance Negro civil rights. Franklin Roosevelt first implanted the provisos into government contracts in World War II. As chief administrator of the executive branch, President Kennedy put new emphasis upon the appointment and advancement of qualified Negroes. Administrative regulation can advance civil rights: the Kennedy administration, for example, successfully pressed the Interstate Commerce Commission to desegregate facilities in terminals serving interstate bus travel. Federal funds are a weapon in the civil rights struggle and are susceptible to the kind of regulation Kennedy imposed in 1962, barring dicrimination in the sale or rental of housing financed through federal assistance. Kennedy employed public appeals, in the form of television and radio addresses to the nation, stressing the moral aspects of civil rights and local responsibilities. Private persuasion was another tactic, involving meetings of Kennedy and his aides with delegations of southern businessmen, theater owners, newspaper editors, and Negro civil rights leaders.

In 1964, a new civil rights law was adopted, incorporating many activities that the President had previously endeavored to promote on his own authority. The new law guaranteed Negroes access to public accommodations and empowered the federal government to file suit to desegregate schools, among other things. But the hard limits of federal authority became starkly apparent in 1965, particularly in events centering upon civil rights marches in Selma and Montgomery, Alabama. Marchers were beaten, and one died from the assault. Local law enforcement authorities bludgeoned and gassed them. Governor George C. Wallace of Alabama informed President Johnson that his state was too poor "to bear the burden" of calling out the Alabama National Guard to protect the demonstrators. The events revealed all too starkly the limited effectiveness of national authority in dealing with recalcitrant state and local governments under the federal system. The rapid, divisive currents of civil rights events will doubtless uncover other weaknesses in our governmental system. The several civil rights questions constitute some of the most difficult and challenging problems ever confronted by democratic leadership.

LEADER OF PUBLIC OPINION

To advance his policies, the President must favorably influence public opinion. Woodrow Wilson measured the unique power of the President's position when he wrote, "His is the only national voice in affairs. Let him once win the admiration and confidence of the country, and no other single force can withstand him, no combination of forces will easily overpower him. His position takes the imagination of the country. He is the representative of no constituency, but the whole people."[11]

Public opinion is a two-edged sword, however; it is both a source of power and a mighty restraint upon the President. In 1947, for example, the huge Soviet army was massed and apparently poised to overrun Western Europe. President Truman and his administration induced the country to accept the Marshall Plan and a new North Atlantic alliance as a response to the situation. These programs permitted Western Europe to build up its military and economic strength, and the Communist threat subsided. But public opinion may also force the President to pursue policies which he believes are inimical to the country's interests. Public opinion forced the President to order sweeping demobilization of our armed forces soon after World War II, thereby encouraging the expansionist tendencies of the Soviet Union. Although the President and his informed advisers well knew the folly of so swift and extensive a withdrawal, they bowed to public opinion.

A contemporary President also has many foreign publics, to which his word and image are brought by the international communications media. American periodicals with foreign editions, the inexpensive transistor radio, and the Telstar satellite that provides access to a world-wide television audience all are at the President's service.

At home, whatever he says or does is news; the front page and the television screen are always within his reach. In asserting their views, Presidents utilize the news conference; the Eisenhower administration first permitted the conferences to be televised, and the Kennedy administration first released the news conference proceedings unedited. Kennedy's responses to reporters' questions revealed his exceptional command of detail and his talent for involvement in policy development from incubation to implementation. Kennedy's brisk assurance and sense of newsworthy material lent zest to his administration. His meetings with some three hundred newsmen in the huge State Department auditorium were not to the liking of his successor, Lyndon Johnson, who fares better with small groups than large and in conversation rather than declamation. In seeking a suitable forum, Johnson has held news conferences in his White House office, in the East Room, and at the LBJ Ranch, among other places. Not all of Johnson's news conferences are televised.

To move his policies forward, the President acts as party leader, working through the party machinery and applying party pressures. Presidents whose administrations are marked by few policy accomplishments, like Tyler and John Quincy Adams, were ineffective as party leaders. Presidents like Wilson and Franklin Roosevelt, whose policy achievements were impressive, excelled in their party roles.

As party leader, the President presides over what at best is a highly uncertain enterprise. President Eisenhower, on the basis of full experience, concluded that "there are no national parties in the United States." The President at most is a chief among chiefs. The state and local party organizations are centers of jealously preserved autonomy and power. They command a formidable corps of workers and followers, maintain their own discipline, possess their own financial resources, and control the selection of senatorial and congressional candidates. The Senate and House of Representatives each has its own party organization. Senators and representatives direct their principal allegiance not to the President but to the state and local organizations to which they owe their nomination and election. A consequence of party pluralism is that legislators of the President's party may both help and thwart the policies he aims to establish through new legislation. The fact that an Eastland and a Humphrey stand under the Democratic banner and a Goldwater and a Case under the Republican one demonstrates how pliable the party label is and how uncertain the President's fortunes are when his party colleagues on Capitol Hill vote on policy questions.

As party leader, the President hand-picks the chairman of the national committee and runs the national party office as though it were his own organization. Notwithstanding these opportunities, the presidential nominee may view even the national party organization as an enterprise of uncertain dependability and conclude that it is wise to build a personal organization to wage his campaign. Kennedy in 1960 and Goldwater in 1964 were assisted by elaborate personal organizations.

In facing the midterm congressional election, the outcome of which is customarily interpreted as a measurement of public confidence in his administration, the President may find cooperation with the congressional and senatorial campaign committees of his party a matter of some difficulty. The difficulty was suggested in a 1958 public statement by then Republican Congressional Compaign Committee Chairman Richard M. Simpson of Pennsylvania. Republican candidates, Simpson declared, should attach no great stress to the President's favor in the 1958 elections, but, instead, should "make known" to the voters any "disagreement with the President's policies." Simpson, a conservative, frequently opposed the President's "Modern Republicanism."

As party leader, the President can apply several pressures to advance his policies and purposes. The oldest of these is patronage. A potent weapon in Lincoln's day, patronage has shrunk to a mere few thousand appointments, thanks to the rise of a civil service merit system. Patronage, or the handing out of jobs in the federal executive and judicial branches, enables the President to strike at the legislator in his home district, to attract or alienate local groups on whose support he depends. But even this weapon is subject to the powerful restraint of "senatorial courtesy," an unwritten rule requiring the President to confer with and secure the consent of the senator or senators of his party from a state before making a nomination to an office in that state. There is also pork barrel—the construction of a veterans' hospital, the letting of a defense contract, and the like— which may be allotted to a district whose congressman has been voting "right" from the President's standpoint. The President can likewise distribute his campaign support, whether in lending his personal endorsement or in embracing the congressman in his own district.

LEGISLATIVE LEADER

Almost any policy of any duration and importance requires money and laws and therefore depends upon the President's prowess as legislative leader. All Presidents who have had a major impact on public policy have thrived as legislative leaders. Andrew Jackson's war on the Bank of the United States was a successful legislative struggle. Theodore Roosevelt's Square Deal, Wilson's New Freedom, and Franklin Roosevelt's New Deal consisted primarily of numerous items of legislation.

In exerting legislative leadership, the President depends considerably upon his messages to Congress. The first of these, his State of the Union message rendered each January, is a presentation of the major outline of his legislative program for the ensuing session. His budget message, to which the executive budget is attached, is a detailed statement of policy objectives and the means for achieving them. The President also makes his economic report in January. In succeeding months, he sets forth his program in even more detail in special messages. Theodore Roosevelt began the practice, which Presidents since his day have often copied, of supplementing his messages with drafts of bills.

The President, in playing his legislative role, is endowed by the Constitution with the veto, which is virtually absolute; the two-thirds vote required in each house to override it is not easily mustered. The veto's grave defect is that it is total: the President, unlike some state governors, lacks the item veto, whereby he can reject particular parts of an appropriation bill and approve the rest; he must accept or reject a bill as a whole.

The President may advance his legislative purposes by various behind-the-scenes activities. He may confer personally with legislators to solicit their support or work out compromises in his effort to put together a legislative majority in support of his measures. Wilson conferred frequently with congressional leaders or sent his "political ambassador," Postmaster General Albert S. Burleson, in his place. He put in a heavy schedule of hours on Capitol Hill, occupying the President's Room there, to confer with legislators. Kennedy was the first President to meet systematically with every major committee. Lyndon Johnson's experience and talent as Senate leader have stood him well in the President's legislative role, particularly his skill at discovering and building consensus around politically feasible compromises. The President may sometimes choose to take his legislative program to the people, a venture which ranges from Franklin Roosevelt's successful "fireside chats" in the 1930's to Wilson's abortive effort to stir the American public into bringing the Senate to support the League of Nations.

ADMINISTRATIVE CHIEF

The President is also administrative chief of the executive branch, the biggest administrative enterprise in the free world. The more than three score departments, boards, agencies, and commissions reporting directly to him present an almost impossible task of supervision. "Even one hour a week devoted to each of them," the first Hoover Commission pointed out, "would require a sixty-five hour work-week for the President, to say nothing of the time he must devote to his duties in developing and directing major policies as his constitutional obligations require."[12]

The President's power to hire and fire is considerably less than that of the usual business executive. Most of his key appointments require the advice and consent of the Senate and are clamored for by factions of his party. The President shares his general personnel powers with Congress and, since passage of the Pendleton Act of

1883, with the Civil Service Commission. His power to make removals, a matter on which the Constitution is silent, is limited by the civil service laws and the courts. In *Myers* v. *United States*,[13] the Supreme Court, reviewing Wilson's removal of a postmaster, seemed to find the President's removal authority unlimited. In 1935, the Court sharply cut back this ruling in *Humphrey* v. *United States*.[14] Humphrey, a Federal Trade commissioner, was removed by President Roosevelt not for causes cited in statute but because of policy differences between the commissioner and the President. The Court, ruling in Humphrey's favor, held that Congress can protect officials such as a Federal Trade commissioner, who wield quasi-legislative or quasi-judicial power, against presidential removal. Even in respect to the departments. the President's removal power may be subject to imposing political limitations. Not all Presidents have been in accord with J. Edgar Hoover, chief of the Federal Bureau of Investigation, who has long possessed a widely favorable public image. A President seeking to remove Hoover would bring down upon himself a great public outcry.

The President delegates duties and authority and, by direction of the Budget and Accounting Act of 1921, develops an executive budget covering income and outgo. He coordinates the agencies, prodding them to work together and settling their quarrels. Almost continuously since the Reorganization Act of 1939, he has possessed limited power to reorganize executive agencies by reallocating functions and revising structures.

Presidents may seek to assert dominion over the executive branch by achieving, as much as possible, a personal impact upon the development of executive policies. Opposing their purpose may be the great bureaucracy and its devotion to routine, and the pressure groups which seek to gain their selfish purposes through the departments. Congressional committees and individual legislators may be more prone to push the departments in behalf of the pressure groups than in behalf of the President.

In his struggle to assert dominion, the President is aided by the White House Staff, the cabinet, and a cluster of agencies composing the Executive Office of the President. The White House Staff consists of a score of assistants such as the press secretary, the appointments secretary, the special counsel, and the special assistants for national security affairs and for science and technology. The staff are extensions of the President—his eyes, his ears, and his legs. They help prepare his messages, speeches, and correspondence; oversee his communications; analyze and refine problems coming before him; and advance his purposes with the executive departments, legislators, executive subordinates, and others.

The cabinet, founded by Washington early in his presidency,

has exercised an uneven role in policy development. Much of the Monroe Doctrine was hammered out in cabinet sessions, but Wilson, Franklin Roosevelt, and Kennedy used it little. Of the several remaining units of the Executive Office of the President, the National Security Council advises the chief executive on national security objectives and commitments and on the integration of national security policy. The Budget Bureau, in addition to its budget function, coordinates proposed legislation for the President and promotes management improvement in the executive branch. The Council of Economic Advisers advises on policy for maintaining a sound and prosperous economy, and the Office of Emergency Planning oversees the mobilization of civilian resources for national security.

PRESIDENTIAL ROLE-SHARING AND DEPENDENCE

The President is not an island unto himself; he shares his several roles with the two other branches, Congress and the judiciary. He depends upon their concurrences and positive acts, which by no means are rendered readily and generously. The Founding Fathers deliberately provided for the duality of independence and dependence for each of the branches, by inserting into the Constitution the basic structural concepts of separation of powers and checks and balances. Essentially contradictory, separation of powers involves division and independence, and checks and balances involves interaction and dependence. Of the two doctrines, checks and balances, or the interaction and dependence of the branches rather than their separation, seems ascendant. Few other governments in the world can equal the functional overlapping of the branches provided for in the Constitution.

RELATIONS WITH CONGRESS

In legislation, the President proposes but Congress disposes. The tendency of Congress to independence may cost the President a substantial part of his program, especially his major measures. This repeated experience drove President Kennedy, as it has other Presidents, to distinguish between a "voting majority" and a "working majority" in Congress. At midyear 1962, the Democratic party possessed a large majority in both houses of Congress; yet the President could not, as he acknowledged in a press conference of June 27, 1962, move difficult measures through Congress and on to the statute books. At that midpoint in his term, despite a generally good box score of legislative successes, he still was denied legislation he deemed of high importance—public school aid, civil rights, medical care for the aged, a cabinet-level urban affairs department, and stand-by authority to lower income taxes.

Congress follows the President's policy guidelines with consistency only in crisis. In the two world wars and in the depression in 1933, Congress filled the President's prescriptions. In the atmosphere of perpetual crisis since World War II, Presidents have, with continuous success, sponsored legislation in the fields of national security and foreign affairs. In crisis, the public expects action and looks to the President for initiative. The best examples of success in more placid times were provided by Theodore Roosevelt and by Woodrow Wilson prior to 1917. Despite the absence of domestic crises, these two Presidents, combining superior leadership with several favorable elements in their circumstances, drove through the substantial social and economic measures comprising their Square Deal and New Freedom programs.

The President encounters trouble in Congress' internal organization, which is full of quicksand for any venturesome social and economic policy. Standing committees can bottle up administration bills or subject them to crippling alteration. Powerful committee chairmen are usually arrayed in substantial degree against the proposals of any presidential administration, Republican or Democratic. A chairman is normally chosen according to the principle of seniority and rises to his place not by demonstrated loyalty to the President but simply by being present year in and year out. Since seniority is best compiled by legislators from "safe" districts or states, chairmen emerge predominantly from the Old South and from northern rural and small town districts. Legislators from such backgrounds tend toward rejection of measures proposed by a President who looks for his re-election to the more liberal voters of the large metropolitan states. The geographic maldistribution of committee chairmanships is suggested by the fact that in 1964 ten of sixteen Senate committee chairmanships were occupied by Southerners. These included such key committees as Finance, Judiciary, Foreign Relations, Banking and Currency, Labor and Public Welfare, and Government Operations, where major legislation of the Johnson Administration reposed.

In the House of Representatives, the Rules Committee is an additional formidable barrier to presidential social and economic legislation. As we saw earlier, the Rules Committee schedules or refuses to schedule the time and conditions under which important bills come before the House. The Rules Committee chairman in 1964, Howard W. Smith of Virginia, had, in over three decades of intermittent service in the post, compiled an imposing record of thwarting presidential legislation. He had bottled up Franklin Roosevelt's wage and hour bill, fought off most of Truman's Fair Deal program, and throttled education and welfare measures of both the Eisenhower and Kennedy administrations.

The Senate filibuster has been the source of occasional historic presidential defeats. Wilson's proposal to arm merchant vessels against German U-boat attack in 1917 was defeated in this way. For years, the filibuster or threat of it has blocked or pared down civil rights legislation. The climax in the long struggle for the Civil Rights Act of 1964 was its escape from the coils of a 75-day filibuster.

CONDUCT AS PARTY LEADER

Because he is dependent on several types of support and approval, the President must temper and restrain his conduct as party leader. He is elected or re-elected to his great office by a popular majority pieced together from voters of his party, of the opposition party, and of the steadily growing body of "independents." His own party may have chosen him as standard-bearer because of his presumed ability to attract broad support. The Republicans, for example, selected Dewey and Eisenhower over Senator Robert A. Taft, "Mr. Republican," who was deemed to lack sufficient appeal to detachable Democrats and independents.

The unreliability of his own party's legislative support makes it imperative that the President cultivate support in the opposition party. History demonstrates that the President's important policies and programs, whether in domestic or foreign affairs, are won with bipartisan support. At the very peak of his political strength in 1933–1934, Franklin Roosevelt was cautious to avoid partisan stances, even to the point of by-passing the traditional observance of the birthdays of his party's heroes, Jefferson and Jackson, lest he alienate the substantial Republican support his legislative proposals were attracting.

For vital decisions affecting his own political future, the President depends upon his party's approval and sanction. Although his party as a rule will grant him the privilege of renomination, the gift is not necessarily automatic. Pierce, Buchanan, and Arthur were denied renomination, and Benjamin Harrison gained it only after a hard struggle. Truman's renomination was jeopardized in 1948 by an attempted revolt by New Deal liberals, labor leaders, and southern Democrats; the revolt was aborted by their failure to find a viable alternative candidate. If the President secures renomination, he will want a platform expressing approval of past policies and outlining his administration's plans, should it continue. While modern Presidents can obtain a platform to their liking, their nineteenth-century predecessors were not always able to. Grover Cleveland dispatched a draft platform to the Democratic convention of 1888 with a moderate plank on the tariff question, the major issue of the day. But the free trade men were so powerful at the convention that the final platform reflected their position more than the President's.

A President depends upon public opinion for re-election, for his party's success in the midterm congressional election, and for day-to-day approbation of his administration's performance. A President may prize popularity and status as a beloved and revered figure, qualities more easily preserved if he pursues policies consistent with patterns of the past. Thus he may avoid proposing major new policies which are apt to bring controversy and to damage at least a part of his popularity. In contrast, an innovative President grapples with problems and undergoes the heat of controversy, the tarnishing of his popularity, and the risk of defeat.

A President may closely tie his policies to the needs and desires of particular economic and social groups. Much of Franklin Roosevelt's New Deal was directed to major disadvantaged groups, such as labor and the Negro. Kennedy's 1960 campaign was pitched to the big urban groups, with promises of expanded social services and reforms in their behalf. Coupled with these promised policies was an electoral strategy that focused upon the large urban industrial states, which eventually proved to be the key to victory. Lyndon Johnson, after his assumption of the presidency, numbered among his earliest callers leaders of organized labor and Negro civil rights groups—the veto groups whose approval was vital to his political future.

ADMINISTRATIVE LIMITATIONS

Although the President is properly typed the "chief executive," his real powers of administrative command over the executive branch are decidedly limited. Congress, too, has substantial administrative powers. The mission and structure of the departments are determined not by the President but by act of Congress. Congress, if it chooses, can vest authority in subordinate officials to act independently of higher leadership; it can specify detailed administrative procedures, rigidly specify a department's internal organization, and require Senate confirmation of designated bureau chief appointments. Congress can create independent regulatory commissions, such as the Federal Communications Commission and the Federal Reserve Board, substantially removed from the President's control. Executive departments require annual appropriations that Congress provides in such amounts and with such strings attached as it chooses. The programs they administer, Congress authorizes and amends. Congress can investigate departmental work in close detail, and its habit is to interrogate not merely top leadership but personnel well down in the hierarchy. As every department head knows, he must respond not merely to his executive superior, the President, but to the standing committees and subcommittees of each house of Congress. Congress makes key decisions on personnel policy in its laws on classification, pay, training, and retirement.

Viewed from the presidency, the executive branch appears not only as a vast array of separate agencies but as a giant bureaucratic monolith. To the President faced with urgent problems on the domestic and international scenes, the bureaucracy may seem slow and unimaginative in coming forth with responses and solutions. Its ways and trappings seem to pose mighty obstacles to policy innovation: its massive paperwork and snail's pace, its layers of specialists, its addiction to negativism and routine, its efficiency in stifling creativity, its typically narrow outlook in contrast to the President's necessarily broader one, and its suspicion (as an enduring center of power wedded to established policies) of a transitory presidential administration as a possible disturbing nuisance.

RELATIONS WITH THE COURTS

The President is also dependent upon judicial approval of the legal aspects of the policies to which his administration is committed. Although the approval is ordinarily forthcoming, the courts on at least several occasions have struck down as unconstitutional key presidential policies. Franklin Roosevelt was distressed when such parts of his New Deal as the National Industrial Recovery Act, the first Agricultural Adjustment Act, the Guffey Soft Coal Act, the Farm Mortgage Moratorium Act, and the Railway Pension Act were ruled by the Supreme Court to be unconstitutional. In time, he launched his court-packing plan, which eventually resulted in a friendlier court. In *ex parte Milligan* (1866),[15] the Court ruled that President Lincoln had unlawfully authorized the trial of civilians by military commissions in an area removed from the theater of war and where the civil courts were open and available. In *Youngstown Sheet and Tube Company* v. *Sawyer* (1952),[16] the Court held that President Truman's seizure and operation of the steel mills on his own authority, in lieu of resorting to available legislation to deal with a strike situation, amounted to a usurpation of the congressional lawmaking power and therefore violated the separation-of-powers doctrine.

RELATIONS WITH FOREIGN LEADERS

Beyond the domestic scene, the President depends for his policy triumphs and failures upon foreign leaders and therefore upon their ambitions and purposes and local political strengths and weaknesses. Since World War II, the President has maintained a string of con-

tacts with foreign leaders that stretches around the globe. The dominant foreign personality in the President's policy calculations since
World War II has been the Soviet premier, who may be a source
of both the most pressing problems and the most impressive accomplishments of a presidential administration. President Eisenhower's
dealings with Khrushchev ranged from the heady atmosphere of good
will at Geneva and Camp David to the collapse of the Paris summit
conference following the Gary Powers U-2 flight. Kennedy's experiences ranged from the raising of the Berlin Wall and the 1962 Cuban
missile crisis, a moment when the nuclear holocaust seemed a real
possibility, to the cooperative undertaking of the test-ban treaty in
1963.

The President's life with the leaders of friendly and allied nations is likewise mercurial, a concomitant not simply of personal
difficulties—indeed, there may be none—but of the clashing political
and policy necessities of two chief executives. Syngman Rhee, the
president of South Korea in the 1950's who was fanatically dedicated
to the cause of reunifying his country, adamantly opposed the efforts
of President Eisenhower and his aides to arrange a truce with the
Communists to end the Korean conflict. Rhee considered his personal
sanction of such a step tantamount to betraying his country. Eisenhower felt that his 1952 presidential campaign and electoral triumph
had committed him to ending the war. Only after weeks of intensive
discussion did Rhee acquiesce. President Charles de Gaulle of France
has been a perennial bee in the American President's bonnet. The
French president persisted with the development of France's own
nuclear capability, thus rejecting the Kennedy-Johnson proposal of
a policy of nuclear interdependence among the NATO countries.

Similarly the American President's pursuit of national policies
may bring consternation to allied leaders. In 1954, for example,
American policy toward the Nationalist Chinese offshore islands of
Quemoy and Matsu put the British into a state of severe nervous-
ness. The Chinese Communists were subjecting Quemoy to intensive
artillery shelling. The Eisenhower administration was pressured by
a large body of American opinion, led by Senator William F. Know-
land of California, to impose a blockade on mainland China. British
Prime Minister Clement Attlee, in contrast, urged President Eisenhower to "neutralize" Formosa and "get rid of Chiang"; Attlee
made it altogether clear, Eisenhower has written, that he "had no
enthusiasm for risking a war over Quemoy and Matsu." Eisenhower
was finally rescued from the vise of the competing pressures of
domestic and international politics, when the clouds of crisis lifted.[17]
When they gathered again in 1955, thanks to Red China's increasingly menacing activity in the area of Formosa, Eisenhower dispatched a draft resolution to Congress authorizing the use of

American armed forces to protect Formosa, the Pescadores Islands, and adjacent territory (which included Quemoy and Matsu) against armed attack. Congress approved the resolution.

STRENGTHENING THE PRESIDENCY

The President's role-sharing and dependence sometimes border on weakness for several of his capacities, particularly for those as party chief and legislative leader. His weaknesses there spawn further difficulties in his roles as chief diplomat and commander in chief: De Gaulle contended in 1963 that the American presidential system was functioning only "in a limping way." What might be done to strengthen the President's several weaker roles, consistent with the nature of the presidency and our political tradition?

To strengthen the President as party leader, we might well endeavor to strengthen the national party organizations. The most comprehensive proposals yet made along such lines are in the 1950 report of the American Political Science Association, *Toward a More Responsible Two-Party System*. The committee included among its proposals recommendations that we revise the size and timing of our national conventions, create a national party council or cabinet, stimulate regional rather than state and local organizations, frame more positive platforms, and encourage closed primaries. Although the report has evoked no great response, several current trends are in accord with its views. For example, the Democratic Advisory Council, which has attempted with mixed success to work out party positions on policy questions, is a firm stride toward the party council or cabinet.

Evident in John Kennedy's brief career as presidential party leader is a formula of some promise for future Presidents distressed by the weakness of their party positions. Kennedy as President did much to subordinate party and congressional politics to urban politics. On the solid foundation of pitching his policies to urban groups, he could confidently cultivate state and local party leaders who determined the selection of, and the support given to, congressional candidates. Local leaders, whose business it is to win elections, presumably would choose congressional candidates responsive to the urban groups being mobilized by the presidential policy proposals. Kennedy, had he lived to follow his formula through, doubtless would have lighted bonfires under congressmen and senators, finding his fuel in the urban groups and local party chieftains.

The urban-group formula admittedly has weaknesses. An individual's identification is more with the group than with the party. Group identifications with the Democratic party were strong in the Franklin Roosevelt era but declined in the Truman-Stevenson era.

The urban-group approach has limited relevance to Republican presidential needs because of the strong tendency for those groups to identify with the Democratic party. Republicans must make a diversified appeal to the urban and suburban voters, the detachable Democrats, the independents, and a goodly breadth of other interests. As for the President's role as legislative leader, whatever changes are ventured must be consistent with Congress' historic status as an autonomous body of considerable power. High on the list of what might be done is the abolition of the uneven terms the Founding Fathers accorded the Senate (six years), the President (four years), and the House (two years). President, Senate, and House should be elected simultaneously for a common term of four years. Data on congressional elections suggests that we might expect an election so conducted to produce a President and two houses of Congress in better harmony on party and policy outlook than their present fragmented election permits. Under the Senate's present six-year term, the Senate is never wholly elected during a President's four-year term, and not until he reaches midterm is a majority of the Senate chosen. The House's election at the President's midterm severely and unfairly tests his administration for its popularity at a time when his administration has barely started. His party's defeat in the congressional election can be badly damaging to the President's prestige at home and abroad. The proposed equal legislative and presidential terms would enable the two branches, elected simultaneously, to reflect a common public mood.

The President's legislative power might be increased to include the item veto for appropriation bills. The item veto would endow the President with a powerful new bargaining weapon which he could employ widely to advance his policy enterprises on Capitol Hill. He could conceivably engage in a kind of "logrolling," exchanging his acceptance of appropriation items for support of his own measures by legislators individually and in blocs. Conceivably, the item veto could give the President a truly commanding influence in legislative affairs. Also, if the treaty provision of the Constitution were revised to require the approval of only a majority of senators present, rather than two thirds, the President would be less vulnerable to pressures for concessions and reservations in the treaty's development and approval. Both the revision of the treaty power and the innovation of a broad item veto would require a constitutional amendment that might awaken the great majority of Americans to the problem of presidential weakness.

Any such alteration of presidential power is bound to raise outcries from critics who might, not without justification, contend that these recommended changes would alter the current balance of power between the legislative and executive branches. Yet if the American nation is to meet its challenges, a presidency of substantial power, with a greater effectiveness than has often characterized it in the past, is indispensable. The restraints upon power known by past Presidents, which prevented the strongest of them from straying long or far in abuses of their office, will operate also on future Presidents.

CHAPTER FOUR

The National Administration

At the outset of George Washington's administration, there were only about 350 federal civilian employees; as late as 1801 there were just 2100.[1] By 1900, the number had climbed to 208,000 and at the dawn of World War I in 1914 to 435,000. The two world wars and the depression-New Deal eras of the 1930's caused great spurts of growth in the national administration, and the challenges and complexities of domestic and international affairs since World War II have helped maintain this growth. The 1940 figure of 1,014,117 was almost double that of 1930, and by mid-1964 the number of federal civilian employees had risen to 2,500,492.[2] The recentness of national administrative expansion is evidenced by the fact that three fourths of the present federal positions were created in the past thirty years. Such major agencies as the Tennessee Valley Authority, the Department of Health, Education, and Welfare, the National Space Agency, and the Central Intelligence Agency, for example, are all products of that era.

Three agencies account for about 80 per cent of all federal

employees. The Defense Department is the largest employer of civilian personnel, with almost half of all federal civilian employees. Another 20 per cent work for the Post Office Department and about 8 per cent for the Veterans Administration.

A glance at the work of the civil service reveals a high degree of specialization and an extraordinary variety of jobs. About one fifth of all civil service posts require a college education, graduate training, and considerable experience. Lawyers and accountants, engineers and doctors, biological scientists and physical scientists, veterinarians, and librarians are but a few of the skilled personnel found in federal employment. No other employer in American society can boast such a variety of talent. Professional and technical employees have, in the 1960's, numbered about 450,000. An almost equal number are devoted to general administrative, clerical, and office services. Approximately one million "blue-collar" employees are engaged in industrial, crafts, protective, and custodial work. A remaining half-million are postal workers.

About 85 per cent of all federal jobs are filled by competitive civil service examinations. In addition, several other merit systems function outside ordinary civil service procedures: the Foreign Service, the Atomic Energy Commission, the Tennessee Valley Authority, the Federal Bureau of Investigation, and the commissioned corps of the Public Health Service. Only about 10 per cent of federal positions are exempted from merit appointment.

The federal service is characterized by high turnover. An average of 300,000 employes a year have left government service voluntarily in the 1960's; another 65,000 in a typical year of this period have been separated by reductions-in-force procedures. The latter are occasioned by cutbacks in programs or termination of activities. Employees with less tenure and without veteran's status may be the first to be separated under such procedures. The consistently high rate of turnover necessitates constant recruitment of qualified personnel.

Less than 9 per cent of federal employees are located in Washington: the United States government is a field-centered enterprise, with employees stationed throughout the fifty states, in our territories and possessions, and in foreign countries.

The greater length of the federal government's personnel experience has taken place under a spoils system rather than under the present predominantly merit system. Merit rules did not make their appearance until the Pendleton Act of 1883, and even then their coverage was limited. In spoils, appointment to federal employment is based primarily upon the appointee's identification with the party that controls the presidency. Historically, spoils has been the cement that unites the party worker to the party organization. It may also serve a vital policy function: it can assure the presence of a national administration whose outlook on policy questions approximates that of the President and his party. George Washington brought into the initial federal service the "best qualified" appointees, who almost invariably were Federalist in political affiliation and outlook. Jefferson, upon his election, felt obliged to dispense patronage to party friends who had worked for "the great victory." Jackson, inheriting a bureaucracy whose loyalty to the policies of his incoming administration was highly doubtful, and being convinced that no man could long hold public office without being corrupted, discharged about 10 per cent of the 10,000 employees in the federal service. Jackson's personnel policies bore a coating of democratic ideology— a faith in the ability of the common man to discharge the duties of government. The Jacksonian view rejected the principle of a career system in government, in preference to "rotation in office" (the use of a limited term for office-holders to forestall an "aristocracy" or other abuse), and scorned the supposition that government required professional preparation. The cycle of spoils, fluctuating as party control of the presidency shifted, endured through the nineteenth century and well into the twentieth. In the first year of the New Deal, 150,000 federal jobs were allotted to deserving Democrats.

President James A. Garfield's assassination in 1882 by a dejected office seeker so outraged public opinion that it assured the passage of the Pendleton Act, or merit law, the following year, thus beginning the break away from spoils as the dominant element of the personnel system. From its small beginnings, the coverage of the Pendleton Act was progressively extended by Presidents who discerned political advantage in particular extensions. The growing importance of government and the increasing complexity of its problems also were undeniable forces supporting the merit principle and the growing professionalization of the federal service. But the merit system has sometimes come in for criticism, even from its friends. Its slowness, due to elaborate hiring procedures, prompts the system to break down in a national emergency such as World War II, when speed is at a premium. The merit system, with the heavy paperwork it often entails, requires the operating administration to devote excessive time to personnel matters. By concentrating on restraints and red tape to keep out spoils, the merit approach has not readily permitted positive personnel management, which stresses developmental tools such as training and counseling, by which a challenging work environment, attractive to the highly competent employee, may be created.

In contrast to European public personnel systems, the American national administration has been the underdog—except at lower levels—in competition with private business and the professions for manpower. Businessmen and members of such professions as medicine have held a position of general veneration in American society; the prestige of government employment, although it has improved in recent decades, still falls well below that of private callings. The career principle, which is still entrenched in European governmental systems, has, at most, received belated and limited acceptance in the United States, as indicated by the high level of federal turnover.

PLURALISTIC ADMINISTRATION: ORGANIZATION

The arrangement of the executive branch is pluralistic in the sense that it comprises a variety of administrative organizations differing in form, in function, and in their policy-making relationship with the President. The oldest organizations are the departments, some of which—State, Treasury, and War—hark back to the earliest days of our government. The Post Office, Navy, and Justice departments, although created later, can also trace their origins to the initial months of the Constitution.[3] The departments are the most traditional source of initiative, plans, information, and expertise in the development of policy and have discharged the major operating responsibilities for its implementation. The neutrality policy of the Washington administration in the Franco-British war was forged largely in the State and Treasury departments and in the conflicts of their respective heads, Jefferson and Hamilton. The Monroe Doctrine evolved with important contributions from Secretary of State John Quincy Adams and his department; Secretary of State John Hay and departmental aides played a similar part in the evolution of the Open Door Policy toward China.

Departments comprise several levels of internal organization. The top command consists of the secretary, under secretary, and assistant secretaries, various assistants, and possibly certain bureau chiefs because of their personal influence, public standing, or the importance of their organization's function. At the next level is middle management, composed of lesser bureau chiefs and such figures of lesser authority as division chiefs and branch chiefs. At the bottom is the rank and file, the great mass of employees whose duties are clerical and whose relation to policy is to carry it out. They are linked to higher-level administrators by the first-line supervisor. Department heads serve in both an individual and a collective capacity: as single administrators of the vast departmental organizations and as members of the President's cabinet. Some secretaries number among the President's intimate, wide-ranging counselors together with members of the White House and Executive Office organization.

The President usually enjoys somewhat greater freedom in choosing department heads than he does heads of other organizations. The Senate seldom objects to his nominations. The courts permit him to fire department secretaries for any cause, as he sees fit. Secretary of Commerce Henry Wallace departed from the Truman cabinet not because of his administration of that department but because of his differences with the President over foreign policy. In choosing department heads, the President weighs factors laden with policy implications. Prominent personalities may be chosen from carefully balanced geographic regions. Departments like State, Treasury, and Defense are usually reserved for appointees with backgrounds relevant to the work of those departments. "Clientele" departments such as Agriculture, Commerce, and Labor are awarded to appointees who are acceptable to, or may even come from, the pressure groups with which they deal. In the Kennedy administration, the Department of Health, Education, and Welfare, whose activities are urban centered, was headed, after the departure of Abraham Ribicoff, by Anthony J. Celebrezze, former mayor of Cleveland and therefore thoroughly schooled in the big-city problems of urban renewal, health, education, and welfare upon which the department concentrates. Foreign born and educated in public schools, Celebreeze was a perfect symbol of the big-city dweller.

HEALTH, EDUCATION, AND WELFARE

Just as the President faces great difficulty in controlling policy-making by his departments, the department secretary is faced with an array of bureaus not uncommonly in a state of incipient or actual mutiny. Consider, for example, the Department of Health, Education, and Welfare (HEW), center of several of the most controversial programs of governmental administration. In the Kennedy-Johnson administration, the department was heavily involved in the major struggles to enlarge programs of aid to education and medical care for the aged. The department consists of a loose confederation of bureaus that cherish their separate identities and the programs and policies under their respective jurisdictions. The department, with 73,000 employees is fifth largest in manpower in the executive branch; its major bureaus are the Public Health Service (with 30,000 employees), the Social Security Administration, the Office of Education, the Office of Vocational Rehabilitation, and the Food and Drug Administration (with a relatively small staff of 2260). Each bureau has a highly professional staff with individual traditions, loyalties, and objectives. In the bureaus' top policy levels are careerists of long tenure and fixed professional viewpoints. Steeped in knowledge of their fields, they well appreciate that their department head comes and goes, and in many subtle ways they can thwart his broad objectives when they do not happen to agree with them.

Conflict may develop not only over specific policy issues but also over organizational questions bearing important policy implications. In the Kennedy administration's final year, a struggle transpired in the Public Health Service over the management of its mental health and mental retardation programs. The National Institute of Mental Health proposed that it be taken out of the larger organization of which it was a part, the National Institutes of Health (NIH), and established as a separate bureau responsible for the administration's program for mental illness. The NIH consisted of five institutes, all research oriented. Its leadership resisted the proposed secession of the Institute of Mental Health. The struggle reached a point where the press reported that the director of the Institute of Mental Health was prepared to resign if an autonomous bureau was not created in the Public Health Service, of which the several health institutes are a part. Arguments were mobilized on both sides of the issue. It was contended that the institute responsible for mental health had become the largest spender of all five health institutes and would expand further. Also, its programs dealt directly with the states, which was not true of the other institutes. A separate bureau, its advocates argued, would provide a visibility vital for obtaining public support for its programs. Defenders of the organizational status quo argued that in the Bureau of Mental Health and Mental Retardation, which advocates of change were proposing, the first category might swallow up the second. Also, it would be more difficult to coordinate the retardation program than the mental illness program. Parts of the former would remain in several institutes of NIH, as well as in the Office of Vocational Rehabilitation, the Office of Education, and the Children's Bureau—all parts of HEW.[4] Presidents Kennedy and Johnson abstained from taking sides, and the struggle drifted on inconclusively, thus assuring the continuation of existing arrangements.

The top leadership of HEW chronically faces a harassed existence because political controversy is inherent in nearly every area of the department's policy responsibilities. Nowhere else in government is the conservative-liberal debate more easily touched off than by HEW activities, actual or proposed. Few of its moves fail to arouse fundamental questions of the citizen's reliance upon government versus his independence, a debate filled with such emotion-laden words and phrases as "paternalism," "creeping socialism," "states' rights," "self-reliance," "socialized medicine," and "centralization." In the past decade, the department has been at the center of the most intense political and policy controversies over compulsory health insurance, the extension of Social Security coverage, the contaminated cranberry episode of 1959, aid to education, and medical care for the aged. The department was even born under a cloud of controversy over its likely role as an engine of the welfare state, a capacity that has marred its entire existence in the eyes of influential legislators. The department's internal functioning has steadily felt the hand of Congress. Influential legislators have carved out for themselves personal fiefdoms of policy-making and operations over which they assert a control that sometimes surpasses the secretary's. Most departments are in the "territory" of at least four legislative committees. Thus the Defense Department is immediately accountable to the House and Senate Armed Services and Appropriations committees. HEW deals, in the House of Representatives alone, with the Ways and Means, Education and Labor, Public Works, Interstate and Foreign Commerce, and Appropriations committees. Year after year, Senator Lister Hill (D., Ala.), chairman of the Committee on Labor and Public Welfare, and Representative John E. Fogarty (D., R.I.), chairman of the Appropriations Subcommittee on HEW, have forced unwanted millions of dollars of research money on the NIH. In 1962, it asked for $583 million, and Congress provided $738 million. The unwanted affluence has brought some NIH research specialists to complain privately of being forced to waste money.

Behind the tireless congressional generosity are a number of alert and skillful pressure groups reflecting the capacity of the welfare field to nourish a host of social service reform organizations. Most bureau chiefs, instead of resisting congressional gifts of money, join in demanding them and otherwise work closely with relevant pressure groups, even to the point of subordinating their allegiance to their department head. Not for nothing did a veteran HEW official once observe that "a Secretary of HEW is never sure his flanks are safe when he goes forth to battle. He can be sure of his troops' competence, but he can't always be sure of their loyalty."[5]

Beyond the departments are the agencies, the largest of which is the Veterans Administration, devoted chiefly to the provision of benefits to a great body of citizens. The Veterans Administration dispenses over $5 billion in benefits each year and affects approximately 80 million persons, consisting of 22 million veterans and their families. The agency's work is not simply routine; it entails innumerable discretionary decisions affecting the individual rights and interests of its clientele.

REGULATORY COMMISSIONS

Further removed from the President's direction and control are the independent regulatory commissions, such as the Interstate Commerce Commission (ICC), the Federal Trade Commission (FTC), and the Federal Power Commission.[6] The commissioners are appointees drawn from both major parties, who enjoy a term of office exceeding the President's and are removable only for cause cited in statute.[7]

The President, nevertheless, has some leverage against the commissions' independence. Most commissioners desire reappointment, an event which cannot occur without the President's initiative. Commissioners are subject to the budgetary and legislative clearance procedures of the Bureau of the Budget and to its studies for management improvement, all of which may be occasions of presidential influence upon commission policy. Commissions, in launching requests for appropriations or for new legislative authority, cherish the President's support as a potent element of political strength. The President, however, often runs a poor third after congressmen and the groups in his influence with the commissioners. Congressional liking for its own influence, particularly in the realm of radio and television licenses, provides a principal obstacle both to greater presidential impact and to reorganization or abolition of the commissions.

The regulatory commissions make policies dealing with industries such as aviation and television, whose technology is unstable and whose economic environment undergoes periodic and sometimes drastic change, such as the introduction of color television and of jet air travel. Since vested economic interests are at stake, the commissions become embroiled in political controversy. A variety of social and economic conditions and changes may serve to produce a fevered atmosphere for commission policy-making. For example, the ICC, dealing with rail and motor vehicle transportation rates, and the National Labor Relations Board (NLRB), dealing with labor-management relations, intrude upon a vital, continuous, and shifting economic struggle. Some commissions act by making rules and regulations to enforce the rules, and conduct adjudication based on their violation. Others, such as the FTC, make few rules, and then largely under special legislation. The bulk of the FTC's work and policy-making occurs in case-by-case adjudication. Many commissions have a kind of split personality as regulators of an industry and as promoters of its welfare. Both missions are likely to be incorporated in the commissions' organic law. The regulatory function assumes that the commissions will be reserved and removed in dealing with industry; the promotional requires close and warm relationships with industry to understand those needs and interests that can be advanced through commission policy.

The oldest of the independent regulatory commissions is the Interstate Commerce Commission, created in 1887 to regulate the railroads as the result of pressures from agricultural and business interests that resented the arbitrary setting of freight rates. Demands for national action mounted after state regulatory bodies, spurred by the Granger movement of the 1870's, failed to relieve the farmer of his economic pressures. The 1887 act began a tendency, long continued by Congress, of vesting in an administrative agency broad responsibilities for policy-making in fields that are vast, novel, technologically and economically complex, and politically hazardous and controversial. Glad to "pass the buck" of laboriously working out concrete policy, but not wishing to vest the policy-making power in the executive establishment, Congress often establishes such regulatory commissions in somewhat of a "no man's land" between itself and the executive. The ICC was therefore charged in 1887 to oversee railroad and water common carrier freight rates and to assure that they are "just and reasonable." Congress did little to specify through guides and standards the meaning of this highly general common-law phrase. Similarly, congressional acts concerning the NLRB and the Federal Communications Commission (FCC) require that their respective activities be conducted in a "just and reasonable" manner, and "in the public interest." The FCC must allocate radio and television channels in accordance with the "public interest, convenience, and necessity."

Various advantages are anticipated from the regulatory commission. Its plural executive permits collective counsel and responsibility and the merging of the insights of different professions and experiences in involved and controversial policy-making. The principle of lengthy, staggered terms for the commissioners (none for less than five years) permits continuity of policy, which the quadrennial turnover of the whole body of department heads does not afford. The commissions, because of their longer term and bipartisan make-up, are presumed to be further removed from politics than are the departments—a circumstance conducive to business confidence and forward planning both by industry and by the commissions. The commissions are more specialized than the departments and therefore have the opportunity to apply concerted effort and skill to difficult industry problems. The commissions are also expected flexibly to bring to bear on a common problem all the powers of government, whether executive, quasi-legislative, or quasi-judicial, thereby overcoming the deficiencies of the separation of powers.

At most, these advantages have been imperfectly realized: the commissions have been the subject of numerous critical studies, some recommending far-ranging changes in their structure and operations. The Brownlow Committee, the first Hoover Commission, Louis Hector of the Civil Aeronautics Board (CAB) in the Eisenhower administration, and James M. Landis, who had been a member of three commissions, in a special study for the incoming President Kennedy, all posed criticisms and recommendations.[8] Chiefly, the critics hold that the commissions' policy-making proceeds on a highly *ad hoc,* case-by-case basis and that policy, therefore, is little planned, is excessively legalistic, and is short-term rather than long-range. The commissions are accused of imposing crushing burdens on the top commissioners, owing partly to ill use of the skills of well-qualified staffs. The commissions fragment executive power and pose difficulties of coordination with the departments. An independent body like the Federal Reserve Board deals with matters of vital concern to the Treasury Department and to presidential economic policy generally. Antitrust policies command the overlapping energies of the Justice Department and the FTC. There can be no national transportation policy so long as the ICC has jurisdiction over railroads, waterways, and motor carriers; the CAB over aviation; the Bureau of Roads over the national highway system; and the Federal Maritime Board in the Commerce Department over ocean shipping. Coordination between the agencies is usually slight.

GOVERNMENT CORPORATIONS

A further form of organization, the government corporation, came into important use during the two world wars and in the New Deal era.[9] The corporation is entrusted with specific tasks and services: insuring bank deposits (the Federal Deposit Insurance Corporation), extending credit to business enterprise (the former Reconstruction Finance Corporation), regional development, including electrical power production (the Tennessee Valley Authority), and the stockpiling of critical and strategic materials (the Metals Reserve Corporation in World War II). Corporations, as an administrative form, have been attractive because of the businesslike character of their operations and because they permit greater flexibility and discretion. Prior to the 1940's, corporations enjoyed wide autonomy in fiscal policy, including the use of income, and in personnel policy. Many government corporations, like private business corporations, were self-sustaining on their own revenues. In the late 1930's, congressional hostility to the corporations began to mount. Legislators resented the lack of accountability of the commissions, an inevitable consequence of their relative autonomy. Conservative legislators opposed the government ownership and welfare tendencies of the corporations. Legislators, restive under strong wartime presidential leadership, found that they could strike at the President by striking at the corporations, many of which were important to his administration's purposes. Still other legislators resented the tendency of corporation witnesses to be stand-offish in testimony before congressional committees. These several sentiments eventuated in the Government Corporation Control Act of 1945, which, while preserving a certain independence in the corporation, made it more accountable to Congress and the President. A corporation such as TVA enjoys such political strength that it was exempted from key provisions of the 1945 act and was able to elude several efforts of the Eisenhower administration—which was markedly less enthusiastic about public power than its Democratic predecessors—to reduce its scope.

DEPARTMENTS AND AGENCIES

A cluster of staff agencies serves the President and his policy needs.[10] The staff are no little part of the President's eyes, ears, tongue, and brain. His most personal staff is the White House Staff, comprising approximately a score of assistants bearing such diverse titles as press secretary, special counsel, special assistant for national security, appointments secretary, and the like. White House aides help prepare the President's messages, speeches, and correspondence; oversee the inflow and outflow of his communications; analyze and digest the problems coming before him; and do the highly consequential detail work in forwarding his purposes with legislators, departments, pressure groups, and party figures. Although White House aides jealously guard their anonymity, they have attained an importance in all presidential administrations since the Franklin D. Roosevelt era, when the staff underwent great expansion, to the point where only several members of the cabinet equal or exceed their influence on policy. The President also has an institutional staff; the oldest and largest unit is the Bureau of the Budget, which prepares and administers the executive budget, clears pending legislation in the President's behalf in the executive branch, and conducts management improvement studies.

The President's oldest organ of collective advice is the cabinet, consisting of the department heads and such other aides as he invites. The cabinet was established by President Washington to help develop policy for the nation's response to the Franco-British war. The cabinet has been an uneven source of counsel in policy-making. Quick, hard-driving Presidents like Wilson, Franklin D. Roosevelt, and Kennedy, who grew impatient with extended group discussion, used it little. Truman and Eisenhower used it more, but with mixed results. The rise of alternative policy organs, such as the White House Staff and the National Security Council, has further circumscribed the role of the cabinet.

The National Security Council, created by the National Security Act of 1947, advises the President on the integration of the many and diverse strands of policy which in their totality comprise our national security policy. The Council of Economic Advisers, established by the Employment Act of 1946, helps prepare the President's economic reports and recommends policies to maintain the economy in a state of maximum productivity. The Executive Office of the President, in which these several presidential agencies are sheltered, also includes the Office of the Special Assistant to the President for Science and Technology, which sifts and tidies up issues emerging from the fast-changing world of science and is a link between the President and the scientific community. The Office of Emergency Planning oversees the mobilization of civilian resources for national security.

The Vice-President, holder of an office long neglected, is playing an increasing part in the President's policy processes. Vice-President Nixon was influential in determining the Eisenhower administration's attitude toward the attacks of Senator Joseph McCarthy, in adapting the Benson farm program to political necessity (Nixon pressed for less drastic reduction of crop supports than the Secretary of Agriculture proposed, in order not to alienate too many farmers), and in contributing to the administration's civil rights policy as chairman of the interdepartmental committee on government contracts. In the Kennedy administration, Vice-President Johnson was chairman of several interdepartmental committees on space, defense, and government contracts. Johnson's importance as a policy counselor in the Kennedy administration is suggested by his membership in the "Ex Com," or executive committee of the National Security Council, a random group of a dozen administration officials who helped the President work out policy in the 1962 Cuban crisis. In the Johnson administration, Vice-President Humphrey has been entrusted with responsibilities in several fields, particularly in civil rights.

Most important policy problems overlap several departments and agencies. Policy is worked out through several kinds of interdepartmental arrangements. The simplest organizational means are personal contacts between officials of the agencies concerned through phone calls, luncheons, business meetings, and correspondence. Where problems are complex or enduring, an interdepartmental committee may be established on which the departments and agencies concerned are represented. Committees customarily employ the bureaucratic trappings of meetings, agendas, memoranda and reports, position papers, and clearances. At their worst, they entail time-consuming negotiation over the minutiae of phrasing of policy statements, leading their victim-critics to designate this as the "age of the comma man." Committees stress negotiation and compromise to the point where they may water down to insipidity what may have begun as a vigorous, creative idea. At their best, interdepartmental committees serve the vital function of building consensus and commitment between departments whose policies must be coordinated and energies combined. Committees have functioned particularly well in such policy areas as foreign aid and government contracts.

The President may also employ *ad hoc* groups to deal with policy problems of special urgency. To consider the nation's response when

Israel invaded Egypt in 1955, President Eisenhower summoned to the White House the Secretary of State, the chairman of the Joint Chiefs of Staff, the Secretary of Defense, the Director of the CIA, and the Assistant to the President. Presidents may establish commissions of distinguished citizens to study and make recommendations on policy problem areas; Truman, for example, created a commission on civil rights from which emerged the report *To Secure These Rights*,[11] forerunner of key federal civil rights policies. In the Eisenhower administration, the adequacy of the nation's military and defense policies was examined by the Gaither Commission. President Johnson widely employs special groups, committees, and commissions to double-check the regular government establishment on serious problems. The assassination of President Kennedy was examined not merely by the regular government agencies concerned but also by a special commission headed by Chief Justice Earl Warren. In deciding whether to proceed with the building and financing of a costly supersonic commercial air transport plane, President Johnson consulted experts from the Pentagon and private banks in addition to the Federal Aviation Authority's report on the question.

PLURALISTIC ADMINISTRATION: PERSONNEL

The national administration can be viewed not only in terms of organization but also in terms of personnel. Federal personnel, like federal organization, is denoted by variety and likewise reflects the essential pluralism of national administration. In their two largest categories, federal personnel can be regarded as "political" and as "merit," each possessing a different method of appointment and different conditions of tenure.

POLITICAL APPOINTEES

Political appointees are chosen for established political offices on the basis of party identification. The appointees involved may become part of the President's immediate official family. For his political appointments, the President may select members of Congress, state governors, big-city mayors, and incumbents of other elective and party offices. His Postmaster General may be his former campaign manager. Harry S Truman, for many of his cabinet appointments, resorted to the Senate. Secretary of State James Byrnes, Secretary of the Treasury Fred Vinson, Secretary of Agriculture Clinton Anderson, and Secretary of Labor Lewis Schwellenbach all hailed from the Senate or the House. Senator Warren Austin was named United States delegate to the United Nations Security Council, and another senator, J. Howard McGrath, became the Attorney General. By resorting to the Senate, Truman, who had just come into the Presidency after some years of service in that body, could better know the calibre of his appointees drawn from its members than from noncongressional sources. Department heads who were former senators or congressmen also might be best equipped to cope with what loomed as a difficult era in executive-legislative relations.

The President's political appointees may be drawn not only from his own party but from the opposition party as well. Indeed, in the case of the independent regulatory commissions, not more than a simple majority of the commissioners may be from the President's own party. The further appointments can be done with a degree of political subtlety. Eisenhower, for example, appointed an "Eisenhower Democrat," Richard Mack, to the Federal Communications Commission; Mack's appointment could not be "charged" against the President's own party, but he came with valued credentials of loyalty.

The President may fill some of his most important policy posts with figures from the opposition party. In World War II, in a quest for bipartisan cooperation for the administration in time of war, Franklin Roosevelt brought in Henry L. Stimson as Secretary of War and Frank Knox as Secretary of the Navy; both were leading Republicans. President Kennedy, victor in a close popular vote in the 1960 election, went to great lengths to create a bipartisan administration in the fields of foreign affairs and national security. His Secretary of Defense, Robert McNamara, and Secretary of the Treasury, C. Douglas Dillon, were both Republicans, as were Allen Dulles, who was held over as director of the CIA, and John McCone, Dulles' successor. McGeorge Bundy, another Republican, was special assistant for national security affairs; and disarmament was the province of two successive Republicans, John J. McCloy and William C. Foster. Each of these fields had at one time or another, in the decade before Kennedy's presidency, been the source of serious political controversy. The ambassador to perhaps the most troubled foreign affairs area in the Kennedy administration—South Vietnam— was the Republican vice-presidential candidate in 1960, Henry Cabot Lodge.

"Political appointee" is a broad term, embracing both those who are professional politicians and former elective officeholders as well as those who are utterly bereft of such experience but who nevertheless are chosen for political office. The President's political appointments reveal much of the quality of his administration and the reality of its philosophical attachments, particularly where the orientation of the appointees may be markedly different from the President's own professed policy objectives. Political appointees range in the depth of their political experience from James G. Blaine, who became Secretary of State in Benjamin Harrison's administration after serving as member and Speaker of the House of Representatives and member of the Senate, to typical members of the Eisenhower cabinet, who brought to their post no significant political experience—most of them hailed from the world of business.

Political appointees with substantial background and influence in party affairs sometimes come into open and serious disagreement with the President on policy questions. An appetite for self-assertion, as well as clashes of viewpoint, may produce the differences. Blaine, who nurtured ambitions for the presidency, regularly disagreed with his chief, Benjamin Harrison, on matters big and small. William Jennings Bryan, Secretary of State in the Wilson administration, broke with that administration on war policy, and James F. Byrnes, Secretary of State in the Truman administration, proved too self-assertive for his chief. Party figures who are appointees, whether or not they assert their own ambitions and policy principles, may represent factions of the party other than the President's. In the Eisenhower cabinet, Secretary Humphrey's attachment was primarily to the Taft wing of the Republican party.

Appointees to political posts may bring not party or electoral experience but relevant professional background, often obtained in the corporations, investment firms, and law offices of the business community. There is some tendency to reserve the principal cabinet posts for those who command relevant technical competence. In the Kennedy-Johnson administration, Dean Rusk brought to the office of Secretary of State experience as head of the Rockefeller Foundation, an organization heavily oriented to foreign affairs, and prior service as an assistant secretary of state. Defense Secretary Robert McNamara, whose department is closely related to industrial production, was president of the Ford Motor Company. Secretary of the Treasury Douglas Dillon possessed a rich background in private investment and finance. Even presidential administrations committed to large-scale social programs and openly critical of private business may resort to it for staff, particularly in the foreign affairs-national security sector. Harry S Truman, who would virulently denounce the "Wall Streeters" one day, had no compunction about appointing them to responsible posts the next. Robert Patterson, James Forrestal, Paul Hoffman, Lewis Douglas, and Robert Lovett were all members of the economic world that Truman on occasion roundly attacked. Appointees with business and professional backgrounds are even more heavily represented at the subcabinet levels as under secretaries, assistant secretaries, and bureau chiefs.

Career employees who are recruited under merit regulations, who possess employment tenure, and who expect to spend their working years in the federal service may also be appointed to political posts. A favorite source of such appointees is active service or retired military personnel. Franklin Roosevelt found military personnel useful in controversial policy areas, such as the administration of work relief in the depression years of the New Deal. Truman was attracted by the military's prestige among legislators in an interlude when congressional attack upon his administration was severe. General George C. Marshall, accordingly, served as Secretary of State and later as Secretary of Defense under Truman. General Walter Bedell Smith was ambassador to the Soviet Union, and General William Draper undertook key missions abroad in connection with the Marshall Plan and NATO.

The President's key appointments may include personal appointees. Although they may possess ample professional and political qualifications, a principal factor in their selection is their acquaintance or friendship with the President, their origin in his home state or region, or their attendance at his school or college—circumstances that may create a special bond. President Kennedy included in his administration a goodly ensemble of Harvard faculty and graduates. President Truman numbered a quantity of Missourians among his appointees: Secretary of the Treasury John W. Snyder was considered a Missourian, although he hailed from Arkansas; Truman's press secretaries were successively Charles G. Ross, a life-long friend and former Washington editor of the St. Louis *Post Dispatch*, and Joseph Short, also of Missouri; Clark Clifford, a St. Louis lawyer, was the President's special counsel who served as speech writer, congressional liaison, and general political strategist; Admiral Sidney Souers, a St. Louis businessman, was executive secretary of the National Security Council. Other Missourians occupied lesser policy posts.

MERIT EMPLOYEES

The great mass of federal employees fall into the several merit systems; a far smaller number of employees at lesser ranks can be counted as political appointees. About 85 per cent of the employees come under the rules and regulations of the Civil Service Commission, chief administrator of the principles of merit, mainly through competitive examinations. Some of the remaining employees come under merit systems separately maintained by agencies such as the Tennessee Valley Authority, the Atomic Energy Commission, the Federal Bureau of Investigation, and the Foreign Service. Federal merit employees come from almost every kind of profession and vocation; they include agronomists, clerks, economists, foresters, custodians, cooks, X-ray technicians, welders, and lawyers.

Congress has empowered the Civil Service Commission to except particular employees from the competitive requirements of the civil service laws. The commission groups the excepted positions under three listings, Schedules A, B, and C. Schedule A includes positions other than those of a confidential or policy-determining character for which it is not practicable to examine. Various protocol officers in the State Department, for example, are listed in this schedule. Schedule B is similar to Schedule A, except that the commission may employ noncompetitive examinations for positions listed with it. Schedule B includes, for example, professional members of the Policy Planning Staff in the office of the Secretary of Defense and technical cryptographic positions in the Communications Security Division, Office of Communications of the State Department. In Schedule C are grouped positions of a confidential or policy-determining character, such as an assistant to the director of the Bureau of the Budget, a special assistant to the assistant secretary of state for Far Eastern affairs, and a confidential assistant to the commissioner of customs. In mid-1964, 108,000 positions were included under Schedule A, 2000 under Schedule B, and 1400 under Schedule C.[12] Although Schedule C is the smallest, it is by its nature the most important in the policy-making processes, and indeed its establishment was intended to enhance those processes.

Schedule C was set up by President Eisenhower in 1953 for personnel in policy-forming or confidential positions that had previously been in the longer-established Schedule A, and in time still other "policy and confidential" positions have been added. In 1955, the second Hoover Commission proposed that Schedule C be the basis of a careful division between "political executives" and "career administrators," or between those who make policy and those who carry it out. Political executives discharge the additional function of explaining and advocating policy before congressional committees and group interests. Career administrators, in contrast, provide the expertise and counsel on which policy decisions are based. The Hoover Commission viewed the two types as complementary but noted that the failure to distinguish between them had often thrust upon career administrators responsibilities for defending policy, which more suitably should fall upon the political executive. The commission also felt that more systematic recognition of political executives might foster greater care in their recruitment, more awareness of their vital tasks, and better heed of the necessary skills and training. Schedule C was subsequently altered to reflect the commission's thinking.[13]

The distinction between political and career executives is clearer on paper than in practice. The Hoover Commission's assumption that those who make policy can be readily distinguished from those who carry it out is not supported by the realities of federal administrative life. For example, the congressional committee habit of interrogating executive officials well down the hierarchical line, in an attempt to discover who is responsible for what elements of a policy decision, precludes the drawing of any hard and fast line between the two personnel categories. The pressure groups, with their keen noses for where power and influences really lie, would hardly be inclined to abide by idealized distinctions.

SOURCES OF PERSONNEL

The personnel system undergoes drastic transformation in the national emergencies of war and economic depression—periods of major policy innovation. In the two world wars and during the New Deal, government expanded enormously. Several sources in society provided the bulk of policy-making personnel in such circumstances. The academic community was the chief source for the New Deal "Brain Trust," for instance; it contributed a cadre of social scientists capable of critical and innovative thinking to deal on the plane of policy with the ills of society. The world wars and the quasi-war environment prevailing since World War II have expanded the roles of scientists, military personnel, and industrial managers. Indeed, so rapidly has their influence enlarged that President Eisenhower was moved to warn, in his farewell address, that public policy might become "the captive of a scientific-technological elite." Such an elite encompasses a variety of specialists, not the least of whom is the operational analyst, who rose from a lesser and earlier status as technician, scientist, statistician, and analyst to the role of an executive who makes decisions and holds the purse strings. Illustrative of the latter elevated capacity is Assistant Secretary of Defense (Controller) Charles J. Hitch, who served previously in the RAND Corporation—a private research enterprise that undertakes analytical studies for the armed forces. The Pentagon, during Hitch's tenure in the Kennedy administration, was heavily stocked with officials from similar backgrounds of graphs, formulas, and quantitative and qualitative analyses, not excepting the Secretary of Defense, Robert S. McNamara.

Operational analysis, which harks back to British military practice in World War I, achieved its highest estate in the United States following the advent of the nuclear age. It enjoys more influence in this country than in any other. The operational analyst, who applies analytical and scientific methods to problem solving, is found in large numbers in the service departments of the Pentagon as well as in the Pentagon superstructure. Various universities, such as M.I.T., the California Institute of Technology, Chicago, and Columbia, also provide intellectual resources—the scientists, mathematicians, and analysts—to study specific problems.

Other major—and more traditional—sources of executive manpower are business and the law. Lawyers are an omnipresent influence in the executive branch. Our government is more legalistic than most, since the substance of policy depends so much on interpretations of regulations, orders, and statutes. Lawyers are not merely legal technicians but often occupy high administrative and policy posts. Their verbal skills and training in dialectic and maneuver make their contributions highly relevant to the work of a cumbrous executive branch, in which policy development transpires in and between giant departments. Lawyers as a class display certain bents in policy-making. They are little inclined to the planning of policy but proceed on an *ad hoc*, case-by-case basis. As a group, they tend to the preservation of the status quo in social and economic policy, although in the Roosevelt era they were a source of major policy innovation. Their contributions to the New Deal, although greater in actual achievements, were conceptually more restricted than the policy innovations proposed by the academicians in the original Brain Trust. Private corporation executives, bankers, and financiers who come into public service are also heavily inclined to the status quo, at least for social and economic policy, and to short-term rather than long-term policy development.

Selection of personnel from one background or source rather than another may be in itself a major policy decision. In 1962, for example, two vacancies arose on the Atomic Energy Commission, the filling of which touched off a spate of intensive maneuvering by administration and congressional forces. Not the least of the several aspects of this matter were the growing misgivings among members of the congressional Atomic Energy Committee that the strong representation of scientists in previous and existing commission memberships had made its programs excessively research directed and university oriented. Congressional committee members proposed to offset the three scientists on the five-member commission with at least one lawyer who would not need long indoctrination into the commission's work.[14]

THE NATIONAL ADMINISTRATION AS BUREAUCRACY

The federal executive branch wears the trappings and displays the habits of bureaucracy. Bureaucratic phenomena are apparent in any sizable organization, public or private, be it the General Motors Corporation, a public school system, or a department of the executive branch. Since any organization, however bureaucratic, also has strongly individual characteristics, which are the product of society, culture, history, the professions, and the individuals composing it, any attempt at generalized description will tread roughly upon specific and important realities.

A leading analyst of bureaucracy, Max Weber, a German economist of the early twentieth century, developed ideal constructs of bureaucratic organization on the basis of studies of western European practice and of the ancient civilizations of China, Egypt, India, and Rome.[15] In all these societies, social mobility was limited, and entry into the civil service and advancement in its ranks were limited and closely aligned with a closed and stratified class and education system; Weber's findings, therefore, must be applied cautiously to the American civil service structure, which is the product of an altogether contrasting social tradition and practice. Notwithstanding this qualification, Weber's observations seem especially applicable to the rational and structural aspects of the American bureaucracy.

ELEMENTS OF BUREAUCRACY

The major elements of the Weber model include the principle of hierarchy, reflected in the line of authority depicted on the organization blueprint. Positions and groups of positions in a department are rationally arranged in relation to one another. Authority extends from the agency head to the base of the organization, with all intermediary positions linked in a superior-subordinate relation to another, each lower office falling under the supervision of a higher office. Hierarchy not only sets the basis of authority but also creates the duty of obedience.

Bureaucratic organization stems from a rational division of labor, or the application of the principle of specialization. Specialization grows as work is increasingly subdivided among positions, and each is vested with legal authority adequate for the task assigned. In the federal executive branch, specialization is the basis of the classification system, incorporated in the Classification Act of 1949, which groups and grades civil service positions according to duties, difficulty, responsibility, and necessary qualifications. The General Schedule provided for in the act contains eighteen grades, with equal pay for equal work set as the ideal for each grade. An employee's rise through the grade structure may betoken the growing importance of his work and skills in relation to policy-making. The higher he is in the grade structure, the greater, normally, is his impact on policy.

Bureaucracy works by processes of formalization. Its members conduct their internal duties and deal with the public according to precedents and rules. The latter are generalized and tend to be applied impersonally and without regard to the differentiating characteristics of individual situations. Neutrality and depersonalization are viewed as aids to efficiency. There is formalization also in the sense that rules are published, records are kept, and files are accumulated and managed.

Bureaucracy functions through a professional administrative class, typified by special training and technical skills relevant to the duties of its positions. Bureaucracy offers a career for one's working lifetime, commenced in a competitive examination. The bureaucrat ascends the career ladder through a blending of merit and conformity to the behavior ideals of the organization. In bureaucracy, "safe men" tend to be best rewarded. The risks of policy innovation are normally shunned, since failure can be costly to career progress and success brings only small—if any—rewards.

Bureaucracy functions within a framework of law, whether in the United States or in western European countries. Law, as Weber noted, contributes to bureaucracy's inflexibility, while simultaneously safeguarding observance of the Anglo-Saxon principle of the "rule of law," which requires that administrative actions affecting individual rights reflect precedents and legal prescription rather than arbitrary personal discretion. In the United States, Congress embodies standards and procedures in legislation to guide officials in their dealings with citizens.

Weber's theory of bureaucracy, derived from European practice, is open to several serious qualifications when applied to the American scene.[16] Most important, American bureaucracy is associated far more with "politics" than is the European model. The relationship is fostered by our system of separation of powers, which diffuses policy-making authority among many centers. Legislators and pressure groups are accustomed to dealing not just with top-level executives; they reach well down into the structure in their quest for those who can take action and influence policy. Members of the bureaucracy encourage these tendencies, since they can be manipulated to build up their own strength to constrain top leadership. The dynamics of administrative politics reduce the routinized flavor that Weber finds in his European model and convert American bureaucracy from Weber's passive, neutral instrument into an active representative of various interest groups.

American bureaucracy has a far higher personnel turnover than Weber's and far freer passage between governmental and private careers. In the United States there is considerable transfer of able young men, after five to seven years of government service, to private business, the professions, and the universities. Likewise, these several recipients provide a strong flow of personnel at various policy-making levels for government employment. Weber's model also fails to reflect the "informal" nature of American bureaucracy—the importance of personal relationships between bureaucrats, which modify routines and established procedures in policy-building; the veneration in American culture of improvisation, innovation, and achievement, which has impact upon bureaucracy; and the sectional, national, racial, and economic variety in the backgrounds of American bureaucrats, which has a leavening effect upon organizational endeavor.

BUREAUCRACY AND POLICY-MAKING

Probably American bureaucracy's most distinct departure from Weber's model is its heavy involvement in policy-making. In the United States the bureaucracy shares with the President and Congress effective power for the initiation, interpretation, and application of major policy. The vast expansion of governmental activity in the twentieth century—in the provision of social services, the regulation of the economy, and the maintenance of the nation's influence and defenses in world affairs—has required the indispensable policy skills of the bureaucracy.

In its policy-making activities, bureaucracy operates from several vantage points. It deals with pressure groups of all sizes, which focus their influence not simply upon Congress but upon the bureaucracy as well and upon the whole range of its policy concerns. Once Congress or the chief executive has decided policy, the pressure groups turn next to the bureaucracy, which, in the course of applying policy received from external or higher authority, makes further policy of more refined detail. The bureaucracy is not a blind automaton acquiescing to pressures. Particular bureaucracies develop skill in resisting special interests and in asserting degrees of public interest. The programs and policies of departments are usually a tempering of private claims with considerations of public interest.

Bureaucracy's part in developing policy is a large one. The bureaucracy is much occupied with recommending policies to Congress. The growing complexity of governmental problems—the intricacies of economic policy, the dependence of the nation's defenses upon a military and scientific technology, the endless host of problems touching upon almost every department of knowledge and learning—make the legislator increasingly dependent upon bureaucratic specialists. Any reading of Armed Services Committee hearings quickly discloses the legislators' dependence upon military experts on questions such as the emphasis to be placed upon missile systems as opposed to long-range bombers, or upon nuclear weapons versus conventional weapons.

The bureaucracy wields several types of influence upon the development of policy in its early legislative stages. It may prepare legislation upon its own initiative, in response to private pressures, or at legislative invitation. A department may draft a bill, render testimony before a legislative committee, or submit a report on legislation that a committee has referred to it. Normally, a department commands the most formidable array of relevant knowledge, and it best knows what has happened to past policy and where its strengths and weaknesses lie. The administrative official is in the position to know why existing policy objectives are not being achieved and to suggest alternative means or policies. The administrator or bureau-crat will often choose to go along with existing legislation, despite its imperfections, and adjust policy to the realities of administrative action, or, in effect, make adjustments within the leeway ordinarily granted in existing law. He is prone to choose this course if asking for new legislation risks an even worse law or a general attack upon his agency and policies. If he asks for a new law, he and his aides are expected to present supporting arguments and facts. More than half the legislation considered by Congress originates in the executive branch.

Consistently since the later years of the Truman presidency, the chief executive has presented an annual legislative package to Congress in his State of the Union, budget, and special messages, followed by drafts of legislation prepared in the executive branch. In 1954, for instance, President Eisenhower presented sixty-five proposals for new legislation covering foreign aid, military defense, farm price supports, social security, housing, and the like. The enterprise involved the cooperation of the departments, the Budget Bureau, and the White House Staff. Originally, the agencies submitted some 300 major proposals, which the Budget Bureau and the White House Staff sifted in order to eliminate items that were politically infeasible and that did not harmonize with the administration's goals and established policies.[17]

When legislation is undergoing congressional consideration, administrators, in addition to testifying before legislative committees in open hearings, appear in executive, or secret, sessions where major dicisions are concluded. Administrators may similarly join conference committees.

In implementing legislation, the administrator also has the opportunity for further policy-making. He can use his opportunity most constructively to the degree that he thinks, and is able to act, in terms of public interest. In implementing legislation, administrators may range between the extremes of ignoring statutory provisions (the Sherman Antitrust Act of 1890 withered on the books for a decade from lack of enforcement until Theodore Roosevelt took it up) and of applying the law with a zealous exactitude well beyond the intentions of its framers (in the manner of a literal-minded customs officer). The choices of acting with vigor or restraint, and of deciding which of several seeming violators to prosecute, are in themselves key judgments of policy. The making of rules to give further detail to legis-lation is also a source of voluminous policy-making. Rules have the status of law, although they must satisfy statutory and constitutional requirements of conformity with legislative standards and impartiality. Administrators engage in additional policy acts, which, although they may not have the force of law, have the force of authority. A speech by a department head or other responsible official, the departmental report to the President and Congress, and the letters and memoranda of administrators all may promulgate policies which department personnel may consider binding.

Administrators, in making policy, are, like the President and Congress, influenced by their own value systems, by their interpretations of their political and organizational environment, and by their ambitions. Secretary of Agriculture Ezra Taft Benson in the Eisenhower administration strove to reduce farm price supports; his objective raised great controversy, but Benson held to his rough course, ruled by a conviction that "We had too much government 'Big Brother' in agriculture," and that there was a "necessity for farmers to stand on their own feet."[18]

Most bureaucrats—the great rank and file—are largely removed from policy-making; they devote themselves to carrying out routine but vital tasks, and thus they daily reaffirm existing policies. The timely delivery of the mails and social security retirement checks, although not policy-making acts, nevertheless vitally affect the welfare of millions of individuals and of society itself and therefore, in the largest sense, the success or failure of established policy.

PRESIDENTIAL USES OF BUREAUCRACY

Policy-making in the executive branch is of necessity a cooperative enterprise. Each of the several main contributors to policy supplies distinctive resources; no one is self-sufficient, each is dependent upon the others. For the President, the vast executive bureaucracy is a storehouse of information, expertise, and—hopefully—ideas. He depends above all upon the agencies for action and implementation of most of his policy decisions. From the viewpoint of his position and needs, that bureaucracy is best that responds in its policy activity to the tone, emphasis, and goals he has set for his administration, that will spare him from error and defeat in the market place of governmental action—that, in a word, will spare him the political and historical embarrassment of stupidity and corruption.

The Roosevelt Technique. Each President has his own ways of dealing with bureaucracy, although within the differences several polarities of choice are discernible.[19] At one extreme was Franklin Roosevelt, whose method was facilitated by the twin crises of depression and war that marked his presidency. Roosevelt aimed to exert a maximum personal control over policy-making and execution. Crisis afforded him a luxury few Presidents have known—the creation of his own bureaucracy to fight much of the depression and war. The bureaucracy he inherited from the previous Republican era entertained predispositions which promised to arouse little enthusiasm and perhaps even hostility toward the New Deal. In both depression and war,

Roosevelt assumed that new organizations possess greater vigor and capacity for innovation than old. Thus the Tennessee Valley enterprise is administered not by the long-established Interior Department but by the specially created Tennessee Valley Authority; the administration's new Wagner Labor Act fell not to the Labor Department but to a new National Labor Relations Board. In World War II, the administration of industrial controls was entrusted not to the Commerce Department but to such new agencies as the War Production Board, the Office of Price Administration, and the War Manpower Commission.

Roosevelt, like other Presidents before and since his time, applied a competitive theory of administration which left his subordinates uncertain and served to keep the reins of decision and policy in his own hands. He often made jurisdictions overlapping, assigning several agencies the same subject: the FERA, WPA, and PWA administered work relief, and the respective responsibilities of the OPA and the WPB for regulating the industrial community were decidedly blurred. The overlapping and uncertainty meant that conflicts arose which only Roosevelt could solve and which therefore served to assure his control. To promote administrative competition, also in the interest of maintaining presidential authority, Roosevelt tended to prefer the use of boards, commissions, and other forms of the plural executive, rather than the single administrator. In the New Deal era, he turned more readily to the creation of new regulatory commissions like the National Labor Relations Board, the Securities and Exchange Commission, the Civil Aeronautics Board, and the Maritime Commission, in his quest for an administrative home for his programs, than to the established single-administrator departments most logically concerned, such as Commerce and Labor.

To maintain his own influence, Roosevelt employed several distinctive types of administrators and aides. He was apt to have an *enfant terrible* or two in his stable, like Hugh Johnson of NRA and Harold Ickes of Interior, whose gifts of piercing invective could puncture the ballooning and unwanted interferences of administrators, legislators, and pressure groups in areas of presidential concern. To foster competition, Roosevelt recruited aides and administrators whose social philosophies were mutually opposing. Budget Director Lewis Douglas and Secretary of the Treasury Henry Morgenthau were economy-minded and conservative on questions of public expenditure. Equally prominent in the ranks were free-spender Harry Hopkins and scores of young lawyers and economists friendly to the doctrines of John Maynard Keynes. Roosevelt was also given to employing wide-ranging assistants who could guide the President's favorite projects through the labyrinthine courses of the executive and legislative branches and into the daylight of established policy.

These assistants made end-runs around the departmental hierarchy, cut bureaucratic red tape, and employed other drastic expedients to produce action when normal government procedures lagged. Raymond Moley, Rexford Tugwell, Thomas Corcoran, and Harry Hopkins all served in this action-forcing, rough-and-tumble capacity. The Roosevelt technique maximizes the President's personal influence in the executive branch, churns up the flow of information and ideas from the bureaus, and magnifies the President's impact on policy. It releases men with ideas and drive in the bureaucracy from the chains of hierarchy and routinization. It is a method of limited relevance, however, to the current era, which is characterized by the soaring importance of foreign affairs whose delicacy is compounded by the dread presence of nuclear armaments. The casual nature of the Roosevelt method bordered at times on the slipshod, and its well-publicized internal strife would be unacceptable today in a world where the executive branch must present a face of unity to other nations. The incalculable expense of error in foreign affairs makes the practice of end-running, which leaves out officials and organizations with contributions of fact and ideas to make, patently unwise.

The Eisenhower Method. At the opposite extreme from Roosevelt's personal, informal, and flexible method was Eisenhower's preference as President for institutionalized relationships with the executive branch. Eisenhower's approach reflected his military background and a conviction, developed in a long governmental career that encompassed the Roosevelt era, that White House administrative practice was lacking in sufficient system. "With my training in problems involving organization," Eisenhower has written, "it was inconceivable to me that the work of the White House could not be better systemized than had been the case in the years I observed it."[20]

The Eisenhower method relied upon a highly developed staff system, at the peak of which was the Assistant to the President, Sherman Adams, a former governor and congressman. Eisenhower expected the staff, as Adams himself has explained, to "boil down, simplify and expedite the urgent business that had to be brought to his personal attention and to keep as much work of secondary importance as possible off his desk." Eisenhower expected his subordinates to reduce lengthy involved documents, requiring his decision, to one page summaries, "which," Adams noted, "was sometimes next to impossible to do."[21]

The lines of communication to and from the President ran through Adams. Cabinet secretaries, except Secretary of State John Foster Dulles, ordinarily dealt with the President through Adams, whose aim, as he has expressed it, was "to resolve specific differences on a variety of problems before the issue had to be submitted to the

President." The departments were expected to take the lead in discovering problems and initiating policy. Since highly influential department heads like Treasury Secretary Humphrey and Agriculture Secretary Benson largely shared Eisenhower's social philosophy, the President could delegate discretion to them with confidence. Equally, Eisenhower's well-known convictions favoring state action to federal and private action to governmental served as built-in restraints upon departmental discretion.

Other Eisenhower innovations promoted the institutionalized presidency. Attached to the National Security Council (NSC) was a Planning Board, which developed policy papers and ironed out agency differences prior to policy presentations to the President and to the agency heads composing the top level of the NSC. Eisenhower created an Operations Coordinating Board, which oversaw the implementation of decisions emerging from the NSC apparatus. The cabinet, too, was systemized. Agenda, heretofore lacking, were provided for cabinet meetings. A secretary was instituted to oversee the preparation of cabinet papers and agenda and to keep a record of decisions the President reached in cabinet. In the Eisenhower era, "teamwork" was a watchword and the noisy internecine brawling of the Roosevelt era was avoided.

Despite this stress on orthodox administrative rationalism, there were occasional human and organizational lapses—the Gary Powers U-2 overflight and the Dixon-Yates contract, for example—the first leaving the President vulnerable in his Paris meeting with Khrushchev and the second exposing his administration to attack from the political opposition. The Eisenhower method seems to afford the President both too little initiative and too little impact upon policy. It depends excessively upon executive subordinates to discover problems, develop alternative solutions, and reach the consensus for decision. Because the President comes in at or near the end of the whole process, his choices are greatly reduced, permitting greater play for the staff and less for himself. The attraction of the method is the assurance it promises that the President will have, in making decisions, the expert counsel and research of all relevant departments and agencies. In the nuclear age, when policy-making more than ever requires many skills and varied knowledge, at least several agencies contain resources bearing relevance to a presidential decision.

The successors of Roosevelt and of Eisenhower have fallen somewhere between the two extremes of administrative technique. Truman, who tended toward administrative orthodoxy, oversaw the beginnings of the National Security Council and encouraged the institutional tendencies of the White House Staff, steps on which Eisenhower had built. Kennedy moved toward the Roosevelt method, although he halted some distance away and indeed seemed to retreat as his administration wore on. Initially, he viewed the White House Staff as a free-wheeling group and shunned fixed staff assignments, rigid jurisdictions, and sharp designations of authority. In time, continuities developed to the point where many of his staff assumed increasingly well-defined spheres of authority. A few remained predominantly utility men, but even they had, as part of their assignment, continuing tasks.

Like Roosevelt, Kennedy attempted to assert a maximum personal impact. He was given to hammering out policy in desk-side conferences with three or four subordinates. He often telephoned subordinates situated rather far down in the hierarchy to discuss with them a policy development in which he was particularly interested. The results, for Kennedy, were often fruitful. He could extract from the bureaucracy fresher information and sharper opinion and could better imbue the governmental structure with a sense of his own purpose. Lyndon Johnson's method borrows from both Roosevelt's President-centered method and Eisenhower's stress on institutionalization. Johnson utilizes the cabinet and the National Security Council and gives wide play to the department head and the bureaucracy. His White House Staff appears to have a more pronounced talent for expediting action than for acting as a leavening force in program and policy development.

BUREAUCRATIC RESISTANCES TO THE PRESIDENT

For the President, the bureaucracy can be a source of tension and friction, a formidable threat to his policy interests. The natural interest of the President is to bring change in policy, particularly if he is of a different party than his predecessor. The natural interest of the bureaucracy is to resist change, to preserve the status quo, notwithstanding any shift in presidential politics. The giant bureaucracy is committed to doing things the way they have been done in the past. Techniques have been mastered and intellectual processes adjusted; rules, regulations, and operating manuals of the organization have been set; and working accommodations with the fiscal and personnel agencies have been established. Life, as much as it can be, is secure and comfortable.

When pressures for change cannot be disregarded, the bureaucracy may openly compete with the President for control of new policy and may outdistance him in the race. This situation is especially likely to occur when the administrative agency involved commands formidable pressure group support. In the 1940's, for instance, the Army Corps of Engineers was able to thwart Presidents Roosevelt and Truman and their stated preference that the Reclamation Bureau of the Interior Department construct and operate the Kings Valley project in California, involving power development, irrigation, and land use, among other things. The Reclamation Bureau reflected a New Deal-Fair Deal policy orientation, while the Engineers were decidedly conservative in social viewpoints. The Engineers ultimately dominated the situation, owing to their strength among the most actively interested local groups in California, especially the land-users associations which reflected the views of larger landowners and business groups. The strong local support of the Engineers was also valued by congressmen from the Kings Valley area, who were mindful of the need for monetary and other support at election time. The Engineers' policy stand derived strength from its harmony with private, local, and congressional viewpoints.[22]

The bureaucracy may resist the President by slowing down implementation of his policy decisions or even by ignoring them. President Truman, upon leaving the White House in 1952 and contemplating the likely plight of his successor, President Eisenhower, remarked, "He'll sit here . . . and he'll say, 'Do this! Do that!' *And nothing will happen.* Poor Ike—it won't be a bit like the Army. He'll find it very frustrating."[23] Truman was forecasting a possible fate not only of Eisenhower but of almost any successor-President.

A department, in asserting an approach to policy, may heavily stress its own expertise and values. The President must view policy through broader lenses. He must consider policy in light of the nation's needs and interests, the requirements of foreign policy, and political necessity, among other things. Agricultural groups, for example, if unchecked, might dump surplus rice abroad, regardless of its impact on foreign policy. The President, in such an instance, must assert the nation's interests and concerns in foreign affairs.

The bureaucracy may also ill serve the President when it provides advice poorly grounded in reality. Such indeed was the fate of President Kennedy in the Bay of Pigs fiasco. An inherited bureaucracy, comprising the Central Intelligence Agency, the Joint Chiefs of Staff organization, and the State Department, was thoroughly committed to the project. The fiasco that followed their recommendations and his implementation of them made the President and his aides considerably more skeptical thereafter of the proposals of the military, intelligence, and diplomatic establishments.

THE EXTERNAL RELATIONSHIPS OF THE ADMINISTRATION

The agencies composing the bureaucracy are involved in a network of external relationships that may determine nothing less than the tenability of their policy positions, the scope of their programs, the availability of money, and even their very existence. Administrative agencies have died because of lack of sufficient external support.

The former Maritime Commission, with indifferent backing from the shipping industry and the President and sharp hostility from key members of Congress, was eventually dissolved as an independent regulatory commission and reconstituted as a subordinate bureau in the Commerce Department.

Agencies compete with one another for dominion over particular policies. In so doing, they often must justify themselves before higher agencies such as interdepartmental committees and the presidential staff, who act as arbiters. In the struggle to prevail, agencies build alliances with one another. In 1962, for instance, a considerable struggle developed in the Kennedy administration over how ambitiously to pursue the development of mammoth solid-propellant (outsized solids) rockets. The Defense Department, with jurisdiction over outsized solids, advocated a relatively modest effort. The National Aeronautics and Space Administration, with support from a subordinate arm of the Defense Department, the Air Force, advocated a bolder program. After inconclusive discussion at lower levels, the issue went to the Defense Department and Space Agency chiefs Robert S. McNamara and James E. Webb. Because the dispute was regarded as fundamental, it could be taken also to the National Space Council, a top-level interagency committee composed of departments and agencies interested in space policy, and to the President himself.

Jurisdiction over large or outsized solids had been the subject of an agreement between the Defense Department and the Space Agency in 1961, which assigned to the Pentagon responsibility for large solids, with the proviso that any resulting program be responsive to the needs of the civilian space program. In 1962, it was generally assumed that sooner or later the nation would need rockets much larger than Apollo liquids—intended for manned lunar landings—for peaceful exploration of space, if not for military systems. At issue was not whether the mammoth rockets were needed but when they should be made available and what kind they should be. Several related questions were at stake in the interagency negotiations. From the standpoint of domestic politics, as well as prudent fiscal policy, what proportion of the nation's resources should be devoted to the thrust into space? What is the best allocation of these resources among competing projects? To what extent are post-Apollo needs likely to be filled by large or outsized solids, and to what extent by liquids or nuclear rockets? In the resulting dialogue, Pentagon officials stressed the realities of budgetary limitations and contended that solid-rocket technology could be advanced almost as quickly with economical tests of scaled-down rockets as with sull-scale tests costing millions of dollars each. Space agency officials countered that they could not decide what missions to pursue with the large solids until "we have obtained some experimental data in a real live situation." The Air

Force contended that the Pentagon was not allowing it to move fast enough in exploiting space for military missions, especially manned missions. It contended that huge solid rockets might well fill key requirements for military space systems. And so it went, as the Secretary of Defense and the Space Agency chief worked to establish a consensus.[24] One pressure that hastened a decision was the Soviet Union's increasing prowess in outer space. In response, American rocket programs were expanded and expedited, including those employing outsized solids.

Agencies must justify their major claims for program and policy before the President and his staff aides. The budget process is a vast judgment day of choice between the policy proposals of agencies as they compete for the limited resources of government. Agencies must support their claims with plans and argument before the Budget Bureau, and before the President and the White House Staff to the extent they intervene. Agencies compete with one another for the priority of policies. The President, faced in 1963–1964 with a looming election, and therefore with the political desirability of a relatively low budget, had to choose to some extent between costly space programs and his announced war on poverty, which presumably involved a considerable stepping-up of educational activity to better prepare workers for the tasks of a technologically complex society. Agencies are subject to presidential double-checking on the validity of their policy claims. When trouble developed in Panama and in Vietnam early in his administration, President Johnson did not rely upon the officials already in those areas but dispatched special missions under his assistant for Latin American affairs, Thomas Mann, and Secretary of Defense McNamara. The White House is also a source of pressure for the adjustment of agency policy to the necessities of politics, from the standpoints of the President and of his party. Secretary of Agriculture Benson, bent upon a policy of reducing farm price supports, faced pressures from President Eisenhower's White House Staff, the Republican National Committee, and Republican legislators from farm states who were fearful of the effect of reduced agricultural price supports upon their political futures.

Agencies must relate themselves to clienteles or pressure groups whose interests are affected by their policies. The relationship is deepened by the diffusion of power throughout the party system, which magnifies pressure-group influence. A reinforcing influence is the increasing need in the conduct of most governmental functions for technical information that specialized groups are in the best position to supply. Agencies therefore exist in a state of more or less continuous negotiation with their pressure groups. Advisory groups, typically including representatives of labor, management, agriculture, and "the public," are attached to most agencies. The official staffs of "clientele" agencies, such as the Agriculture and Labor departments, include representatives that the private groups themselves choose. The AFL-CIO, for example, usually designates from among its own numbers two of the assistant secretaries of labor. Often the officials chosen from the pressure groups do not regard themselves as primarily responsible to the administration but continue to act responsively to the private interests they represent.

The several pressure groups may pursue contrasting approaches to policy, permitting the agency leeway for manipulation and self-assertion. Secretary Benson, in furthering efforts to reduce farm price supports, drew his most approving response from the Farm Bureau, the largest of the general farm organizations—which, as Benson described it, was "consistently wary of government controls [and] opposed to government price fixing, farm income grounded in Federal subsidies, and government production controls as a means of 'stabilizing' the farm economy," The National Grange, whose policy orientation was more to the center, "generally supported our policies, but less strongly than the Farm Bureau." The National Farmers Union "consistently opposed our position on price supports; the NFU holds to the theory that farm prices are, and should be, 'made in Washington,'—that the agricultural economy must depend on Federal subsidies to give farmers their 'share' of the national income."[25]

Congress, its committees, and its members engage in a variety of acts vital to the interests of the agencies. Congressional appropriations determine the strength or impoverishment of agency programs. Congress sets the agency's overall administrative structure and allots its major functions among its bureaus—determinations which frequently bear a policy significance. Congress passes new laws and therefore has a life-or-death hold over new policies and programs. These basic powers give Congress, its committees, and its key members great leverage over various lesser aspects of agency functioning. Some of the varieties of congressional involvement are suggested by the agenda of a breakfast meeting between Benson as Secretary of Agriculture-designate in the Eisenhower administration and Senator Richard B. Russell of Georgia, Senate Agriculture Committee chairman. The subjects discussed included the desirability of renewing the International Wheat Agreement, by which the United States, Canada, Australia, and Argentina sold to wheat-short countries predetermined quantities at stipulated prices. The United States government was subsidizing the sales. Senator Russell expressed the view that the agreement should be revised and rebudgeted. "It costs too much, the losses are too heavy," he said. Russell also urged the incoming secretary "to move rapidly on the reorganization of the Department" and had definite opinions on the functioning of the Agricultural Advisory Commission that the President had pledged to establish. "Don't give it statutory authority," Russell said. "Make it nebulous, keep it in-formed, but make sure it remains *advisory*."[26]

The appointment of key agency officials, which requires the Sen-ate's approval, may be the occasion of a great political struggle that turns not so much on the nominee and his qualifications as on the policies, past and future, that his career symbolizes. A case in point is Leland Olds, President Truman's nominee for a third term on the Federal Power Commission. The Senate Interstate Commerce Com-mittee, to which the nomination was referred, witnessed a fierce struggle to beat down Olds' reappointment. Magazine articles he had written some twenty years earlier, disclosing a strong philosophical commitment to public power projects, were brought forward, and private power advocates made much of certain "objectionable" testi-mony he had rendered to the committee. President Truman himself joined the fight by charging in a letter read before the Senate that "powerful corporation" were blocking Olds' appointment. "We can-not allow great corporations to dominate the commissions which have been created to regulate them," the President declared.[27] In further pronouncements, Truman made support for Olds a matter of honoring the Democratic platform, but party members on the Senate committee were unimpressed and joined with Republicans to reject the nomi-nation 7 to 0.

Far more typically, however, a large measure of unity prevails between an agency and its group-interest clientele, creating a com-bined pressure on Congress. A most powerful agency weapon is the manufacture of grass-roots pressure group support for legislative meas-ures it wants. An agency's field offices, scattered about the country, may excel in such undertakings. For example, the National Rivers and Harbors Congress, a powerful water-use lobby, is a frequent partner of the Corps of Army Engineers in promoting legislative projects. Likewise, the Extension Service of the Agriculture Depart-ment works closely with the Farm Bureau Federation, most powerful of the farm lobbies.

STRENGTHENING THE NATIONAL ADMINISTRATION

Study of the executive branch, with a view to its improvement, has been a frequent undertaking in the twentieth century. In modern times, at least four distinguished study groups have addressed them-selves to sweeping reviews of the subject: the Brownlow Committee (1937), the first and second Hoover commissions (1949 and 1955), and the Subcommittee on National Policy Machinery (1960's), with Senator Henry Jackson of Washington state as chairman. The reports of these study groups provide a mine of information on the functioning of the executive branch and of ideas and recommendations for its improvement.[28]

The Brownlow Committee was most drastic in its recommendations for a simplification of administrative organization in the executive branch, in the interests of strengthening the President's administrative direction and control. The Brownlow group proposed to abolish the independent regulatory commissions and to vest their legislative and executive functions in departments whose duties were related to the commissions' work. The judicial activities of the commissions would be conducted by separate bureaus attached to a department for "housekeeping," or finance and personnel needs, but otherwise detached. The Brownlow committee also advocated the absorption of all government corporations into the departments, in the expectation of simplifying the President's direction and control. Toward the same end, the committee recommended that the President be given a chief personnel assistant in lieu of Civil Service Commission (a rearrangement that has not occurred) and assistance for policy planning (which, to a degree, has been provided by the Council of Economic Advisers, the National Security Council, and other staff resources).

The first Hoover Commission and its Task Force on Departmental Management offered an array of proposals to enhance the unity of the executive branch and to strengthen the President's leadership. Congress was urged not to break the President's line of command by delegating authority directly to bureau chiefs, and its habit of requiring senatorial confirmation of bureau chiefs was lamented as a kind of erosion of presidential authority. The commission proposed the consolidation of the fifty-odd agencies that at the time reported to the President into a more manageable number. To reduce the power of the triple alliance of bureaus, pressure groups, and congressional committees, the Hoover group urged the strengthening of top-level departmental management. Stronger arrangements of under secretaries, assistant secretaries, and staff and policy assistants, proposed by the commission, were designed to tie the departments more closely into the functioning of the presidency, into the development of national policy to which the departments are obliged to contribute, and into the management of international affairs, to which the relating of departmental work becomes increasingly important.

The several study groups have been attentive to personnel policy. The first Hoover Commission stressed the need for a "positive" personnel policy, one that would build a working environment and arrange career opportunities attractive enough to induce able talent to remain in the service for a working lifetime. The second Hoover Commission urged the creation of a mobile career corps, a "senior civil service," chosen from upper-level civil service employees on the basis of their judgment, leadership, adaptability, and promise for higher responsibilities. The Jackson Subcommittee on National Policy Machinery has urged both private and governmental employers to facilitate the transfer of strong talent in business, the universities, and the professions for limited-period service in government in middle- as well as higher-level positions. This expedient could regularly infuse the Washington bureaucracy, to a greater degree than at present, with new ideas, new blood, and a heightened zest for accomplishment—qualities that would provide insurance against several of the worst bureaucratic ills.

CHAPTER FIVE

Policy-Making Processes

Policy in a democracy is rarely created by a single act or by a single individual; more commonly it is the product of several or more individuals and of protracted procedures. It is seldom the inspiration merely of the present but is rooted in past thought and act, in the nation's ideals and historic traditions, and in individual and group experiences and commitments.

For convenience, a distinction may be drawn between policy activity that is *developmental* and activity that is *authoritative*. Developmental activity in the legislative and executive branches covers a wide range of acts, gestures, and words. Legislators and high executive officials make speeches urging new policy and arrange and support party platforms to the same end. Members of the bureaucracy apply their knowledge and analytical skills to the production of policy recommendations in reports and memoranda supported by fact and reasoned opinion. Legislators introduce bills and resolutions, conduct investigations, and rouse constituents, groups, and general opinion. Developmental policy activity deals in ideas, the selection of problems, research, the formulation of alternatives for possible action, and selection of some alternatives over others. Developmental activity may follow a measured course, or it may occur in fits and starts. It may transpire over days or even over decades. It may have small, almost imperceptible beginnings, yet eventuate in explosive action and importance. The origins of Franklin D. Roosevelt's court-packing plan of 1937, which involved him in probably the most engrossing political struggle of his career, can be traced at least as far back as 1932— to an offhand remark in a speech at Baltimore, in which he termed the Supreme Court a mere annex of the Republican administration. When the Court subsequently ruled the National Recovery Act, a key measure of the New Deal, unconstitutional, Roosevelt, in an agitated mood, called in his occasional counsellor Professor Felix Frankfurter, of the Harvard Law School, and Hugh Johnson, the NRA administrator. He would bring the court into line, Roosevelt emphatically asserted, and he outlined two specific ways for doing so: "packing" the court, by adding to its present members new appointees presumably favorable to New Deal legislation, or cutting back its appellate jurisdiction, which the Constitution empowered Congress to do by statute. When the Court persisted in striking down legislation, Senator George Norris urged still a further alternative upon the President: to center his 1936 campaign for re-election upon the Court issue and thereby secure support for a broad constitutional amendment sanctioning the New Deal. Roosevelt rejected this counsel and in 1937 moved to "pack" the Court.

Policy activity in its most authoritative form takes on the aspect of law, with its attributes of legitimacy, command of obedience, and possible sanctions, including coercion. There are degrees of authoritativeness. The Constitution and its amendments are the fundamental law from which all other laws derive and with which policy actions, particularly if they are challenged in the courts, must be in accord. a variety of formal, legally binding policy acts emanate from the legislative and executive branches: the statute, the treaty, the joint resolution, the executive order, the proclamation, and the administrative rule and regulation. All can be lawfully binding upon the private citizen. In addition, within the legislative and executive branches are a variety of policy forums and actions which, although not binding on the private individual, possess the full quality of authority for members of a particular branch. A legislative committee report may in reality be the key to the fate of a policy project, owing to the general tendency of the houses of Congress to adopt the recommendations of committees. In the executive branch, an expression of opinion or desire by a superior may evoke from a subordinate the same fidelity of response as a ringing command. The party platform, to which both legislative and executive policy-makers resort, may fluctuate between blatant emptiness and the reality of commitment. Senator Everett

Dirksen, the Senate Republican leader, suggested something of this range in rallying his party colleagues to support cloture to speed the civil rights bill of 1964. He recalled that his party had had strong civil rights planks in its platform for many years. "Were these promises on civil rights but idle words for vote-getting purposes," he asked, "or were they a covenant to be kept?"[1]

For the executive and legislative branches, the policy-making process can be either an individual or a cooperative interbranch enterprise. It was President Kennedy, not Congress, who determined the nation's response in the 1962 Cuban missile crisis. It was the House Rules Committee, implicitly supported by its legislative chamber, which determined that the nation should not have a broad-gauged program of federal aid to education in 1961—not the Senate, which had approved it, nor the President, who had recommended it. In refusing to report out the bill, the Rules Committee prevented the House from voting upon it. Much policy, particularly major policy, is made by Congress, the President, and the executive branch jointly. For most of the things they do, the President and his colleagues of the executive branch require laws and money, which under the Constitution only Congress can provide. But Congress, for its part, depends in large degree upon the executive to enforce and administer the laws it enacts. Congress passed the Sherman Act in 1890 to limit the growth of economic monopoly, but for a full decade, until the advent of Theodore Roosevelt, the executive branch largely ignored the law.

LEGISLATIVE-EXECUTIVE POLICY-MAKING

Legislative-executive interaction in policy-making may cover a wide range, in the developmental as well as in the authoritative stage. What each branch does or can do in the present is influenced by what both have done in the past. Such was the case with the development of what became the Social Security Act of 1935, a landmark policy enterprise that marked the beginning of the federal government's undertaking of a broad range of social insurance and public welfare programs, an act with implications for nearly every American family and for many other social institutions.

The Act of 1935 had been anticipated by the Wagner-Lewis bill of 1934 and similar bills of the day which were designed to induce the states to enact unemployment compensation laws. President Franklin D. Roosevelt, after endorsing the Wagner bill in a public letter, weakened in his support, impressed with the counsel of individuals from the business world who pointed out flaws and from New Dealers who deemed the time to be ripe for a more comprehensive social security measure than one dealing merely with unemployment insurance. Rarely can social legislation be enacted without the President's strong backing, and the Wagner-Lewis bill was no exception. Both in the executive branch and in Congress, there was growing feeling that an old-age insurance plan should be included. A powerful influence upon this general attitude was the Townsend movement, comprising several million members, mostly old people, which proposed to give every American over the age of sixty $200 a month—a sum which in those years of economic deflation seemed outrageously large. "Without the Townsend plan," the then Secretary of Labor, Frances Perkins, has written, "it is possible that the old-age insurance system would not have received the attention which it did at the hands of Congress."[2]

The President by midsummer 1934 had disclosed to administrators and legislators his purposes and tactics in the months ahead on social security. He wished to push a measure through in the first weeks of the next session of Congress. The President declared that he had come to the view that everybody should be covered for every contingency in life—from the "cradle to the grave," he termed it—under a social security system. While those of his aides most devoted to social security were gratified, they also questioned the practicality and wisdom of too ambitious a scheme. He took other steps to launch his policy initiative firmly. Surrounded by administrators of varying political views, with whom clashes on social security were altogether foreseeable, he secured from the cabinet an agreement that all its members would support the program that a committee to be appointed by the President might prepare. In a special message to Congress, Roosevelt attested to his commitment to broad-gauged social security, pointing to the necessity of governmental measures for "the security of men, women and children," which, he said, should embrace three elements: "a decent home to live in, development of natural resources to afford maximum opportunities for employment, and security against the hazards and vicissitudes of life."[3]

Some three weeks elapsed between the President's message and his creation of the cabinet committee.[4] Roosevelt, at this juncture, was preoccupied with the wind-up of the current congressional session and the myriad important matters it involved. The planning of the organization and composition of the committee was done by Harry Hopkins, the Federal Emergency Relief Administrator and a presidential confidant; by Secretary of Labor Frances Perkins; and by Dr. Arthur Altmeyer, Second Assistant Secretary of Labor. The upshot was an Executive Order, approved and issued by the President, providing for a cabinet committee and a supplementary organization of several levels. At the top was the Cabinet Committee on Economic Security, composed of the Secretary of Labor as chairman, the Secretary of the Treasury, the Attorney General, the Federal

Emergency Relief Administrator, and the Secretary of Agriculture. The latter was substituted, at the President's expressed wish, for the Secretary of Commerce, who had been included in the original draft of the Executive Order. In addition, the order authorized the setting up of an Advisory Council on Economic Security, a Technical Board on Economic Security, and an executive director and a staff to assist the Committee on Economic Security. All this was done.

The purpose of this seemingly elaborate structure was to develop a proposal that would reflect a consensus of individuals and organizations, both inside and outside government, with different lines of responsibility and consequently different outlooks: labor and management; the Treasury Department and the Labor Department, each with contrasting interests; and various experts in the social security field, each with a distinctive approach to the subject.

The Cabinet Committee on Economic Security held thirteen formal and several informal meetings over an eight-month period. The "most important" of all meetings, according to E. E. Witte, the committee's executive secretary, was an informal evening session of more than six hours at Secretary of Labor Frances Perkins' home midway in this period. The meeting was unscheduled; no minutes were kept, and only three members of the committee were present— Secretary Perkins and Harry Hopkins, whom Witte termed "the two most active members of the committee," and Secretary of Agriculture Wallace. Also present were Arthur Altmeyer, the Second Assistant Secretary of Labor, Assistant Secretary of the Treasury Josephine Roche, and Witte. Pressure for the meeting had been generated by a deadline the President had imposed for his own receipt of the committee report. Because the written report was not yet ready, the group agreed that there should be an oral presentation to the President by Secretary Perkins and Mr. Hopkins. In a discussion that continued well into the night, the group hammered out a consensus on major issues that had been blocking completion of the written report. To be sure, that report still confronted formidable hurdles.

The Technical Board was appointed by the Committee on Economic Security from experts on various social security areas from the departments and agencies. Labor, Treasury, Justice, Works Progress Administration (WPA), and the National Labor Relations Board were among the agencies represented, and the board set up its own structure, comprising an executive committee and committees on unemployment insurance, old-age security, public employment and relief, and medical care. The board members tended to be at the assistant secretary and bureau chief level, such as the chairman, Altmeyer, and Miss Roche, both assistant secretaries, and Isador Lubin, chief of the Bureau of Labor Statistics. The most important of the board's several reports to the Committee on Economic Security concerned "Major

Alternative Plans for the Administration of Unemployment Insurance" and approved recommendations made by the director and staff concerning old-age security and medical care, and aid for children. The extent of participation of individual Technical Board members varied, as it did for the cabinet committee.

The final part of the structure comprised a staff of experts and technicians, with Edwin E. Witte, an economics professor of the University of Wisconsin, as executive director. Previously, Witte had served as secretary to the Progressive Republican congressman John M. Nelson, as statistician and secretary to the Wisconsin Industrial Commission, and as chief of the Wisconsin Legislative Reference Library. In the latter capacity, he had drafted pioneering social legislation for which Wisconsin was distinguished. He had also been acting director of the state's unemployment compensation law (Wisconsin and Ohio were the only states with such laws) and had studied social insurance methods in Europe.

As executive director, Witte recruited a staff, chiefly from the universities, of experts in such social security areas as health insurance and medical care, old-age security, and unemployment insurance. The Children's Bureau in the Labor Department was tapped for staff work on security for children. A staff from the Federal Emergency Relief Administration (FERA) did studies in public employment and relief, an enterprise that was soon curtailed by a decision that the immediate relief problem was outside the committee's jurisdiction. Witte became aware that the FERA staff was using the committee as a means to bring their views, embodied in the committee's report, before the President. Witte's most trying task was that of finding social security experts willing to subordinate their professional preferences to the necessity of establishing consensus and to put aside their customary standards of perfection so the committee's reports could hold to a tight time schedule. In addition, he consulted nearly two score individuals in the government and outside, among them experts in the universities; Supreme Court Justice Louis D. Brandeis, whose influence on social legislation during Woodrow Wilson's presidency had been profound; Abraham Epstein, a private authority on social security systems; and several prestigious business figures known to be either neutral or open-minded toward administration policies. The President had suggested two of these figures himself: John J. Raskob of General Motors and Walter C. Teagle of Standard Oil. "Very contradictory advice was given me by the people consulted," Witte wrote, "but I still regard these conferences as having been distinctly worthwhile, as they served to rapidly acquaint me with the widely varying views entertained within the Administration circle and the difficulties to be overcome."[5]

Members of the White House Staff and various presidential assistants gave Witte and his colleagues guidance concerning the President's own thinking and needs. Roosevelt discussed his views, which were numerous, with his secretary, Louis Howe, and his general assistant, Raymond Moley, who passed them on to the committee. Hopkins and Secretary Perkins had ready access to the President, both to present their views and to pick up his reactions. At one juncture, at Moley's request, Witte prepared a lengthy statement on the problems of economic security for inclusion in a presidential speech to be given at Green Bay, Wisconsin. Although only two sentences of Witte's write-up were used, they had a marked effect on the stock market, which dropped five points, and brought Treasury officials to demand that social security be soft-pedaled.

The President himself played a continuous and far-ranging role in the development of social security policy. In the weeks prior to the cabinet committee's creation, Roosevelt had explored social security problems with Miss Perkins and with his general advisers, Raymond Moley and Rexford Tugwell; with Harry Hopkins, who was close to the President; and with Louis Howe. As he was wont to do in exploring major new policy areas, Roosevelt also looked for counsel outside government circles—in this instance from Gerard J. Swope and Owen D. Young of General Electric and from John J. Raskob of General Motors. Once the cabinet committee had been created, Roosevelt provided the fullest expression of his views midway in the enterprise in a meeting with Miss Perkins, Altmeyer, Witte, and Thomas Eliot, the committee's counsel, bill draftsman, and adviser on legal questions— a critical assignment in an era when the Supreme Court was striking down many New Deal measures as unconstitutional. Roosevelt, in offering his views, stressed that the committee should not necessarily recommend what he at this point deemed desirable. He felt committed to both unemployment insurance and old-age security, and he hoped the committee would explore thoroughly the possibilities of a "single package" social security system providing protection against all major personal hazards leading to poverty and dependency. He expressed decided preferences for state administration of unemployment insurance, although reserve funds, in his view, had to be handled by the federal government. Unemployment insurance, he felt, would encourage the stabilization of employment. All forms of social insurance, in his view, should be self-supporting, without subsidies from general tax sources. He contended, as he had as governor of New York, that the only long-term solution of the problem of old-age insurance lay in a compulsory plan. All these views were incorporated in the final administration proposal.

The widest-ranging influence upon the social security plan's development was Executive Secretary Witte, whose almost agonizing experiences occurred when he shepherded the final committee report, which he and specialists prepared, through a lengthy process of clearance, seeking the approval of each department represented on the committee. Several committee members refused to sign the report without having every word of it and the accompanying draft bill scrutinized by subordinates in whom they had absolute confidence. Witte's worst troubles occurred in the Treasury Department, where two groups opposed social security: One group, conservative, aimed to hold down expenditures and avoid any stir that might trouble business; the other, radical, contended that the nation's severe unemployment involved deeper maladies than any that social security could deal with, and hence the program would have little value. Eventually the report was cleared; an important factor carrying it over the difficult hurdle of securing unanimity was the circumstance that the President had announced in a message to Congress on January 4, 1935, that he would send a special message on social security within ten days. "The committee had 'gotten the President out on a limb,'" Witte noted, "and simply had to reach an agreement without further delay."[6]

The Bureau of the Budget, the President's regular advisory agency on finance and legislation, forcefully entered the picture after the committee's report was in the President's hands. At that juncture, Hopkins, in a private conversation with Roosevelt, had induced the President to combine the draft social security bill with his own work relief program. The work program had been encountering rough handling in Congress, and Hopkins by this maneuver hoped to have some of the aura the social security measure would attract rub off on his own work program. But D. W. Bell, the acting budget director, objected to this procedure, and the two measures were thereupon separated.

JOINT CONGRESSIONAL POLICY-MAKING

The policy-making process in Congress also embraces many units, each capable of speeding up, slowing down, or even stopping policy development, at least for a given session. Congressional policy-making processes lack both the flexibility of the executive branch processes and the forceful influences for unity and action which the President and his White House aides can impart. The House of Representatives, particularly, works according to rather set procedures which facilitate slowdown or stoppage in policy development. But House procedures can be modified, and policy development can be speeded up and assured. The manipulation of House rules and the dodging of procedural obstacles cause policy-making in the House—and only to a lesser degree in the Senate—to become a tactical game that is centered upon parliamentary maneuver and procedural rules. Although the Senate's procedures are freer and more flexible then the House's, the filibuster can be invoked in the higher chamber, a tactic which has been fatal to many a bill, particularly in the field of civil rights.

The Civil Rights Act of 1964, but one of several civil rights laws passed in the century since the Civil War—and easily the most comprehensive and far-reaching of them—was steered successfully through the innumerable shoals on which any controversial legislation is apt to founder in Congress. The 1964 victory centered upon several intense procedural struggles in Congress, whose outcome was a life-or-death determination of the fate of civil rights policy.

Sweeping civil rights legislation had been promised by President Kennedy in his 1960 campaign, but it was long withheld (to the dismay of civil rights groups) in the belief that the legislation could not pass Congress and that, indeed, it might endanger other legislation the administration was pushing. Early in 1963, Kennedy finally recommended enactment of a mild bill. The rising civil rights demonstrations and boycotts in the North and South, however, brought the President to submit a new and far stronger bill in 1963 which, among other things, would guarantee Negroes access to public accommodations, allow the federal government to file suit to desegregate schools, and permit federal programs to be cut off in any area where discrimination was practiced in their application. Kennedy put the highest priority tag upon passage of the new bill.

Nearly a year elapsed between the introduction of the new bill and its enactment. Its successful passage through the treacherous parliamentary reefs was in no small measure a product of cooperative enterprise between the presidential administration and congressional leaders of both political parties. It also illustrated that congressional policy processes are essentially exercises in constructing majorities in both houses—sometimes very large majorities—in order to surmount procedural obstacles.

Several types of parliamentary maneuver can be discerned in the 1964 civil rights story.[7] The manner in which the legislation was introduced, its sponsorship, and its provisions, possessed a calculated significance. In the Senate, the administration bill was introduced by the Democratic leader, Mike Mansfield. In a companion move that demonstrated the bipartisan concern for civil rights, Mansfield, with Everett Dirksen, the Senate Republican leader, as co-sponsor, introduced a bill with all of the administration's recommendations except the controversial public accommodations section. Thereupon Mansfield and Senator Warren G. Magnuson (D., Wash.) introduced as a separate measure the public accommodations section.

These several maneuvers reflected the realities of the Senate standing committees, which, like those of the House, have life-and-death power over bills. Most bills die in committee, in the sense that they are never reported out or are reported out negatively. Committees have great power to delay, and, with the mounting street demonstrations in summer 1963, time was of the essence to the administration. The most ominous reality in the Senate was the Judiciary Committee, to which civil rights legislation is traditionally referred. The Judiciary Committee was chaired by Senator James Eastland of Mississippi, whose adamancy against any and all kinds of civil rights legislation had long been proven beyond any doubt. The Mansfield-Magnuson maneuver of a separate bill for the public accommodations provision was aimed to remove from Eastland's jurisdiction what was both the most symbolic and the most controversial feature of the civil rights proposals. The maneuver succeeded, and the public accommodations bill was referred by the presiding officer of the Senate, the then Vice-President Lyndon Johnson, to the Commerce Committee, which Magnuson headed and which presumably had the votes to report out the bill favorably. In the House of Representatives, no similar problem existed. The House Judiciary Committee was chaired not by a southern Democrat but by a northern liberal, Congressman Emanuel Celler of Brooklyn. Celler himself introduced the full civil rights bill, including the public accommodations feature, which was then referred to his committee.

Since a national election was approaching, the initial maneuvers in the House centered upon interparty competition for credit for any achievement which might be brought off. In the House, unlike the Senate, these early maneuvers did not center upon the problems of the conservative southern Democrats. Some days prior to the introduction of the administration bill, twenty-nine House Republicans (including John Lindsay of New York but not including William McCulloch of Ohio, ranking Republican on the Judiciary Committee) introduced a bill, based on Fourteenth Amendment guarantees, outlawing segregation in various public accommodations.

Republican and Democratic differences in both houses did not turn simply on political maneuvers geared to the coming election. There was a constitutional issue which, in turn, was joined to a historic idealized issue that had long divided the parties. Republican proponents of civil rights legislation—and particularly of the public accommodations feature—contended that its constitutional base should rest upon the equal-protection clause of the Fourteenth Amendment. They argued that many public accommodations required the sanction of the state governments, usually in the form of a license, and that this fact provided the best basis for outlawing segregation. The administration and its legislative spokesmen, in contrast, proposed to rest the public accommodations provision upon the commerce clause, a clause broadly interpreted by the Supreme Court in behalf of federal action. An extant Supreme Court decision, handed down near the close of the nineteenth century, threw some doubt, in administration eyes, upon the serviceability of the Fourteenth Amendment.[8] The constitutional debate had relevance to the question of committee referral in the Senate. Basing the public accommodations feature on the commerce clause created a kind of logic for referring it to the Commerce Committee rather than to the Judiciary Committee and took the edge off any asserted arbitrariness in the choice. Many Republicans, however, opposed reliance upon the commerce clause, owing to its image as a kind of octopus that had justified federal controls over matters left traditionally to state regulation or private action. These matters ranged from minimum wages to drug prices; to add public accommodations was to gorge the federal monster further.

Another kind of maneuver at the introduction-of-bills stage was the injection of measures suited to the views of Negro civil rights groups. The administration bill was some distance removed from their expressed desires. In the House, consequently, Congressman Robert W. Kastenmeier (D., Wis.) introduced a bill that included, among other things, voting guarantees in both federal and state elections and a special temporary voting referee procedure. The procedure was designed to assist qualified Negroes to register and vote by providing voting referees to serve while civil suits were pending. This kind of bill became a fulcrum for pressure—a possible bargaining weapon for legislative spokesmen for the Negro groups.

Given the power of standing committees to throttle or rewrite legislation, the stage of committee hearings and reports was crucial. In the Senate, affairs proceeded much as the initial maneuvering anticipated. The Judiciary Committee, under Eastland's leadership, held nearly two months of hearings and then took no action to report out the administration bill. The Commerce Committee held twenty-two days of hearings, with witnesses whose views ranged from those of the Secretary of State, Dean Rusk, that failure to enact the administration bill would cause the world to question "the real convictions of the American people," to those of Governor Ross Barnett of Mississippi, who contended that the bill was aiding a "world Communist conspiracy to divide and conquer" the United States.

The Commerce Committee prepared and agreed upon an amended version of the administration's public accommodations bill. The alterations included adoption of the so-called "Mrs. Murphy clause," which exempted from the bill's coverage owner-occupied private homes in which not more than five rooms are for rent. For weeks, the committee delayed filing a formal report on the bill, a decision based on strategic considerations. Once the report was filed, the bill could be brought up by any member of the Senate, an eventuality the Democratic leadership wished to avoid. A Senate debate, the leadership feared, would quickly become a filibuster, resulting in a general shutdown on the progress of other legislation. The leaders wished to postpone that unwelcome but seemingly inevitable development at least until the House passed its bill and sent it to the Senate. Meanwhile, by keeping the bill in committee, Senate leaders were keeping their chamber's tracks clear.

The strategy succeeded; the Senate committee report was held back, and on February 10 the House, by a vote of 290 to 130, passed a civil rights bill. In one view, this was the culmination of a long, intensive enterprise in building a majority. True to the traditional process by which proposals for most economic and social legislation become laws, the civil rights bill was an enterprise in bipartisan cooperation. The House bill, the most sweeping measure to clear either house in the twentieth century, was supported by 152 Democrats (with 96 opposing) and 138 Republicans (34 opposed). The victorious majority was a bipartisan coalition of Republicans and northern Democrats. Although dozens of amendments were considered, some severely limiting, not a single amendment was adopted that was opposed by the bill's managers, who included the House Republican leader, Charles Halleck. Behind the bill's managers was a juggernaut of major lobby groups: the Leadership Conference on Civil Rights, an alliance of Negro groups; the various major Negro civil rights organizations; the top AFL-CIO industrial unions; and Protestant, Catholic, and Jewish church groups, all of whom waged an aggressive, carefully formulated campaign. Probably the most critical stage in the bill's progress in the House was the period of negotiations between the Democratic and Republican leaderships to work out a bill that could command the support of the many Republicans whose votes would be needed in concert with those of northern Democrats to defeat southern Democrats and nonsouthern conservatives who might combine in whittling down and possibly killing the bill.

This majority-building enterprise was imperiled by the distance between, on the one hand, Republicans who wanted more stress placed on the Fourteenth Amendment and on state action in the public accommodations section, and, on the other hand, Democrats who were the legislative spokesmen of civil rights groups pressing for a stronger bill than the administration favored. The differences between the two opinion wings reached climactic proportions when the civil rights groups induced six northern Democrats on the House Judiciary subcommittee considering the bill to write a measure that went beyond that of the administration. The problem facing the administration's legislative leaders was how to modify the subcommittee bill when it reached the full committee and put it into a form that might be acceptable to a bipartisan coalition on the House floor, without forcing the civil rights advocates of either party to appear to back down. This hazard was enlarged by signs that Southerners on the Judiciary Committee were maneuvering civil rights advocates into sending the strong subcommittee bill to the floor.

Several hazardous decisions were made and maneuvers taken to combat the mounting dangers. The administration decided to run the political risk of asking publicly, through the testimony of Attorney General Robert Kennedy before the full House Judiciary Committee, for a milder bill. The Attorney General declared that the subcommittee bill had provisions which either were legally unwise or were so sweeping as to provoke unnecessary opposition to the bill. He especially objected to Title II, which barred discrimination in any business authorized or licensed by any state or locality, and to a new Title III, which gave the Justice Department almost unlimited powers in filing suits to halt deprivations of civil rights. "What I want is a bill, not an issue," the Attorney General declared. His views brought cries of "sellout" from the NAACP and other civil rights groups.

The realignment of congressional forces stirred by Robert Kennedy's move was soon apparent. Congressman Celler announced that he would put aside his own feelings and support a moderate bill in order to win congressional approval. The ranking Republican of the House Judiciary Committee, William McCulloch, termed Kennedy's testimony "very useful, very constructive." But the strong civil rights liberals on the committee, such as Jacob Gilbert (D., N.Y.) and Robert Kastenmeier (D., Wisc.), were adamant against any modification of the subcommittee bill. The machinery of maneuver and behind-the-scenes negotiation began turning at full speed. Celler cancelled a scheduled Judiciary Committee meeting for two days while administration representatives and McCulloch, Halleck, and other Republican leaders hammered out an agreement on a compromise bill. The process entailed, as it usually does, extensive bargaining. In exchange for blocking the subcommittee bill and supporting another, the Republicans insisted on dropping provision for a temporary voting registrar formula for special three-judge federal courts, for making the Civil Rights Commission permanent, and for adding to the commission's authority to investigate voting frauds. The Republicans also insisted upon eliminating the proposed Community Relations Service as unnecessary, adding a fair employment section with court—rather than administrative—enforcement of decisions, and a modified Title III. The Kennedy administration and its legislative spokesmen accepted these demands. The Judiciary Committee thereupon rejected the subcommittee bill—with Southerners and some liberals, interestingly, joining to support it—and substituted the new and milder bipartisan version. Vital to this victory was the switch of four northern Democrats who had supported a strong subcommittee bill. Attorney General Kennedy hailed the bipartisanship of Halleck and McCulloch. "In my judgment," he said, "if it had not been for their support and effort, the possibility of civil rights legislation in Congress would have been remote." The new bill, he added, was a "better bill than the administration's in dealing with the problems facing the nation." By dint of further struggle, the bill eventually passed the House.

The second crucial venture in bipartisan majority-building occurred in the Senate and focused on a formidable issue of parliamentary procedure. The filibuster, both the symbol and the logical result of the Senate's proud tradition of free debate, was a weapon that Southerners time and again had employed with fatal effect on civil rights legislation. Passage of the Civil Rights Act of 1964 required the imposition of cloture upon debate, which cannot be done, under Senate rules, without an imposing vote—two-thirds of the senators present and voting. Prior to 1964, cloture had been invoked successfully only five times. The 1964 civil rights bill eventually became the sixth time when, with all 100 senators present, the Senate by vote of 71 to 29— four more votes than necessary—invoked cloture. The imposition came after a 75-day filibuster on the bill, the longest ever experienced under the cloture rule. The practical problem faced by advocates of the House bill was that its provisions were considered too strong by conservative Republicans whose votes were necessary if cloture were to be imposed. Again, the bill's provisions were recast, this time with Senator Everett Dirksen, the Senate Republican leader, in the crucial policy-developing role. In essence, Dirksen worked out with the Justice Department amendments which did not vitally affect the substance of the legislation but which were sufficiently responsive to states' rights and gradualist sentiment to produce the necessary Republican votes. Dirksen's efforts at persuasion were not limited to the Senate. He first had to convince President Johnson, who at the outset of the cloture venture was reportedly pessimistic of its success, that cloture could be obtained by astute amendment of the House bill.

The problem of majority-building facing Dirksen and Democratic Senate leaders was a problem of simple voting mathematics. A tally of the predispositions of senators on the question of cloture revealed that 30 members were unalterably opposed, leaving 70 possible votes in favor—27 Republicans and 43 Democrats. Of these, nine—seven Republicans and two Democrats—were deemed by the party leaders to be, at best, on the fence. The heart of the politico-mathematical problem was to win over five or six of these nine "swing votes" to establish cloture. Dirksen had good access to the Republican senators involved, since he had always been diligent in keeping his lines open to both the liberal and the conservative wings of the Republican party which those senators represented. In approaching the "swing" senators he could draw upon the personal loyalties built up over the years and upon the pressures implicit in his position as leader over committee appointments and over the scheduling and support of bills in which senators and their home states were interested.

In the enterprise of majority-building, both Presidents Kennedy and Johnson were always central figures, working from various vantage points and by various methods. They committed their prestige by making public statements in behalf of civil rights legislation—President Johnson by his outspoken commitment to Negro rights, for example. In his first address to Congress, following President Kennedy's assassination, Johnson named civil rights as a priority item for Congress' consideration. If he had been lukewarm in his advocacy, which included a speech on the subject in Georgia, success with cloture would doubtless have been unlikely. Johnson apparently took little part in the parliamentary maneuvering, despite his skill in such endeavors. When Republican spokesmen charged that Johnson was on the brink of a "deal" with Southerners on civil rights in order to pick up votes for his tax bill, the administration found it necessary to deny that the President would engage in any "deals" or compromises on the civil rights bill. Following a weekly meeting of Democratic congressional leaders at the White House, Hubert Humphrey, the assistant Senate majority leader, declared that the President was "committed" to the bill passed by the House and would make "no wheels and no deals" to water it down in the Senate.[9] Johnson's chief contribution in the Senate struggle seems to have been his successes in buttonholing and convincing several Democratic legislators. Senator Howard W. Cannon (D., Nev.) was believed to have voted for cloture upon the strength of a presidential appeal which doubtless shored up other wavering Democrats as well.

PRESIDENTIAL APPROVAL OR REJECTION

After legislation is enacted by the two houses of Congress, it comes to the President for his approval or veto. The President's approval is a routine final act in the drama of lawmaking when the bill coming before him mirrors the views for which he has previously pressed. His signing then becomes something of a ceremony; the press snaps pictures as the President affixes his signature, and the legislators who contributed to the victory are gathered about his desk. The President may offer a statement of commendation, as President Johnson did in hailing the 1964 Civil Rights Act as "a major contribution to meet a national responsibility."

Paradoxically, in signing a bill into law the President may approve policy with which he actually disagrees. Because the President has a general veto, he must approve or reject a bill in its totality; in approving, therefore, he often accepts provisions he deems objectionable. He may couple his approval with a statement pointing out the features of which he disapproves, as Franklin Roosevelt did in reluctantly accepting a requirement in the extension of the Selective Service

Act, just prior to the nation's entrance into World War II, limiting the use of troops raised under its provisions to the Western Hemisphere.

For the President, whether to approve or to veto may be an arduous policy and political decision, and in making it he may seek counsel in many quarters. The Bureau of the Budget regularly provides such counsel on the basis of its legislative clearance function, by securing opinions from interested departments and agencies and sometimes from key members of the White House Staff. President Truman, faced in 1947 with the question of whether to approve or to veto the Taft-Hartley labor bill, consulted widely.[10] His cabinet was divided. Some secretaries considered a veto a useless gesture in view of the likelihood that both houses would override it. Others considered a veto politically ill-advised, since a coal strike was looming with possible severe public consequences. The Secretary of Labor and Clark Clifford, the President's special counsel, pressed for a veto. The Democratic National Committee and the chairman and vice-chairman of each state committee were polled regarding the action the President should take; the result was two to one in favor of a veto. For most of two days, the President was closeted with his advisers and had available their exhaustive written analyses of the bill. The Secretary of Labor provided an overall review, the Attorney General dealt with the legal aspects, the Secretary of Commerce with the industrial aspects, and the National Labor Relations Board chairman with the administrative problems. Presidential counsel Clifford generally guided the group and studied the legislative history of the bill and the many committee reports.

Truman ultimately chose to veto—a course finally recommended by most of his advisers. His veto message was drafted with the help of his special counsel, the White House labor adviser, his press secretary, and the National Labor Relations Board chairman. Its language was vehement, and it served not simply as a congressional message but as a political document, stating in stark terms what was to become a major issue of the approaching 1948 presidential election. Although presidential vetoes are seldom overriden, the record-breaking number of strikes in the Truman era brought Congress to sustain the Taft-Hartley Act against the President's disapproval.

ADMINISTRATIVE IMPLEMENTATION

Policy that has survived the rigors of executive formulation and legislative and presidential approval must face the final hurdle of administrative implementation. This phase can constitute a full fruition of policy embodied in enacted legislation; the administration of the Peace Corps, for example, fulfills the objectives incorporated in the legislation establishing it. But administration can also be a period of diversion and retreat from policies previously adopted.

Administrative implementation involves several phases critical to the future of policy. One is the appointment of key officials, such as the members of a regulatory commission, bureau chiefs, and others. The attitudes, values, and ambitions of the persons appointed illuminate the likely shape of future policy. Since the President initiates most top appointments, he is the focus of pressures which were present but did not prevail in the legislative phase of policy but which aim to do so in the appointive phase. The Federal Reserve Act, passed after long struggle in the Wilson administration, required the appointment of a Federal Reserve Board. President Wilson, anxious to win the support of the banking and business community for the new regulatory venture, nominated such a preponderance of bankers and businessmen that a progressive of that era was driven to exclaim, "Why, it looks as if Mr. Vanderlip [president of the National City Bank of New York] has selected them."[11] Similarly, the Federal Trade Commission, also created during the Wilson administration, presumably to limit monopoly and restore competition, at first seemed to move in the opposite direction under the businessmen-commissioners whom Wilson had appointed. Louis D. Brandeis, who had been influential in the initiation of the Federal Trade Commission Act, openly declared that Wilson was ruining the commission by his choice of commissioners.

Administrative implementation may involve sublegislation or rulemaking by the administrative agency and administrative adjudication based on these rules or on the basic statutes. The law under which an agency acts may provide it broad discretion in its sublegislative activity. The National Labor Relations Act of 1935, for instance, authorized the board created by the act to determine the "appropriate unit" for collective bargaining. Both the long-established AFL and the youthful CIO had great stakes in the NLRB's definition of the bargaining unit. The AFL focused upon a craft approach and the CIO upon the inclusion of unskilled and semiskilled as well as skilled labor in its drives for union membership and collective bargaining. The Board proceeded to define the appropriate unit in rule-making and adjudication with conspicuous partiality to the shop-wide and plant-wide approach to which the CIO was devoted. Friendly NLRB policy was a major factor in the phenomenal growth of the CIO in the 1930's.

The moment of truth for much public policy occurs in its enforcement. Policy incorporated into legislation, with presidential and bipartisan support, can wither and die from lack of enforcement—or, with sufficient attention, it can flower and thrive. Thus the Sherman Antitrust Act, which commanded impressive enforcement resources in the Taft administration, received abysmally little in Calvin Coolidge's.

INDEPENDENT CONGRESSIONAL POLICY-MAKING

Congress' most affirmative policy-making is done in cooperation with the President. Because of the very nature of the lawmaking process, such policy-making requires coordination and agreement productive of a majority of votes in both houses and action by standing committees and conference committees able to develop the consensus which the new legislation represents. In this sense, legislation such as the Civil Rights Act of 1964 is the outcome of cooperation and consensus by members, leaders, committees, and parties.

But Congress also can act negatively, and indeed much of the time it does. Instead of cooperating with the administration, Congress sometimes engages in conflict with it. Congress can reject legislation the President proposes; it may or may not substitute a positive policy of its own. Although its principal function is to make laws, actually it performs with greater relish and skill a countervailing function: keeping laws from being made. In this sense, Congress is a highly negative body whose policy often is to have no policy. According to a contemporary critic of congressional policy-making, Senator Joseph S. Clark (D., Pa.), the national legislature is controlled by a minority, conservative in orientation, heavily southern in the Senate and rather less so in the House, an alliance of conservative southern Democrats and conservative Republicans, the latter chiefly from rural areas and small towns. Members of this conservative alliance hold strategic positions of power in Congress and are thus able to block policy.[12]

In 1963, Senator Clark contends, the controlling congressional minority, or the "Establishment," could undertake, by astute use of delaying tactics, to defeat nothing less than President Kennedy's complete program. As 1963 ended, the civil rights bill which Kennedy had presented at midyear with the most emphatic urgency, was stuck in the House. His tax bill, to which he had accorded an equally high priority, was becalmed in the Senate Finance Committee. A dozen appropriation bills remained unenacted a full six months after the fiscal year for which they were intended had expired.

It was not that Congress as a whole or its individual houses were engaging in acts of corporate negation. Indeed, neither Congress nor its individual houses, acting as bodies, had engaged in any rejections. Rather, the power of Congress to kill, block, and delay—to respond to national problems by inaction—is exercised by numerous and scattered organs of power. The power to act negatively in Congress is diffused among standing committees and steering committees, fortified by the seniority rule. The committee system and the seniority rule vest an effective negative power in a group of elder statesmen who, Senator Clark contends, are unrepresentative of dominant public and congressional opinion. The patriarchs of the Establishment are Senator

Richard Russell of Georgia and Representative ("Judge") Howard Smith of Virginia. Establishment members are almost invariably charming, amiable, and popular men who mean to keep the Republic safe from what they regard as unsound social and economic innovation. In its affirmative actions on policy, the Establishment supports the military, calls for vigor in foreign affairs, and generally shows more devotion to property than to human rights.

The Establishment's power centers in the standing committees. In 1964, for example, Southerners controlled the chairmanships of nine out of sixteen committees. It was not the 87th Congress that rejected Kennedy's proposal for medical care for the aged but the House Ways and Means Committee, by a margin of five votes. By one vote, the same committee refused to report out an extension of unemployment compensation.

The Establishment controls policy through manipulation of a power structure emanating pressures on individual legislators. The congressional electoral campaign committees of the two houses, which the Establishment also dominates, distribute campaign money with noticeably greater prodigality to candidates who conform to the Establishment's ideological standards than to those who do not. Another pressure is committee assignments, doled out as punishment or reward. Assignment to the right committee may enable a senator to do more for his state and thereby to impress his constituents, particularly pressure groups among them. In 1963, of fourteen nonfreshman senators who proposed to weaken the existing filibuster rule and who applied for new committee seats, only one got what he wanted in committee assignments. Of eight nonfreshman senators who supported the rule, seven were satisfied.

In addition to lawmaking and its substages of committee hearings and reports, votes, and the like, Congress or its parts can engage in other policy activity. Its committees can launch investigations of sectors of the executive branch. These investigations may be the forerunners of legislation, or they may derive from Congress' responsibility to oversee the chief executive in the discharge of his obligation to take care that the laws are faithfully executed. Equally, Congress may probe the executive to see that the funds it appropriates are expended properly. Investigations may be conducted in a fashion stressing harmony and cooperation between the executive and legislative branches in the manner of Senator Harry S Truman's investigations of domestic wartime administration in World War II.[13] But during the Civil War one of Lincoln's heaviest crosses was the Congressional Joint Committee on the Conduct of the War, which concentrated upon the Army of the Potomac and harassed its generals indiscriminately; it employed wild rumor and irresponsible publicity and became the factional instrument of its members.

Congress also acts by means of resolutions. These may serve as expressions of internal policy which may have important consequences for external policy. By resolution, for example, the individual houses create, empower, and finance investigating committees. By resolution, the individual houses can censure individual members, as the Senate did Senator Joseph McCarthy, whose investigations had injured the executive branch. Resolutions may be by an individual house, or the two houses may combine in concurrent resolutions. Resolutions may be a prelude to lawmaking or a show of congressional feeling which has the force of publicity rather than of law. As the 1962 Cuban missile crisis mounted, and prior to any substantial overt response from the executive branch, Congress passed a resolution invoking the Monroe Doctrine and the 1947 Rio Pact for joint Western Hemispheric defense against foreign intervention. The United States, the resolution declared, was determined to prevent, by "use of arms" if necessary, any Cuban military build-up threatening American security. The resolution served a double purpose for the bipartisan majority which produced it: to warn Khrushchev and Castro, and to jog certain administration policy-makers who seemed to the legislators to be taking an excessively detached view of Cuban developments.

PRESIDENTIAL POLICY-MAKING

In certain sectors of policy-making, the President can make policy with Congress playing little, if any, part. Particularly as chief diplomat and as commander in chief, the President enjoys broad powers to engage in executive-centered policy-making. A classic instance is President Kennedy's policy-making in the Cuban missile crisis in 1962, the first nuclear confrontation between the United States and the Soviet Union.[14]

In mid-October, a United States U-2 reconnaissance plane discovered the presence in Cuba of Soviet medium-range missiles, capable of reaching every American city within minutes, and sites under construction from which to fire them. The discovery touched off fourteen days of diplomatic maneuver, military build-up, and policy decision. In this period, President Kennedy engaged in lengthy consultations with his staff, exchanged numerous communications with the Soviet premier, and eventually chose to impose a blockade on Cuba to prevent more missiles from coming in. In addition, he sought removal of the missiles already there. The blockade was imposed, the nation was informed of the nature of the crisis, and Khrushchev agreed to removal of the missiles and refrained from adding to their number. Our allies had to be informed and rallied, and the blockade administered.

In view of the vast consequences of policy in the missile crisis, the President's personal role in its resolution was central. It was he who set the atmosphere within which his administration worked—the composure which governed the policy-making deliberations. He had to choose the staff aides to provide counsel, and, as was typical with Kennedy, he dealt not merely with department heads but with under secretaries and assistant secretaries as well. When he eventually had to make the awesome and lonely choice among policy alternatives, he settled upon a blockade. Kennedy exchanged communications with Khrushchev, himself composing many of the messages and choosing at times which of the premier's contradictory statements of view and intent to rely upon for further policy-making. He had to receive Soviet Foreign Minister Andrei Gromyko on October 18, and, in the interest of preserving secrecy so that his eventual policy choice might gain momentum, he abstained from revealing the fact that he knew of the presence of Soviet missiles in Cuba. Kennedy informed the nation of the crisis in a radio and television address that was beamed around the world. He oversaw the administration of the blockade, the location of American naval vessels and approaching Soviet and Soviet-satellite vessels, and personally gave the order for the boarding of one of the latter. Simultaneously, he carried on his other presidential duties, including a full schedule of speeches in the ongoing congressional election campaign.

Kennedy relied for policy advice on a group soon known as the "Ex Com," or Executive Committee of the National Security Council. The Ex Com was a kind of improvisation, enabling the President to meet with those staff members in whose judgment he had particular confidence and whose functional specialty in policy-making was strongly relevant to the crisis. In meetings of the Ex Com, the President, when present, presided; his fellow conferees included Vice-President Johnson, Secretary of State Rusk, Secretary of Defense McNamara, Secretary of the Treasury Dillon, Attorney General Robert Kennedy, Under Secretary of State Ball, Deputy Secretary of Defense Gilpatric, CIA Deputy Director Carter (CIA Director McCone was away from Washington in the first days of the crisis), Assistant Secretary of State for Inter-American Affairs Martin, General Taylor (Chairman of the Joint Chiefs of Staff), McGeorge Bundy, presidential assistant for national security affairs, and Theodore Sorensen, presidential counsel and principal speech writer.

The group's essential task was to weigh the alternative responses the United States might make to the Soviet challenge. Several possibilities were considered. If the United States did nothing, its prestige would be undermined and its security threatened, since the missiles would radically alter the military situation. Latin America might fall under Soviet sway. As a second possibility, the United States might invade Cuba, or subject it to air strikes, or both. Ex Com discussions of this alternative stressed that such action would taint our moral position, disturb our allies, agitate the neutral nations, and risk a Soviet countermove in Berlin or elsewhere. A third possibility was a blockade, but it, too, might provoke a Soviet response and offend our allies, especially the maritime powers. The choice between the second and third alternatives occupied some days, although the initial meeting of the President with the Ex Com produced two immediate policy decisions: that the existing air surveillance the United States was maintaining over Cuba should be intensified and that any other action the United States might take should occur as close as possible to its public disclosure of the Soviet bases. As the crisis wore on, Kennedy went outside the government to bring into the discussion former Secretary of State Dean Acheson and former Secretary of Defense Robert Lovett. United Nations Ambassador Adlai Stevenson and Ambassador-at-Large Llewellyn Thompson, Jr., a former ambassador to the Soviet Union, were also brought in.

While the Ex Com was deliberating, the vast executive machinery was at work preparing the means of action to support the several possible alternative policy decisions, thereby preserving the President's opportunity to choose among them. The Defense Department estimated the kinds of units, numbers of men, and time factors necessary for various military actions. The State Department explored the possibilities of Latin American and European support, and its experts on Soviet behavior weighed the effects of various actions on the Russians and their likely responses.

The President and the Ex Com were rushed to the climax of policy decision by the speed with which Soviet technicians were bringing the Cuban missile installations to completion. In addition, the passing of time increasingly endangered the preservation of the secrecy of the policy-making venture. The Ex Com, with the President, had been developing a consensus that the blockade was the best of the several alternatives. Once this policy choice had been made, it had to be "articulated" in the several ways in which the United States government under the circumstances might act. A television and radio address had to be prepared for the nation—or, in reality, for the world, what with the magic of the Voice of America and Telstar. Even before the President had reached a final decision on the blockade, his special counsel and speech writer, Theodore Sorensen, had prepared a draft of the address upon the assumption that a blockade would be imposed; the final speech emerged after five drafts. The blockade decision had to be articulated in legal terms. In Ex Com meetings, Llewellyn Thompson had stressed the need for a foundation of legality for any action taken. The Russians, he believed, had a feeling for "legality," and action soundly based in law would impress world opinion. The State and Justice departments developed the legal justification for a blockade which they instilled in the presidential proclamation imposing the blockade; they also drafted that document. The blockade decision required elaborate preparations by the Navy and the other armed services bearing responsibilities for supporting it. The State Department prepared a statement of the Cuban problem and of the American response for use with the Organization of American States, NATO, and our major allies. Under the supervision of Alexis Johnson, Deputy Under Secretary of State for Political Affairs, a "master scenario" was worked up, depicting every necessary step prior to the President's speech—briefings of Adenauer, Macmillan, and De Gaulle, orders to embassies, ship movements, and the like. A Kennedy-to-Khrushchev letter had to be prepared to accompany a copy of the television speech announcing the blockade.

Before launching his policy, the President "touched base" with several sources of domestic political power or influence whose favorable response to the chosen policy was prized. Former President Eisenhower was brought to Washington for a briefing. Twenty congressional leaders of both parties met with the President for what was by no means an occasion of routine acquiescence. Senator Russell, the Armed Services Committee chairman, and Senator Fulbright, the Foreign Relations Committee chairman, bluntly asserted their disagreement with the President's policy, arguing that a blockade was too slow and therefore involved great risk—but the President was not to be dissuaded.

President Kennedy provided the first and also the fullest statement of his policy decision in his televised speech. He blamed not Cuba but the Soviet Union for the crisis and announced that he had ordered a "quarantine"—a word he had substituted for "blockade." (Franklin Roosevelt had in 1937 employed the term "quarantine" against aggression in international relations.) The quarantine, Kennedy said, would apply to all offensive weapons destined for Cuba. Ships carrying them would be turned back. Furthermore, he added, preparation of the missile sites must cease; if it did not, "further action" would be taken. The United States would maintain air surveillance of Cuba, and the President called upon Khrushchev to withdraw "all offensive weapons" from the island. To preserve his option of "further action," Kennedy engaged in a large-scale military mobilization. American missile-launching sites were put into a state of final alert. A 100,000-man force was readied to invade Cuba. Naval ships and submarines hurried out to sea, and three Polaris-firing submarines left their berths in Scotland.

The crisis continued; messages passed between Kennedy and Khrushchev; Soviet and Soviet-satellite ships were intercepted in the waters off Cuba. Finally, Khrushchev, in the fifth exchange of communications with Kennedy in seven days, said that he had ordered work on the bases stopped and the missiles crated and returned to the Soviet Union. Representatives of the United Nations, he promised, could "verify" the dismantling. In return, the President was asked to make a no-invasion pledge. Kennedy did so and issued a statement welcoming Khrushchev's "statesmanlike decision," and the blockade was lifted.

Kennedy, both in his observable conduct and as reflected in the commentary his aides have provided concerning the crisis, followed several principles in making policy.[15] Although he relied heavily upon his aides, he himself made the ultimate decision—which, in view of the awesome responsibility it involved, could not be delegated. Policy-making in nuclear confrontation is, to say the least, a grueling test of presidential self-confidence. Kennedy rightly insisted that he could act only upon hard fact and not merely upon rumor and report. He held to this course despite the prodding legislative resolutions and the criticisms of his inaction by individual legislators. Kennedy, in choosing to act, aimed always to give Khrushchev an option or choice— to avoid, above all, backing him into a corner, where his only resort would be military. An American military attack upon Cuba, whether an air strike or an invasion, would have left the Soviet Union with the choice of either a military response or humiliating surrender. The attractiveness of the blockade was that it gave Khrushchev acceptable options. He did not need to subject his ships to being stopped and searched but could divert them—as he did. The blockade, consequently, left a way out for the Soviet Union, which for the Kennedy administration was an elementary principle of policy-making in nuclear confrontation. Another operative principle is evident in the efforts of Kennedy and his aides to slow down the escalation of the crisis to permit Khrushchev time to consider his moves. Deliberation, it was hoped, might produce more measured and less drastic responses than swift exchanges. Hence the value of notes and ambassadorial visits, and the blockade—gradual procedures as compared with a precipitate invasion or air strike.

The President is mindful of his several "constituencies" in framing and promulgating his policy choices. He may have to act against the disapproval of certain of these constituencies. Kennedy thus engaged in dialogue with legislators and leaders of both parties, with mixed success. He sought and won the approval of allied leaders—De Gaulle, Macmillan, and Adenauer—and the countries of NATO and the OAS. But it is also clear from available evidence that he was prepared to pursue his policy without allied approval. In making his policy choices, the President must weigh and assess factors which no staff aid, ally, or allied leader can perceive, owing to the simple circumstance that he alone occupies the presidential place and only he, therefore, can weigh and balance its unique information and manifold responsibilities.

ADMINISTRATIVE POLICY-MAKING

Although the preponderance of major policy innovation occurs at the initiative of the President and his political and personal aides and subexecutives, administrative and bureaucratic initiatives are numerous and important within the framework of established major policy. In regulatory agencies, policy innovation can be launched in the making of new rules or the amendment of old ones, or in ignoring or violating, through agency practice, those that are formally established. Policy may be initiated in inquiries that are commended or prosecutions that are launched, in the outcome of administrative adjudication, and in enforcement.[16]

The possibilities of some of the latter kinds of initiative are suggested by the administrative career of Dr. Frances O. Kelsey, a research scientist and chief of the drug investigation branch of the Food and Drug Administration. In 1961, Dr. Kelsey's suspicions were aroused over thalidomide, a tranquilizer, before its adverse effects were revealed by mounting statistics of deformed births in Europe. Her suspicions led to the launching of prosecutions and close regulation of the product. In 1964, her attendance at professional meetings where the adverse effects of Dornwal, another tranquilizer, were discussed led her to question the application of a pharmaceutical company to change the time limit on the usage of Dornwal. Her investigations suggested that the company had willfully withheld information from the FDA concerning reported cases of serious side effects associated with the drug. The company was soon indicted.[17]

In general, policy activity in departments and agencies at lower levels is more specialized and narrower in scope than that at higher levels. The higher in an agency's hierarchy that policy is made, the greater are the number of specialities that enter into it and that must be coordinated and reconciled. Particularly at the uppermost levels of a department, policy proposals are related to considerations of international affairs and to the political necessities of the President and his administration. Often the role of the department secretary, under secretary, assistant secretaries, and their political and administrative assistants is to instill these external factors of foreign affairs and presidential political necessity into internal department policy-making.

Administrative policy activity is ordinarily conducted within the confines of hierarchy and specialization. The rigidity of these channels may be modified by the practice of an administrative chief, such as a branch chief, who may choose to apply the method of policy-making advocated long ago by Mary Parker Follett.[18] In her view, policy is most efficiently developed through the freest and most genuine exchange of ideas. To further this efficiency, she proposed that authority and hierarchy be de-emphasized and contended that a group idea developed through such interchange is superior in quality to the ideas of individual members.

This writer viewed something of this procedure in application in the development of the rules and regulations of a small rationing program in World War II. For several days, seven senior and junior members of the branch met together and were skillfully encouraged by the branch chief to contribute and weigh ideas. The procedure seemed to evoke more ideas than regular channels could possibly do and enhanced the interest and sense of participation of junior staff. On the debit side, the procedure is expensive in terms of man-hours consumed; it reduces the responsibility of the specialist; and it is difficult to apply when pressures of time are great.

APPLYING POLICY

In the application of policy, contingencies which may not have been anticipated may arise; failures and successes of the chosen policy may evoke pressures and needs for further policy. Policy exists in a kind of continuum, in a chain of cause and effect. It is not isolated but is enmeshed in other events and occurrences which it both influences and is influenced by.

For the application of policy, the legislature is heavily dependent upon the administration and its unique command of manpower, skills, physical resources, and money. The President has a similar dependence, tempered by his intimate association with administration, his far-reaching power of command, and the fact that certain acts of policy application can be performed only by the President himself. Only Kennedy could have invoked his policy in the Cuban missile crisis in his televised speech. But while the President was speaking, a vast administrative machinery was in motion. The Assistant Secretary of State for Latin American Affairs, Edward Martin, briefed Latin American ambassadors and Secretary of State Rusk, and Intelligence Director Hilsman briefed the neutral nations, including Yugoslavia. Under Secretary Ball briefed the diplomatic correspondents, and Defense Secretary McNamara the military correspondents. Ambassador to the United Nations Adlai Stevenson presented the American case in a televised session of the United Nations Security Council. The blockade was applied by the Navy. Communications were exchanged between Khrushchev and Kennedy. The State Department drafted forty-three presidential letters to the heads of government of all our alliances and to Willy Brandt, mayor of West Berlin. The Soviet ambassador at Washington was called to the State Department, and General Lauris Norstad, the NATO commander, was alerted. The American military mobilization continued, and the U-2 surveillance of Cuba was intensified. Robert Kennedy has attributed the resolution of the crisis to an event in the latter enterprise and the President's response to it. Major Rudolph Anderson, Jr., one of the two U-2 pilots whose photographs touched off the missile crisis, was shot down over Cuba during a subsequent surveillance flight. Major Anderson's death, Robert Kennedy has said, "led the President to notify Mr. Khrushchev that strong and overwhelming retaliatory action would be taken unless he received immediate notice that the missiles would be withdrawn."[19] The President's tough message and vast military preparations are credited with bringing Khrushchev around to agreeing to remove the missiles.

Whether policy succeeds or fails is a matter that is judged not only in the ultimate court of history, but in the daily operations of political and administrative affairs. Policy, like any other human endeavor, can be judged from various vantage points. What it has done can be measured against what it has set out to do. More often than not, the record is a mixture of successes and failures. Did Kennedy succeed in his professed objective in getting Soviet missiles out of Cuba? He evoked a pledge from Khrushchev to remove them, but because Castro balked, Khrushchev's pledge permitting United Nations inspection of sites in Cuba to determine whether the missiles had been removed remained unfulfilled. Although Soviet vessels were observed and photographed, apparently withdrawing missiles from the island, and U-2 flights disclosed the dismantling of missile sites, no close-up on-site inspections in Cuba have ever been made.

Policy can also be judged in terms of its ability to create or contribute to equilibrium. Equilibrium can be viewed in two senses: as a relationship between the nation and other nations or as a relationship of lesser political entities with one another—the executive with the legislature, the President's party with the opposition party, and the like. The equilibrium between the United States and the Soviet Union, however troubled it was, deteriorated to the peril point in the Cuban missile crisis. Although there can yet be no certainty that Kennedy's policy got all Soviet missiles out of Cuba, it did, in its eventual effects, snatch United States-Soviet relations out of the nuclear confrontation and back to the easier equilibrium that preceded it.

For all policy-makers, legislative or executive, equilibrium can be viewed as policy that produces satisfaction, acquiescence, or approval in the majority of the constituency concerned. An administrator whose agency has several groups of clientele, for example, can ill afford to pursue for long policies which alienate all or most of them. Equilibrium, in this sense, is a reasonable serenity in the relationship with constituency—the absence of outcry or other acts of opposition.

Responses to the success or failure of policy likewise cover a wide gamut. The Social Security system, established in 1935, achieved such a measure of success that both major political parties have endorsed it and have worked to increase its coverage. Indeed, the largest of two major expansions occurred in the Republican administration of President Eisenhower. In 1939, survivors' benefits were added; in 1956 in the Eisenhower era, disability insurance benefits were added, and the coverage, size, and duration of benefits for unemployment compensation and old-age retirement programs were extended. The successes and failures of policy and the responses to them also have political and personal dimensions. When President Thomas Jefferson brought off the Louisiana Purchase, he achieved more than a policy success; he also scored a political triumph. "The acquisition of Louisiana and the peaceful manner of possession," the American representative of France, Pichon, reported to his government, "have raised Jefferson and his friends to a high point of popularity and regard. His re-election must be considered assured."[20] How policy fares, whether well or badly, has consequences for its maker's self-image. Franklin Roosevelt, when his proposed court-packing legislation languished for weeks in Congress, stalled by the tactics of the opposition, underwent a noticeable decline in his accustomed aggressive leadership. Harold Ickes, Secretary of the Interior, noted that the President "has acted to me like a beaten man."[21]

Elected policy-makers, whether the President, senators, or congressmen, face a periodic review by their constituents of their total performance on policy in an election year. Why constituents vote as they do is a mosaic of many factors, none of which may be decisive but all of which are significant. Representative John Lesinski of Michigan, the only northern Democrat to vote against the Civil Rights Act, had reason, in view of subsequent events, to consider whether his policy decision was a success or failure in light of the reactions of his party and constituency. His negative vote drew the censure of the state Democratic organization, and by dint of a realignment of his state's congressional districts, he drew as his opponent in the Democratic primary Congressman John D. Dingell, an arrangement also suggesting penalization. Dingell won, with superior organization and endorsements from labor and other key voting groups.

The ultimate judge of a policy's success or failure is History itself. But we have had enough experience with that fickle and changing muse to know that none of her judgments is ever really final.

Elements of Policy

Policy, if put under the probing lens of a microscope, would appear as a mosaic of many interacting particles. So involved is the process and so many are the elements that produce policy that it is useful to distinguish the elements of input from those of output.

INPUTS

ENVIRONMENTAL FACTORS

The elements of input derive from the environment—the universe, the world, the nation and its subdivisions, the minds and characters of the policy actors, their relationships to one another—and from the political art itself—its style, timing, vocabulary, and the like. Policy cannot exist except as it is called into being by situations, events, problems, and issues. These needs may be genuine, but they also may be contrived or exaggerated. Political actors (e.g., legislators, Presidents, and administrators) may encourage pressure groups to increase their demands; a diffused popular disgruntlement or concern may be seized upon, focused, and spurred by a climbing political careerist.

Every policy actor lives in a political environment containing events and actual or potential issues, problems, and situations which may enhance political opportunities or threaten the progress and even the survival of the policy actor. Clement L. Vallandigham, an Ohio congressman and Copperhead with a large midwestern following in the Civil War, thrived politically on Union military defeats in the early war years, to the point of holding a seat in the House of Representatives, seeking the governorship of his state, and thinking seriously of the presidency, all the while opposing and obstructing Lincoln's policies and urging that the war be brought to an end. Both his obstructionism and his political career collapsed in the later stages of the war, when Union victories began to mount.[1]

Legislators, Presidents, and upper-level administrators view the environment through political lenses. From their standpoint, the environment and its elements may pass through several developmental stages. Initially, there may be situations that are somewhat diffuse and fragmentary but concentrated enough to be visible and forceful. The Louisiana Purchase, for example, materialized from several kinds of situations—Spain, which originally owned the territory, was declining in strength; New Orleans, by its location, could control the Mississippi, upon whose traffic the American western farmer depended; and Napoleon, who had acquired the territory from Spain, was involved in European war, with its towering demands upon French treasure and strength. These circumstances harbored potential consequences of great magnitude for the American nation and for President Jefferson and his administration. The several parts of the total situation fused into an event: France's expressed willingness to sell the Louisiana Territory to the United States.

Events may achieve a further significance by becoming political issues. The events that were rushing toward what was to become the Louisiana Purchase quickly emerged as the nation's leading political issue. The opposition Federalist party, which had been pressing for military conquest of the territory, greeted Jefferson's moves to purchase it with cries that he was bankrupting the treasury to buy a desert. But the preponderance of the country's opinion hailed the purchase as a great boon. Indeed, so popular was the event that the several political factions of Jefferson's own party scrambled to claim credit for it. Northern Republicans, sniffing hungrily for a strong presidential candidate to rid them of the "Virginia succession" to the presidency, aimed to establish one of their own as the hero of the Louisiana miracle. Lavish efforts were launched to prove that Robert Livingston of New York, who with James Monroe had negotiated the transaction, deserved the lion's share of credit.[2]

Policy-making is also influenced by another sector of the environment: the world of ideals and ideas, values and attitudes. The relation between office-seeking policy-makers and ideals is often a point of cynical jest. It was also a matter of resigned confession by Oscar Underwood, a distinguished House floor leader who wrote that "the desire to win the immediate battle, the apprehension lest the failure to yield to organized pressure may sacrifice a political future, or a score or more of less creditable motives, have often-times blinded the eyes of the public representatives to the great prinicples of free government. . . ."[3] Yet most of the heroes of John Kennedy's *Profiles in Courage* did defy political expediency, at a high price, to be sure, to pursue ideals. President Andrew Johnson, facing the problems of the Reconstruction era, was largely governed in policy decisions by his cherished ideal of the old Union and the old Constitution, a commitment which had long guided his political career. The Union was not to be revised and reconstructed; it was to be restored. As President he maintained, as he had as legislator, that there were too many federal laws and that the general government must not supplant the states.

Ideals are shaped by values which are more numerous and often more explicit in their influence on policy. Values may silence a policy-maker in controversy or hurtle him to the front lines of combat. They are the controlling analytic tools that enable him to choose among policy alternatives. Policy actors have personal values which determine their deportment toward problems, issues, colleagues, and adversaries. Loyalty is a personal value that often stands high in the politician's code. Harry S Truman, both as senator and as President, persevered in his loyalty to associates against the severest tests. Roy Roberts, editor of the Kansas City *Star*, who knew Truman well, catalogued his several personal qualities at the outset of his presidency. Near the top of Roberts' list was "loyalty, perhaps excessive loyalty that sometimes gets high officials into trouble,"[4] a prophesy that unfortunately came true in the "mink" and "deep freeze" scandals involving subordinates who served the President ill in exchange for his unwavering support of them.

The value pattern of policy actors may be highly idiosyncratic. Education ranked high and religion low in the values President Grant applied to policy questions. Education he viewed as a boon to the Republic which merited the utmost emphasis in public policy. "We are a republic," he declared, "whereof one man is as good as another before law. . . . Hence the education of the masses becomes the first necessity for the preservation of our institutions."[5] Grant's conviction led him to propose a constitutional amendment requiring each state to "establish and forever maintain free public schools" for all children irrespective of "sex, color, birthplace, or religion." What troubled Grant most about churches was their vast tax-free property holdings, which he proposed be taxed.

The arrangement of a policy actor's values in a hierarchy is determined no little by his attitudes toward morality and power. Andrew Johnson, both as legislator and as President, stressed morality and neglected power. Convinced of what was right, he pursued it with little attention to power—to the winning of allies in Congress and in the parties, to the construction of compromises that would assure that at least part of what he deemed right would prevail while lesser parts were sacrificed.

Johnson's predecessor, Abraham Lincoln, in contrast, viewed morality and power as complementary. As a congressman in 1858, he could speak in northern Illinois in one vein before abolition-minded audiences, but farther south, where voters of southern extraction were dominant, he spoke in another. In Chicago, on July 10, 1858, he urged, in referring to the Negro, that we "unite as one people throughout this land, until we shall once more stand up declaring that all men are created equal." In Charleston, South Carolina, on September 18 of the same year, he declared, "I am not, nor ever have been, in favor of bringing about in any way the social and political equality of the white and black races: that I am not, nor ever have been, in favor of making voters or jurors of Negroes, nor of qualifying them to hold office. . . ."[6] As President, Lincoln could rise to heights of moral splendor in his Gettysburg and Second Inaugural addresses and yet perceive and act upon the assumption that what he proposed to achieve required a bold, resourceful assertion of all available—and sometimes unavailable—constitutional powers. Hence his suspension of the writ of habeas corpus, imposition of censorship of the mails, use of unappropriated Treasury funds, and other actions initiated on his own authority and without it if necessary. All this he did prior to any statutory sanction by Congress.

The environment of the mind in policy-making abounds with assumptions as to what is and what should be in the conduct and purposes of colleagues, rivals, voters, and leaders and peoples of other nations. Assumptions may shut out certain policy decisions and shape and control others. Assumptions are also fragile things, easily crushed by the weight of events. The unanticipated explosion of war in Korea in 1950 smashed an assumption generally embraced by top American military authorities and sanctioned by Presidents Roosevelt and Truman. United States ground forces, the operative assumption went, should not and must not ever be engaged on the Asiatic mainland, lest they be pinned down there when they might be needed in other, more strategically vital parts of the world. Least of all should they be committed to an area like Korea, slight in military value and difficult to defend. This assumption was an early casualty of the Korean War; its violation intensified as the conflict dragged on, until eventually some 250,000 American troops were dispatched to that unhappy land.

The environment of the mind also includes ideas existing in various stages of formulation and in various relations to one another. Stealing other people's ideas is a steady and unashamed preoccupation of policy-makers. In Congress, it is commonplace for ideas for some politically promising legislative enactment, developed by members of junior status, to be snatched up by senior members whose names are almost invariably associated with the legislation that ultimately is enacted. Basic ideas that appear in the Monroe Doctrine were anticipated some years earlier by the utterances of Henry Clay and Thomas Jefferson. Of the incipient South American revolts, a crucial event in the Doctrine's development, Jefferson said in 1808, "We consider their interests the same as ours, and the object of both must be to exclude all European influence in this hemisphere."[7] Beyond Jefferson and Clay, the roots of the Doctrine reached back to the initial years of the Republic, to the pronouncements of Washington, particularly his Farewell Address.

Goals are concretized ideals, linking the personal value-choices of the legislator or executive with the needs and possibilities of the political environment. Some professed goals of politicians, like "honest government" and "national unity," verge on the platitudinous. Personal goals may shape or control policy goals. The desire for re-election, the President's wish for a vote of confidence in a congressional election, and his ambition to choose his successor may determine his course on policy.

For a President, particularly, choosing goals is a crucial act that affects his administration's tone, the level of its striving, its mission to which his aides and supporters may subscribe their loyalties and energies. "The President's got to set the sights," Harry S Truman observed. Goal-setting reflects the President's instinct for the future, his understanding of the past, and his mastery of the present. It serves best if it captures the nation's needs and yearnings, engages the potential of its resources, and reflects the direction in which the world is moving.

Presidents vary in their manipulation of goals. John Kennedy contended that presidential goals should always be inspiring, despite the rigors and delays in their achievement. Some Presidents excel at choosing solid, feasible goals. In domestic politics, Woodrow Wilson displayed an impressive knack in choosing objectives for his New Freedom program of social and economic reform projects that were notably ripe for realization, and he carried them out with extraordinary shrewdness and skill. Some Presidents have resorted to diversionary goals, in the manner of James Buchanan, much of whose administration was beset by the crashing tempest of Kansas, where the winds of northern and southern sectionalism warred. Buchanan, in his second annual message to Congress, chose to convey a series of foreign affairs goals to which the nation might turn its united effort for years to come. His announced objective was to enable the United States to "attract to itself much of the trade and travel of all nations passing between Europe and Asia" and thereby to become the wealthiest and most powerful nation on the globe.[8] For his own administration, Buchanan proposed a string of measures: purchase Cuba to assure United States dominance in the Caribbean; expand the Navy; endow the executive with special authority to protect transport routes through Panama, Nicaragua, and Mexico; conclude commercial treaties with China, Japan, and other countries of the Far East; revise the tariff; and construct a Pacific railroad.

ALTERNATIVES

Having established a goal or chosen an event, problem, or situation to act upon, the policy actor will normally canvass the possible courses of action. These can be discovered, invented, or formulated—pursuits which Herbert Simon terms "design activity."[9]

Before the alternative courses of action can be mustered, raw information must be extracted from the environment and studied for meaning. Policy-makers are especially concerned with the clues that past or present fact may give to future circumstances. President Truman and his counselors, faced with the surprise North Korean invasion of South Korea, easily and unanimously agreed that the Soviet Union was behind the move. The far more difficult problem was to interpret the Soviets' motive and purpose, on which the nature of the American response would considerably depend. Truman solicited the interpretations of General Omar Bradley, chairman of the Joint Chiefs of Staff; George Kennan, chairman of the State Department's policy planning staff and an authority on Soviet behavior; and John Foster Dulles, then the negotiator of the Japanese peace treaty. Each of these counselors, and others Truman consulted, had his own interpretation of the meanings of events in Korea—that the North Korean attack was a diversionary gambit, preparatory to a major Soviet blow, possibly against Iran; that the Communists were "soft-spot probing" and that therefore the appropriate American countermove was to create "situations of strength" wherever the Soviets probed, including Korea. Others held that the Soviets were "testing" the will of anti-Communist nations to resist open aggression, in the manner of Hitler's reoccupation of the Rhineland; that the Korean maneuver was a "demonstration," by which the Soviet Union expected to make a show of its strength and of allied impotence, with world-wide repercussions; that the Soviets were promoting a general "Far Eastern strategy," part of which was to block American efforts to bring Japan into the free world. Interpretation of the environment, as the Korean example demonstrates, is often an inexact enterprise.

Having made their interpretation as best they can, the policy

actors move on to the next hurdle: formulating alternative responses
to the problem, event, situation, or issue. Faced with a badly deteriorating military and political situation in South Vietnam in the
summer of 1964, President Johnson and his counselors had several
alternatives to choose among: to make a commitment of American
forces to the area well beyond the estimated 16,000 United States
military "advisers" already there; to make a modest further increase
in the American forces; or to give up South Vietnam as a lost cause
and gradually withdraw American forces. For a time the second
alternative was chosen. But as events in Vietnam further deteriorated
during 1964 and 1965, the President was driven to adopt the first
alternative. In 1965, again in light of the worsening situation, the
President ordered air strikes against North Vietnam, an alternative
that had not been strongly considered the preceding year.

Alternatives possess variant relations with each other. They may
be mutually exclusive—to choose one is to preclude the other. They
also may be mutually reinforcing. The policy-maker then does not
choose between alternatives but instead determines how many possible paths of action to combine into a policy. Lincoln, pursuing his
purpose to free the slaves, viewed his alternatives as complementary
rather than exclusive. Dubious that whites and freed Negroes could
live together peaceably, he weighed the possibility of achieving emancipation through colonization or shipment back to Africa. He was
also impressed with the legal and political necessity of compensating
the slaveowners. At one point, in late 1861, he drafted two bills for
compensated emancipation in Delaware. In an experiment which, if
successful, could have been applied to other states, Lincoln proposed
the issuance of $700,000 in federal bonds to finance the emancipation
of Delaware's slaves. Some months later, he was urging Congress to
underwrite emancipation in all states that freed their slaves.[10]

The climactic phase of policy-making is "choice activity," or
selecting a particular course of action from among the alternatives
available. Although the policy-maker can delegate the earliest steps
in policy-making—such as the discovery of problems and the framing
of alternatives—to skilled subordinates, the actual choice among them
cannot be delegated. Subordinates can recommend the choice, but
the policy-maker must make the final determination, either by ratify-
ing the choice his subordinates recommend or by making another one
himself. Presidents are under no illusion concerning the high and
solemn nature of their choice activity. President Truman reminded
himself of his momentous task by posting on his desk a sign that
read, "The buck stops here." President Eisenhower counseled the
incoming President Kennedy, "There are no easy matters that will
come to you as President. If they are easy, they will be settled at a
lower level."

How and why a policy-maker chooses as he does is often a mystery at all but the deepest level of his thoughts. Occasionally, however, policy-makers will offer explanations for choosing as they did, which may or may not be the operative reasons. Senator Howard W. Cannon (D., Nev.), whose late-hour commitment to cloture in behalf of the 1964 civil rights bill was important to the success of the venture, explained his vote to reporters by saying, "I just felt we had to bring an end to this matter after a reasonable time and get on with the business of the Senate."[11] But in the post-mortem analyses, there were other explanations of why Cannon voted as he did. One was that organized labor back home had applied considerable pressure. Another view was that a personal appeal by President Johnson brought Senator Cannon around. Whether either or both of these were in fact decisive, only Cannon knows.

Even more than individual decision, the whole style of a policy actor's choice-making may be involved and inscrutable. Franklin Roosevelt, both to those who worked with him and to those who have studied his career, continuously exuded such mystery. In making policy choices, he seemed to weigh a whole complex of factors—political timing, consequences to his personal political fortunes, likely pressure-group reactions, partisan advantage, impact on Congress and the public. He permitted situations to intensify and crystallize, opposing forces to pull in conflict, until through some means of "unconscious calculation," as his aide Rexford Tugwell termed it, policy finally emerged. Roosevelt, according to Tugwell, made it seem that "no choosing had taken place."[12] Policy was not systematically thought out; rather, the President's intuitions seemed to converge to produce a result. Roosevelt, like many other policy-makers, both legislative and executive, preferred to avoid making affirmative policy choices in troubled situations. He liked to procrastinate, to give swirling contentious forces an opportunity to settle and the pressure of events to slacken.

How a policy-maker chooses may be determined largely by his own and the nation's commitments to policy. Early in the Cuban missile crisis, President Kennedy sent for copies of all his earlier statements on Cuba, on its threat to vital American interests, on the distinction between offensive and defensive weapons, and on American armed intervention. "These earlier decisions," noted Theodore Sorensen, the President's counsel, "made it unlikely that he would respond to the October crisis by doing nothing and unlikely that his first step would be an invasion."[13]

POLICIES

The end product of choice is policy. Policy tends to have several attributes. It is *novel*, in the sense that nothing identical with it exists, or else there would be no need to create it. Policy has the quality of *importance*, often even of controversy. It is *authoritative*, in that it commands or claims to command the observance of others—whether they be the general body of citizens, in the case of policy embodied in legislation, or subordinates, in the case of policy established by the President or a department head. Policy is ordinarily greater than mere decision—more comprehensive, more novel, and more important. Policy springs from decision or from an accumulation of decisions. Policy seldom emerges from a logical and orderly progression of decisions proceeding to their objective in the manner of soldiers marching on parade. Rather, policy is apt to develop in a halting, irregular march, in fits and starts, and even from a confusing accumulation of contradictory decisions.

Policies are not coins of common value; in their relationship to one another there are the greater and the lesser. Lesser policies are aften the product of superordinal policies. The greatest or broadest policies are comprehended in a presidential administration's central purpose, vision, or grand design, which has a shaping and often determining effect on lesser policies. Indeed, some Presidents have endeavored to convey the central purpose of their administration through a popular and memorable phrase—a particularly recurrent attempt in the public relations era of the twentieth century. Theodore Roosevelt spoke of his administration as the "Square Deal," Woodrow Wilson provided the "New Freedom," Franklin Roosevelt the "New Deal," Harry Truman the "Fair Deal," Dwight Eisenhower "Modern Republicanism," and Lyndon Johnson a vision of the "Great Society." The phrases themselves are sometimes almost accidental in their origin. "Fair Deal" did not gain currency until 1949, nearly five years after Truman became President; it first appeared, although not in capital letters, in a State of the Union address of January 5, 1949: "Every segment of our population and every individual has a right to expect from his government a fair deal." The belated appearance of the label may be attributed to the fact that Truman had not decided what the central purpose of his administration was to be. His commitment to a fair deal at home and abroad, although heralded by his reconversion address of 1945 and by the Marshall Plan of 1947, did not come into clear relief until his inaugural address of 1949. Woodrow Wilson long wavered between Jeffersonian agrarianism and urban progressivism and between Bryan pacifism and internationalism. Eventually he chose progressivism and internationalism.

President Kennedy discerned the controlling effects of central design upon both foreign and domestic policy in a speech at Ann Arbor, Michigan, in October 1960, hailing the achievement of several Democratic forebears. What they did abroad harmonized with their central purpose, he declared, "because it fitted in exactly with what they were trying to do here in the United States: the Fourteen Points were the international counterpart of the New Freedom; the Four Freedoms of Franklin Roosevelt were directly tied to the aspirations of the New Deal; and the Marshall Plan, NATO, the Truman Doctrine, and Point Four were directly tied to the kind of America that President Truman was trying to build."[14]

THE POLITICAL SEASONS

A policy-maker's attitude, approach, and effectiveness are shaped by what might be called the "political seasons." Political or policy-making effectiveness is not a constant, and a considerable factor in its fluctuations is political time. New Presidents and newly appointed administrators are apt to know the policy-making bliss of a post-electoral or postappointive "honeymoon." In the first months of tenure, a President, bearing his fresh electoral mandate, is likely to command better support from Congress and a new administrator greater responsiveness from both his superiors and his subordinates. Policy-makers choose to concentrate upon more ambitious projects and efforts in the initial period of their tenure. President Kennedy was often said to act according to the belief that a presidential administration's strongest and most lasting impressions are made in its first months.

There is also the season of political decline, when the policy-maker's influence and effectiveness slacken. The loss of an election or the approaching end of term or tenure bring on this unpleasant phenomenon for legislator, chief executive, and administrator alike. The 1946 congressional elections were a black day for President Truman. The Republican party had captured both houses of Congress, bringing to an end fourteen years of uninterrupted rule of the national legislature by the Democratic party. There were ominous signs of the President's waning political, and therefore policy-making, influence. There was much talk in the press of a legislative stalemate that would bar any major laws and of the likelihood that the highly successful bipartisan foreign policy of the past would be replaced with bitter inaction. Such anticipations brought Senator J. William Fulbright (D., Ark.) to suggest that Truman appoint a Republican as Secretary of State, resign as President, and permit the Republican to succeed him. The dark forebodings soon eventuated in Truman's worst policy (but not political) defeat, when Congress passed the Taft-Hartley Act over his veto. Truman's stock, beginning to fall as early as the first months of his second term, fell even in Russia. The official newspaper, *Pravda,* concluded that the President and his fellow Democrats had "squandered the political capital" inherited from Roosevelt.

Truman's successor, Dwight Eisenhower, experienced the debilitating effect of the Twenty-second Amendment, limiting the President to two terms, upon the influence of the incumbent in his second term. In effect, the amendment establishes a long season of political and policy decline by posing a definite terminal date to presidential tenure. Before the Twenty-second Amendment was passed, Presidents typically would not disclose the fact that their tenure was ending until the latest possible moment. For Eisenhower, the amendment meant a noticeable weakening of his grip on Republican legislators and a softening of his previous strong support from the press and business.

PERSONNEL

Policy can be viewed as the product that emerges from the contributions of a complex of personnel, each applying a distinctive skill or expertise. Policy-making, in this sense, is based upon specialization much as is the industrial process in American society.

Among personnel, as among policies, there are the greater and the lesser. At the apex of any policy-making venture is authoritative leadership, where the real power to establish the policy in question reposes. The power involved may be legal, political, or administrative; one and more, or all, of these kinds of power may be possessed by the leadership. In the executive branch, leadership is arranged by hierarchy, with each level—President, bureau chief, or branch chief— specializing in certain kinds of policy-making. The specialization is based partly on function—in the sense that certain kinds of health policy are made in the Department of Health, Education, and Welfare—and partly on importance. Policies of topmost political and/or substantive significance are made by the President; those of little, if any, political cast and those of middle substantive importance will be authoritatively settled well down the hierarchical line. In the legislative branch, where authority is more diffused, authoritative leadership is more difficult to identify. Ultimately, it rests with the majority of the individual houses and in concurrence between the houses. Each legislator, with his vote, is theoretically an authoritative leader. In reality, however, as we have seen, this leadership often rests with the standing committees and with their powerful chairmen.

Beyond authoritative leadership are a variety of skills whose contributions are of the "doing" and "thinking" variety. Policy-making requires ideas, research, and formulation; it also entails advocacy and implementation. Some personnel, in actual policy-making situations, are involved in both doing and thinking; others are confined to one or the other. One or both of these functions are represented in the following categories of personnel who support authoritative leadership.

Advisers. Legislators, the President, and lesser executives may draw upon the ideas and knowledge of advisers in developing policy. Advisers may make sizable contributions well before their chief takes office. Woodrow Wilson, preparing for the 1912 presidential campaign and looking for a new and solid issue, turned for help to Louis D. Brandeis, a distinguished private lawyer with definite views on public policy. A foe of concentrated economic power and a champion of regulated competition and of economic freedom for the small businessman, Brandeis led Wilson into the kind of thinking that produced the Federal Trade Commission Act and other laws of Wilson's New Freedom. A President such as Franklin Roosevelt may resort in his pre-office preparation not merely to single advisers, but to whole teams of them, such as his famous Brain Trust, recruited from several universities while he was still governor.

Advisers may be distinguished as "insiders" and "outsiders." Insiders are on the payroll of the legislator or the executive branch; outsiders derive their economic sustenance elsewhere. Insiders are the legislator's administrative assistants or other staff members. Thus Senator John Kennedy utilized considerably the counsel of his assistant, Theodore Sorensen. For the President, insiders may include a special assistant on the White House Staff, in which capacity Harry Hopkins served Franklin Roosevelt during World War II; a department head such as Martin Van Buren, who, while Secretary of State, counseled President Andrew Jackson on a great variety of affairs; or an appointee well down in the executive hierarchy such as Amos Kendall, who, as fourth auditor of the Treasury, had similar breadth in the Jackson era. Insiders, by their presumably more frequent association with the President, are more familiar with his current thinking, with the status of existing policy developments, and with the administration's various tendencies. Outsiders, since they come from a different environment than the insiders, offer a fresh perspective. Since they are not identified with existing policy, as insiders may be, they have no vested interest in the status quo. Outsiders are more easily gotten rid of than are insiders.

Experts. Most public policy rests upon the concepts and data of various branches of knowledge. Indeed, modern-day public policy, in its several parts, more or less corresponds to the diversity of specialization found in our universities. Knowledge of the social and natural sciences, of law, medicine, engineering, and a host of other learned disciplines, is required in public policy-making. Experts in the executive departments and agencies, recruited heavily from the universities, are in their contribution to public policy applying and extending their previous academic preparation. Among experts, as well, in their influence upon policy, there are the lesser and the greater—from the researcher who merely collects data to men like Edwin Witte who, in the course of his efforts to bring the Social Security system into being, dealt directly with department heads and the President and put in a week of testifying before congressional committees.

Promoters. Policy, in order to pass from the stage of development to the stage of adoption, requires advocacy. It must be "sold" to higher authority, where decision on its fate ultimately rests. Top-level leadership may engage in promotion: President Kennedy, in a national television address, sought to rally the public behind his program of tax reforms; Senator George Norris, in floor speeches and in private cloakroom persuasion, sought his colleagues' support for public power development at Muscle Shoals.

The President and the executive departments and agencies have aides whose chief activity is promotion of policy projects. The President's assistant for congressional affairs and the latter's several assistants promote on Capitol Hill the full breadth of the administration's legislative program. Individual departments may have an assistant secretary for congressional relations aided by a large complement of legislative liaison officers. The Defense Department numbered some 400 of these officers in 1963. There is also the dimension of public liaison serviced by the White House and departmental press secretaries and assistants.

Administrators and Implementers. The heads and operating staffs of the departments and agencies, at both the highest and lesser levels, do the vital work of carrying out policies and of proposing their revision and extension. The President, too, is an administrator who applies policy, by order and supervision or by direct personal act. The legislator who launches a committee investigation to determine how efficiently policy is administered, or the line official in a Social Security field office who passes on the rights under the old-age and survivors program of the citizen before him, are both dealing with policy in its most ultimate and meaningful sense: its application.

Allies and Adversaries. The pluralistic distribution of policy-making power in the executive branch, in Congress, and between the branches fosters the presence of adversaries and necessitates the cultivation of allies. The prevalence of the pluralistic system in international affairs, with many nations and policy-makers, makes for striking similarities between domestic and international policy-making.

Each ally or adversary is responsive to his own constituency and his career ambitions—in a word, to his self-interest, whether he be a civil servant, legislator, department head, President, or chief executive of another nation. In view of their capacities for independent decision and the pressures of self-interest, the participants convert policy-making into a process of struggle, compromise, and accommodation. The designation of a particular policy actor as an ally or adversary may shift from one policy project to the next. Thus French President Charles de Gaulle supported Kennedy's policies in the Cuban missile crisis but opposed his policy of NATO-centered nuclear armaments. For a policy-maker such as the President, dealing with policies of the variety and importance which he does, the roster of allies and adversaries may be considerable. President Kennedy in 1962 jousted openly or quietly with such adversaries as a majority of the House Ways and Means Committee and its chairman, Wilbur Mills, who bottled up the administration bill of medical care for the aged, among others; with the United States Steel Corporation, whose price rises threatened his anti-inflation policy; with Governor Ross Barnett of Mississippi, who blocked the enrollment of Negro student James Meredith in the state university; with Khrushchev and Castro over the installation of Soviet missile sites in Cuba; with Prime Minister Diefenbaker of Canada on NATO nuclear policy; and with the United States Air Force and British Prime Minister Macmillan on the future of Skybolt, a United States-built missile-carrying aircraft, which the Air Force championed and on which British military planning relied. A listing of President Kennedy's policy "allies" in the same period would present a similar variety.

STRATEGIES AND TACTICS

Policy-making is an enterprise in strategies and tactics. In choosing his policy goals, the executive or legislator is engaging in strategy. A senator from an industrial-urban state, in deciding to push for legislation particularly in accord with the needs of that kind of state, has made a basic strategic choice that provides a framework for much subsequent activity. An administrator preparing his budget is forced by that process to make strategic choices—what major policies to pursue, upon which the limited resources of his organization, its manpower, and matériel will be concentrated. All makers of public policy in choosing strategies also indulge in the setting of priorities, determining which are the greater and which the lesser among policy projects. President Lyndon Johnson in the first months of his administration made an apparent attempt to concentrate upon the building of policy achievements in domestic policy. The top efforts of his administration focused upon the passage of tax, civil rights, and other domestic legislation; upon the prevention of a national railroad strike; and upon quieting the troubled domestic climate engendered by President Kennedy's assassination. Johnson tended to aim at "holding the line" in foreign affairs rather than undertaking bold new policy initiatives. Behind this strategic choice were considerations of the greater pressures of the domestic scene, the approaching elections of 1964, the need for concrete policy accomplishments which seemed more attainable on the home front than in foreign affairs, and the likelihood that domestic achievements would build his international prestige and improve his chances for later policy gains in that arena. Policy-making involves tactics of seemingly endless variety. A President, to effect his legislative strategies, may resort to both open and behind-the-scenes politics.[15] The legislative managers of the 1964 Civil Rights Act, for example, maneuvered to keep the act's public accommodations provisions out of the Senate Judiciary Committee, chaired by James Eastland.[16] Franklin Roosevelt maneuvered to give top legislative priority to his court-packing bill, which put behind it in the policy-making assembly line legislation concerning agriculture, labor, and the creation of "T.V.A.'s." Roosevelt apparently hoped to spark farm labor and conservation groups into pressing legislators to expedite his court plan—which was lagging badly in committee—by postponing consideration of their legislation until his own had been acted upon.

Tactics also include rationalization and advocacy. President Kennedy, particularly in the area of public policy and labor-management relations, was given to rationalizing, in public and private pronouncements, that his policies were in the "national" or "public" interest. When the steel union and management negotiated a new contract in 1962, the administration, through its Council of Economic Advisers, calculated a maximum percentage of increased labor costs which the industry could absorb without increasing its prices. The percentage—which, in effect, was a proposed ceiling on labor's demands and industry's pricing, was termed by administration spokesmen "noninflationary" and in the "national interest." Likewise, when the International Association of Machinists walked out of two California plants of Aero-Jet-General Corporation in 1962, despite the President's pressures on the union to postpone the strike, Defense Secretary Robert McNamara termed it "a callous disregard of the national and public interest."

Rationalizing and advocacy also require skillful choice of vocabulary to secure maximum effects. On many occasions no weapon is more powerful than the memorable phrase, such as William Jennings Bryan's "cross of gold" sentence in a dramatic speech that swept the Democratic convention of 1896 off its feet and literally captured him the presidential nomination.[17] He was encouraged to devote his campaign to the silver issue, to which he gave top priority.

Since policy-making is often highly controversial, its vocabulary is sometimes severe. Policy expressions on the Taft-Hartley Act brought on a deluge of verbal brimstone. President Truman, in vetoing the act, termed it "unworkable" and "burdensome." The act's sponsors retorted in kind. Senator Robert A. Taft in a radio address said that the President had "completely misrepresented" the character of the act. Congressman Fred A. Hartley, the act's co-sponsor, declared that the veto consisted of "double-talk, sham, distortion, abuse; far-fetched, strained, and tortured interpretations of clear, simple clauses; hysterical grasping at any argument, however invalid, to thwart the will of Congress."[18]

Advocacy involves gestures as well as words. Franklin Roosevelt, in promulgating policy, loved to instill surprise. It added momentum to policy and threw the opposition off guard. He sprang his court-packing plan by supervising personally the details of its launching—endeavoring, above all, to keep its substance a secret. He had the White House secretarial staff report to work on the day of the launching at 6:30 a.m. to mimeograph the several presidential papers announcing the plan. The papers were distributed to a hastily summoned meeting of the cabinet, with Joseph T. Robinson of Arkansas, Democratic Senate floor leader, and Speaker William B. Bankhead also present. The meeting lasted ten minutes, with everyone reading the material and Roosevelt asking for no comments and hurrying off to a press conference. Both the extraordinary substance of the policy and its well-guarded preparation gave its ultimate appearance the effect of a bombshell.

OUTPUTS: THE POLICY PRODUCT

The policy machine of the legislative and executive branches yields an output whose diversity can be viewed from several vantage points. There is a hierarchy of laws, through which policy is expressed and which authoritatively makes a given policy inferior or superior to others. Supreme policy, in the legal sense, is embodied in the Constitution, the fundamental law. All policy must ultimately be based upon authority derived from the Constitution. The next level of the legal hierarchy of policy is of two parts. One part, statute, brings Congress with the chief executive to enact laws incorporating policies, both general and specific, which in turn provide the basis for further policy. The other part, the President's prerogatives, such as the power he holds as commander in chief by direct conferral of the Constitution and without legal necessity of congressional concurrence, are also the basis of further policy. The President issues Executive Orders and Proclamations, founded in statute or prerogative, to effectuate a particular policy. The order or proclamation serves as the administrator's mandate; its publication in the *Federal Register*, issued by the National Archives, is viewed as putting the public on notice and subjecting it to its provisions.

The departments, agencies, and regulatory commissions issue rules as a kind of quasi-legislative activity on the basis of an authorizing statute or Executive Order. These administrative rules have the force of law and are published in the *Federal Register*. The Commerce Department, for example, may issue rules regarding various United States exports, and the Interstate Commerce Commission may issue rules regulating safety on railroads.

The departments, agencies, and commissions may conduct adjudication based upon alleged violations of their rules. The decisions made in adjudication take the form of orders which are binding upon the private parties concerned. Like the courts, the agencies tend to follow their own precedents in adjudication.

In making rules and orders, the agencies must follow guidelines or standards, set forth in statute. These standards may be both procedural and substantive. If a statute lacks standards or provides them only generally or incompletely, the agency may develop and express them in formulating its rules and orders. Thus, when Congress by statute authorized the Interstate Commerce Commission to require the railroads to charge freight and passenger rates that are "just and reasonable," the ICC, to effectuate this general mandate, had to formulate standards which helped determine the permissible rates. This it did in its rules and orders, as it set up allowable returns on investments, methods of computing amortization and depreciation, and the like.

Administrative actions, both rule-making and adjudication, are subject to review by the courts for their conformity with the Constitution and the statutory authority on which they are based.

Administrative agencies utilize the "instruction," based on the general lines of policy set out in statute, Executive Order, and administrative rule. The instruction specifies to administrative personnel what they are to do, usually in a recurring situation. The instruction stipulates policy, although with more emphasis on procedure than on substance. Poor procedure can vitiate good policy. The information bulletin, circulated among the department's or agency's employees, provides background on policy, explaining its purpose, rationale, or procedure. This is a nonauthoritative document which lacks the force of law, although it is important in enabling administrative personnel to understand and accept particular policy.[19]

The hierarchy of administration helps assure that everyone contributes to the shaping of policy. When a section head who has received a directive from his branch chief chooses to give it little notice because he disagrees with it, he is affecting policy.

Policy, like a building, can be viewed from various vantage points. It can be understood as an accommodation and reconciliation of several antithetical concepts and influences. For instance, policy may be a relating of special interest to public interest. The American polity is a vast concentration of special interest groups: the mass groups of nationality, race, religion, and labor; economic entrepreneurial groups; moral groups; and professional and bureaucratic groups. All seek to advance their purposes or to hold their advantage by shaping public policy. Final policy is largely the outcome of the clash and struggle, the convergence and divergence of power-wielding special interests. Yet there also is, or should be, the countervailing ingredient in policy-making of general interest or public interest. These are not so easily identified as special interests but are nevertheless asserted by many a legislator and administrator, the political parties, and the executive. In one sense, general interest is a kind of consensus or balance that emerges from the clashes of special interests and the mediation effected between them by the official policy-makers. This mediation is fostered by the nature of policy-makers' constituencies. A senator or congressman has varied interests in his state or district; if he is overly devoted to some, he risks alienating others and thus destroys the base of variegated political support he requires for election. Even more, the President and the political party must command support from a nation-wide structure of special interests and provide a balance between their individual demands.

General interest can be viewed as both substance and procedure. The President, in the substantive sense, may have quite definite views formulated by his economic advisers concerning the limits to which labor costs may rise in the steel industry without warranting a price increase. He can confront the labor unions with a ceiling beyond which their demands cannot penetrate without injury to the public interest. He can admonish industry on the ground that a price rise is unwarranted by the limited character of increased labor costs and add that any such increase would impair the nation's interest in holding down inflation, increasing foreign trade, and improving the balance of payments. In the procedural sense, general interest is a kind of standard which the administrator or legislator takes into his calculations of what policy should be. It is not a specific decision or policy but a way of formulating policy.[20]

The policy product can be viewed as national policy, which is often a blend of domestic and foreign policies. A frequent argument made by advocates of the Civil Rights Act of 1964 was that the act was necessary to improve our civil rights standards at home in order to improve the nation's image abroad and therefore the credibility of our foreign policy among other nations. The view of national policy as a blend of domestic and foreign policies means that policy cannot be made adequately in either subdivision without weighing its impact upon the other. Hence the Kennedy administration, in formulating its views about wage and price policy in the steel industry in 1962, related its domestic policies concerning inflation, employment, and economic growth to its foreign policies concerning the balance of payments, then a severe problem. More and more, policies in traditionally domestic fields have assumed an international dimension. This trend heightens the necessity of viewing national policy as a process giving due weight to both.

Policy-making can also be viewed—particularly in a nation such as the United States, with its sharp sectional differences—as a reflection of local and national factors. In 1961, for example, President Kennedy dispatched to Congress a message asking that the minimum wage be increased "to keep pace with the higher cost of living." The minimum wage law had served the historic function of affording protection to the unorganized worker and presumably, therefore, to millions in the work force across the nation. In the legislative proceedings that followed, the administration, in order to build up the majority necessary for legislative passage, had to pick up in the House of Representatives, where the bill's progress was more difficult than in the Senate, a dozen Republican or southern Democratic votes. The bait was set for the latter in the form of changes in the bill making concessions to their local political circumstances. The bill was altered to eliminate 140,000 laundry workers and 15,000 cotton-gin employees from its coverage. The laundry workers, mostly Negroes, were the key. Some ten southern congressmen were under strong pressure to keep these workers out. It also happened that these same Southerners really wanted to vote for the administration bill, because they thought it would help them at the White House. With laundry workers eliminated, they could satisfy home pressures by citing that accomplishment as a southern victory and a justification for their ultimate vote for the bill.

Policy can also be arranged hierarchically, according to its importance. A presidential administration may have a grand design, such as the professed commitment of Franklin Roosevelt's first two terms to economic recovery and reform. The specific policies his administration developed tended to fit within that broad, determining framework. Policies may be adaptive or innovative. Adaptive policy is the adjustment of existing policy to changing circumstances or to new problems without a change in its vital substance. Raising the national minimum wage in 1945, 1949, 1955, and 1961 were adaptations to, among other things, economic inflation. On the other hand, a policy such as the Emancipation Proclamation was innovative: it represented a clear departure from previously prevailing policy, which was predicated upon the legal existence of Negro slavery. Policy activity may also be repetitive and routine; established policy may be effectuated and perpetuated by the supporting activity of administrators and subadministrators, in the manner of the clerk in the Social Security office who computes the death benefits of an individual insured under the system. The most important policy choices are sometimes nonpolicy choices, in the sense that it is decided to maintain existing policy rather than to adopt new policy. Thus, each year in the period 1957–1960, Congress considered the question of whether to raise the minimum wage and extend its coverage but each time decided not to alter the existing law. Policy must also be distinguished between word and deed, between what is said and what is done. A presidential speech and an act of Congress ordinarily are only promises of what shall be. It is the specific actions—usually of administrators, subadministrators, and appropriation committees—that determine what really *is*.

Public policy-making in the United States proceeds on a pluralistic basis, the only possible basis in a democratic society. Above all, such policy-making is founded on a fundamental law—a Constitution—which provides for key political liberties. Provisions of our own federal Bill of Rights—guarantees of freedom of speech and press, the right to petition and assemble, due process, the right of trial by jury, and other rights—in effect subject governmental action to review in the light of a fundamental law. Pluralistic policy-making, by definition, requires the free organization of opposing opinions and public expression of those opinions—essences of "the open society." Policy-makers can therefore be voted out of office in periodic elections and replaced by new policy-makers committed to different platforms, policies, and programs. Pluralistic policy-making leaves government and the policy-makers dependent upon public or electoral opinion which can make and unmake Congresses and presidential administrations.

Pluralistic policy-making, as practiced in the United States, relies upon the competitive principle. Competition arises from the creation of the two political branches and the investing of overlapping powers in them, encouraging struggle for dominion over policy. There is competition in the bicameral legislative system and the power of one house of Congress to check the other. Many a President instills competition into administrative policy-making by resorting to several quarters for advice on the same policy question or by handing out administrative jurisdictions on an overlapping, and therefore competitive, basis. By its very nature, the fact that policy of importance overlaps several or more departments encourages competition among them.

Pluralistic policy-making in the United States also rests on the representative principle—on the assumption that a variety of opinions, groups, and geographical sections can legitimately and effectively contribute to policy-making. Policy-makers therefore represent a variety of constituencies—the President, a national constituency; the Senate, the states; and the House, the smallest and most local constituencies. Even more important, our political system encourages the formation of numerous and diverse pressure groups who vie with one another in the struggle to influence policy-makers in the executive and legislative branches. Administrative policy-making also is often deliberately representative. President Washington, forming his first cabinet, deemed it wise to include representatives from each of the principal sections of the country—the North, the South, and the middle states. Departments resort to advisory committees, representing diverse economic interests, sections, and professions, which contribute their counsel and, hopefully their support. Many agencies and bureaus have close, even symbiotic, relationships with outside groups and thus function in part as their representatives. The Veterans Administration, for example, is in no small way the advocate of the interests of veterans' organizations.

Pluralistic policy-making, as practiced in the United States, has proceeded on the basis of several conceptions of the role of the majority. American policy-making, in contrast to British, for example, does not assume the use of an enduring legislative majority. The majority that passes most important laws in any one session of the House of Commons is relatively fixed and stable. In the United States it shifts; it is different for every legislative question. American legislative majorities tend to be limited-purpose majorities rather than disciplined and enduring majorities. Our political parties tend to minimize their differences; each appeals to a broad sweep of groups of varying policy outlooks instead of presenting clear-cut contrasts, policy choices between liberalism and conservatism.

POLICY ANALYSIS

Policy-making has become increasingly subject to several kinds of systematic analysis which draw upon the tools of the social and mathematical sciences. The tools are put to at least two kinds of use: first, they are utilized by the policy-makers themselves to facilitate and enhance the efficacy of their work; second, they are employed by students seeking explanations of how and why particular policies have been made.

THE GAME ANALOGY

Policy-making can be studied as a kind of game.[21] The game is played within a defined arena: in this present study, the federal legislative and executive branches. The game also has goals: making or establishing a chosen policy. For its participants—the legislators and administrators—the process, like any game, imparts a sense of success or failure. There are established roles, and strategies and tactics are formulated. The approval of constituencies must be courted and won. There are indeed at least several games transpiring at once—a legislative, a presidential, and an administrative game—each with its own rules and players. Players in one game collaborate with players in another to achieve overall or shared policy goals. Thus the administrator may relate himself to the legislative game, observe its rules, and indulge in tactics and strategies to secure its prizes. The games and their respective players mesh their particular efforts to achieve joint results. One's view of policy questions is affected by his particular game. A legislative or executive office seeker or officeholder will gauge his approach to policy according to his political game or on a calculation of votes and interests that might contribute to his side's success.[22]

In the Cuban missile crisis, something of the game analogy was applied as President Kennedy's Ex Com weighed the several alternative responses the United States might make to the Soviet's installation of missile sites in Cuba. Each alternative was worked on a "track" of the likely Soviet response to the American move, the subsequent American response, and so on, until a final resolution of the interplay was conceivable. In working out the track, the American policy-makers endeavored to anticipate the Soviets' policy objectives, their likely strategic and tactical choices, and their own definitions of success or failure in the encounter.

GROUP STUDIES

We may learn much about how public policy is made, or about how it might be made more efficiently, through group studies. These vary widely in emphasis and method.

The member of the House or Senate is a member of a face-to-face group. To win status in the group, the member must adjust his behavior to it and show ample regard for the Senate or the House as an institution. Thus he is more than a Democrat or Republican, more than the congressman of a particular district or the senator of a particular state. The Senate is often spoken of as a "club," complete with an "inner circle," signifying the primacy of acceptance that some members have over others. To win acceptance is to conform to several standard expectations concerning the conduct of the members—chiefly, to serve an apprenticeship with cheerful unobtrusiveness, leaving the glory to the senior members. The junior, or newer, member is expected to perform routine legislative tasks rather than to reach for publicity by proposing important policies or by shining in committee hearings or floor debate. He is expected to concentrate on the fields of legislation with which his committee or constituency has particular concern rather than to pry into other legislative fields— a step that would be regarded as a challenge to the leadership and the domain of interested colleagues. He does well to compromise rather than to insist on fixed principles or ideology. The expectations of conformity are accompanied by rewards—better committee assignments, more preferment for their states, and friendlier consideration of their bills. Such conformity helps assure the performance of vital duties, distributes the work load, and encourages specialization and the habit of compromise as the key to consensus.[23] But the outsider, or nonconformist, also has a useful role—as the achievements of such legislators as George Norris, Wayne Morse, and Estes Kefauver suggest. The legislator whose career aspirations exceed the possibilities of his own house may need to resort to nonconformist behavior to attract necessary public attention. Kefauver caught the nation's eye during his crime investigations, but he trod on political toes in the course of enhancing the national reputation he had to develop to compete seriously for the presidency. The nonconforming legislator may also serve society's occasional requirement of more drastic approaches to policy than the legislature's ordinary pace and tolerance can provide; the publicity-getting nonconformist, if he can bestir public support, can then become a spur to his house of Congress.

VOTING BEHAVIOR

Analysis of voting behavior has been applied far more rigorously to the private citizen participating in national elections than to the legislator as voter in the House or Senate. Voting analyses provide the policy-maker with a penetrating profile of the condition of electoral opinion. Indeed, it is standard practice for legislators and Presidents, both while in office and during campaigns, to watch carefully polls of the electorate's opinions on policy.

Voting analyses thus far have been quantitative rather than qualitative, fact-centered rather than value-centered, and have relied heavily upon the methods of statistics and social psychology. The more intensive studies of citizen voting have utilized several techniques. The Opinion Research Center, for example, has relied upon a "national sample" of several thousand voters chosen as a cross section of the nation as a whole. Questions are answered tersely— "yes," "no," "no opinion," "approve strongly," and the like—which facilitates tabulation but which can overlook subtleties of opinion. Another approach is the "panel method," whereby a sample, chosen at random from a community, is interviewed several times during a campaign to ascertain changes in individual responses and to correlate them with concrete events. This method, which has been applied in particular communities, in the manner of the Paul F. Lazarsfeld study of Elmira, New York, can also be administered on the basis of a national sample. The latter has been done by the Survey Research Center at the University of Michigan for the 1948 and 1952 presidential campaigns. The Center's study, *The American Voter*, is the most comprehensive of all voting studies. In general, the studies indicate that a complex of factors in the individual voter's background—

his personality, family, religion, ideals, education, and friends—affect his responses to the personality and policy promises of the presidential candidate.[24]

Since husbands and wives tend to vote similarly, children are apt to be raised in a one-sided political atmosphere and, at least in their early voting, tend to vote as their parents did. Studies show that the higher the education and income and the more professional the nature of employment, the more likely is the voter to be a Republican. In contrast, the lower a voter's education and income and the more his occupation centers upon manual, unskilled labor, the more likely is he to be a Democrat. Religion seems to correlate with partisan identification. Northern white Protestants tend to vote Republican, and Jews and Catholics Democratic. In recent elections, the Catholic vote has been volatile, shifting to the Republican Eisenhower in 1952 and 1956 and swinging heavily to Kennedy in 1960. The Negro vote has been massively Democratic since Franklin Roosevelt broke it away from its traditional Republican moorings. Farmers respond differently to politics than do city folk; according to the Michigan Survey Center, since 1958 the voting distribution of farmers outside the South has shown the widest fluctuation of any major occupational group. Age is a stabilizing factor in party preference. Although from one fourth to one third of the electorate consider themselves independent voters, data show that many of this group support one party frequently.

Not only have the research techniques differed in studies of voting behavior; different researchers have sometimes drawn different conclusions from the same evidence, and still others, after further consideration, have altered their earlier interpretations. At the same time, however, there is a large measure of agreement in their findings. One area of agreement is that the voter's exercise of choice at the polls on candidates and policy issues does not follow a steady, rational course.

THE FUTURE OF POLICY-MAKING

What does the future hold for legislative-executive policy-making? Certainly, it holds a store of problems no less severe than those that have faced American government in the past. A vital difference, however, may be the necessity of new policy to move faster in the future than in the past, thereby imposing new strains on a policy-making machinery that is by no means renowned for its speed.

On the basis of present indications, policy-makers in the future will have to address themselves to at least three great revolutions. One is the *human rights revolution*—the striving of great numbers of our own citizens, and of whole nations abroad, to secure basic rights and freedoms. We face also the *automation revolution*, which in future decades may make such severe inroads into employment that we may need to redefine our attitudes toward work and leisure; in any such redefinition, the official legislative and executive policy-makers must take a leading part. In foreign affairs, we are deep in the *weapons revolution*, whose prospect becomes more ominous as mastery of nuclear weapons production and use spreads to other nations.

The serious issue concerning our policy-making machinery is whether it is capable of sustained promptness in supplying responses to growing problems—indeed, to crises. There is much that is balky in the present machinery: the bureaucratic habit of becoming laggard and unimaginative; the frequent recourse of Congress to sheer negativism and its tendency to turn down policy initiatives without offering substitutes; and the formidable obstacle course that policy must traverse—the Senate filibuster, the seniority principle of selecting committee chairmen, the strangling power of the committee bottleneck, the diffusion of leadership and responsibility. The President stands atop the great behemoth of the executive branch and, notwithstanding growing numbers of energetic executive aides, encounters ever more difficulty in controlling it.

In light of the formidable problems confronting the policy process in the future and the several ailments afflicting the machinery, it behooves us to examine seriously and particularly its several parts and to weigh the means of possible improvement. We should apply measures that seem promising to strengthen congressional organization and methods and administrative structures and practices and to improve the President's powers where they show weakness. In a society of pluralistic policy-making, every citizen has a stake in the quality of governmental machinery.

FOOTNOTES

CHAPTER ONE

1. C. P. Snow, *Science and Government* (Cambridge, Mass.: Harvard University Press, 1961), p. 1.

2. See *The Federalist*, No. 10. Of the several editions of this work, particularly recommended are those of Benjamin F. Wright, *The Federalist* (Cambridge, Mass.: Harvard University Press, 1961) and Jacob E. Cooke, *The Federalist* (Middletown, Conn.: Wesleyan University Press, 1961).

3. Karl Mannheim, *Ideology and Utopia* (New York: Harcourt, Brace & World, Inc., 1936), p. 99.

4. John Adams, *Defence of the Constitution of the United States of America Against the Attack of Mr. Turgot*, in Charles Francis Adams, ed., *The Works of John Adams* (Boston: Little, Brown & Co., 1856), VI, 218.

5. See *The Federalist*, No. 5.

6. Quoted in Richard Hofstadter, *The American Political Tradition* (New York: Alfred A. Knopf, Inc., 1948), Vintage ed., p. 191.

7. Oliver Wendell Holmes, "Ideals and Doubts," *Collected Legal Papers* (New York: Harcourt, Brace & Co., 1921), pp. 303-304.

8. Quoted in Ralph H. Gabriel, *The Course of American Democratic Thought* (New York: The Ronald Press Company, 1940), p. 376.

9. 4 Wheat. 316 (1819).

10. Radio-television address, August 23, 1954; see *The New York Times*, August 24, 1954.

11. *Proceedings and debates of the Virginia Convention of 1829–30*, p. 66.

12. K. Cralle, ed., *The Works of John C. Calhoun* (New York: Appleton-Century-Crofts, Inc., 1957), VI, 33.

13. Quoted in Alpheus Thomas Mason and Richard H. Leach, *In Quest of Freedom: American Political Thought and Practice* (Englewood Cliffs, N.J.: Prentice-Hall, Inc., 1959), pp. 297-298.

14. See, for example, James MacGregor Burns, *The Deadlock of Democracy* (Englewood Cliffs, N.J.: Prentice-Hall, Inc., 1963), and Joseph S. Clark, *Congress: The Sapless Branch* (New York: Harper & Row, 1964).

15. Quotations from Hofstadter, *The American Political Tradition*, pp. 187-196.

16. Charles M. Wiltsie, *John C. Calhoun, Nullifier, 1829–1839* (Indianapolis: The Bobbs-Merrill Co., 1949), p. 429.

17. Hofstadter, *The American Political Tradition*, p. 176.

CHAPTER TWO

1. Donald R. Matthews, *U.S. Senators and Their World* (Chapel Hill: University of North Carolina Press, 1960), Chapter 7.

2. Charles L. Clapp, *The Congressman, His Work as He Sees It* (Washington: The Brookings Institution, 1963), p. 214.

3. William S. White, *Citadel: The Story of the U.S. Senate* (New York: Harper & Brothers, 1956), p. 57.

4. Clapp, *The Congressman*, pp. 35ff.

5. 376 U.S. 1 (1964).

6. Matthews, *U.S. Senators and Their World*, pp. 16-26.

7. White, *Citadel*, p. 117.

8. Clapp, *The Congressman*, pp. 35ff.

9. A. Robert Smith, *The Tiger in the Senate: The Biography of Senator Wayne Morse* (Garden City, N.Y.: Doubleday & Co., Inc., 1962), pp. 239-241.

10. Oscar W. Underwood, *Drifting Sands of Party Politics* (New York: The Century Co., 1928), p. 158.

11. Arthur H. Vandenberg, Jr., *The Private Papers of Senator Vandenberg* (Boston: Houghton Mifflin Company, 1952), p. 55.

12. Tom Connally, *My Name Is Tom Connally* (New York: Thomas Y. Crowell Co., 1954), p. 111.

13. Vandenberg, *Private Papers*, p. 93.

14. Matthews, *U.S. Senators and Their World*, p. 221.

15. Clapp, *The Congressman*, p. 89.

16. Joe Martin, *My First Fifty Years in Congress* (New York: Harper & Brothers, 1960), p. 55.

17. Clapp, *The Congressman*, p. 77.

18. Transcript of an interview of Sam Rayburn by William Lawrence on the American Broadcasting Company's radio and television network, July 16, 1961, p. 12.

19. Martin, *My First Fifty Years in Congress*, p. 9.

20. Champ Clark, *My Quarter Century of American Politics* (New York: Harper & Brothers, 1920), II, 337.

21. Quoted in Neil MacNeil, *Forge of Democracy: The House of Representatives* (New York: David McKay, 1963), p. 93.

22. Martin, *My First Fifty Years in Congress*, p. 183.

23. Quoted by MacNeil, *Forge of Democracy*, p. 94.

24. Clapp, *The Congressman*, p. 286.

25. Burton K. Wheeler, *Yankee from the West* (Garden City, N.Y.: Doubleday & Co., Inc., 1962), p. 323.

26. Quoted by Clapp, *The Congressman*, p. 323.

27. Quoted by Clapp, *The Congressman*, p. 328.

28. Quoted by MacNeil, *Forge of Democracy*, p. 114.

29. See *The New York Times*, September 29, 1963.

30. Martin, *My First Fifty Years in Congress*, pp. 47-48.

31. Wheeler, *Yankee from the West*, p. 276.

32. See Robert Bendiner, *Obstacle Course on Capitol Hill* (New York: McGraw Hill Book Co., 1964); James MacGregor Burns, *The Deadlock of Democracy* (Englewood Cliffs, N.J.: Prentice-Hall, Inc., 1963); and Joseph S. Clark, *Congress: The Sapless Branch* (New York: Harper & Row, 1964).

CHAPTER THREE

1. For Washington's conduct of the presidency, see Douglas S. Freeman, *George Washington* (New York: Charles Scribner's Sons, 1954–1957), Vols. VI and VII.

2. For an evaluation of presidential contributions, see Clinton Rossiter, *The American Presidency*, rev. ed. (New York: Harcourt, Brace & World, Inc., 1960), Chapters 3 and 5.

3. See his *The President: Office and Powers*, rev. ed. (New York: New York University Press, 1957), Chapter 1.

4. For a deft and extended analysis, see Richard E. Neustadt, *Presidential Power* (New York: John Wiley & Sons, Inc., 1960).

5. Quoted in Theodore C. Sorensen, *Decision-Making in the White House* (New York: Columbia University Press, 1963), p. 13.

6. See Nelson W. Polsby and Aaron B. Wildavsky, *Presidential Elections* (New York: Charles Scribner's Sons, 1964).

7. For an extended discussion of presidential roles, see Louis W. Koenig, *The Chief Executive* (New York: Harcourt, Brace & World, Inc., 1964).

8. Harry S Truman, *Memoirs* (Garden City, N.Y.: Doubleday & Co., Inc., 1955–1956), II, 449.

9. *Youngstown Sheet and Tube Co. v. Sawyer*, 343 U.S. 579 (1952).

10. Grant McConnell, *Steel and The Presidency—1962* (New York: W. W. Norton and Co., Inc., 1963).

11. Woodrow Wilson, *Constitutional Government in the United States* (New York: Columbia University Press, 1908), p. 68.

12. Commission on Organization of the Executive Branch of the Government, *Report on General Management of the Executive Branch* (Washington, D.C.: Government Printing Office, 1949).

13. 271 U.S. 1 (1926).

14. 295 U.S. 602 (1935).

15. 4 Wall. 2 (1866).

16. 343 U.S. 579 (1952).

17. Dwight D. Eisenhower, *Mandate for Change* (Garden City, N.Y.: Doubleday & Co., Inc., 1963), pp. 464-465.

CHAPTER FOUR

1. American Assembly, *The Federal Government Service: Its Character, Prestige, and Problems* (New York: Columbia University Press, 1954).

2. United States Civil Service Commission, *1964 Annual Report* (Washington, D.C.: Government Printing Office, 1964), p. 28.

3. For an account of the origins of the earliest departments, see Leonard White, *The Federalists* (New York: The Macmillan Co., 1948).

4. See *The New York Times*, August 28, 1962.

5. *The New York Times*, August 5, 1962.

6. For discussions of the independent regulatory commissions, see Marver H. Bernstein, *Regulating Busi-*

ness by Independent Commission (Princeton, N.J.: Princeton University Press, 1955), and Robert E. Cushman, *The Independent Regulatory Commissions* (New York: The Macmillan Co., 1941).

7. See *Humphrey v. United States,* 295 U.S. 602 (1935). The case is discussed in Chapter Three, p. 79.

8. See President's Committee on Administrative Management, *Report with Special Studies* (Washington, D.C.: Government Printing Office, 1937), pp. 39-42, and Commission on Organization of the Executive Branch of the Government (first Hoover Commission), *The Independent Regulatory Commissions* (Washington, D.C.: Government Printing Office, 1949). The views of Louis Hector are incorporated in his letter of resignation; see *The New York Times,* September 17, 1959. An extensive summary of the Landis report is found in *The New York Times,* December 27, 1960.

9. For discussions of the government corporation, see first Hoover Commission's *Report on Federal Business Enterprises* (Washington, D.C.: Government Printing Office, 1949), and C. Herman Pritchett, *The Tennessee Valley Authority* (Chapel Hill: University of North Carolina Press, 1943).

10. For discussion of the President's staff, see Edward H. Hobbs, *Behind the President* (Washington, D.C.: Public Affairs Press, 1954).

11. President's Committee on Civil Rights, *To Secure These Rights* (Washington, D.C.: Government Printing Office, 1947).

12. Data from United States Civil Service Commission, *1964 Annual Report,* pp. 28 and 83-93.

13. Commission on Organization of the Executive Branch of the Government (second Hoover Commission), *Personnel and Civil Service* (Washington, D.C.: Government Printing Office, 1955).

14. See *The New York Times,* July 28, 1962.

15. H. H. Gerth and C. W. Mills, *From Max Weber: Essays in Sociology* (New York: Oxford University Press, 1946).

16. For perspectives on Weber, see John M. Pfiffner and Robert V. Presthus, *Public Administration,* 4th ed. (New York: The Ronald Press Company, 1960), Chapter 3; Peter Blau, *The Dynamics of Bureaucracy* (Chicago: University of Chicago Press, 1955); and Peter Woll, *American Bureaucracy* (New York: W. W. Norton & Co., Inc., 1963).

17. Richard E. Neustadt, "Presidency and Legislation: Planning the President's Program," *American Political Science Review,* XLIX (December 1955), 980.

18. Ezra Taft Benson, *Cross-Fire* (Garden City, N.Y.: Doubleday & Co., Inc., 1962), p. 66.

19. For an account of the practice of different Presidents, see Louis W. Koenig, *The Chief Executive* (New York: Harcourt, Brace & World, Inc., 1964), Chapter 7.

20. Dwight D. Eisenhower, *Mandate for Change* (Garden City, N.Y.: Doubleday & Co., Inc., 1963), p. 87.

21. Sherman Adams, *First-Hand Report* (New York: Harper & Brothers, 1961), pp. 52-53.

22. See Arthur Maass, *Muddy Waters: The Army Engineers and the Nation's Rivers* (Cambridge, Mass.: Harvard University Press, 1951).

23. Quoted in Richard E. Neustadt, *Presidential Power* (New York: John Wiley & Sons, Inc., 1960), p. 9.

24. See *The New York Times*, October 28, 1962.

25. Benson, *Cross-Fire,* p. 156.

26. Benson, *Cross-Fire,* p. 27.

27. See *The New York Times*, December 19, 1946, p. 34.

28. See President's Committee on Administrative Management, *Report with Special Studies* (Washington, D.C.: Government Printing Office, 1937); Commission on Organization of the Executive Branch of the Government (first and second Hoover commissions), *Reports* (Washington, D.C.: Government Printing Office, 1949 and 1955); and Senate Subcommittee on National Security and Staffing and Operations of the Committee of Government Operations, *Hearings* and *Reports* (Washington, D.C.: Government Printing Office, 1959 and after).

CHAPTER FIVE
1. *The New York Times*, June 11, 1964.

2. See her Foreword to Edwin E. Witte, *The Development of the Social Security Act* (Madison: University of Wisconsin Press, 1962), p. vi.

3. Witte, *Social Security Act*, pp. 17-18.

4. This account relies upon Witte, *Social Security Act.*

5. Witte, *Social Security Act*, p. 17.

6. Witte, *Social Security Act*, p. 73.

7. This account of the Civil Rights Act of 1964 is based upon the *Congressional Quarterly Almanac* for 1963 (Washington, D.C.: Congressional Quarterly, Inc., 1963); the *Congressional Quarterly Weekly Reports* for 1963 and 1964 (Washington, D.C.: Congressional Quarterly, Inc., 1963 and 1964); and *The New York Times* for 1963 and 1964.

8. See the Civil Rights Cases, 109 U.S. 3 (1883).

9. See *The New York Times*, February 19, 1964.

10. See Louis W. Koenig (ed.) *The Truman Administration* (New York: New York University Press, 1956), pp. 240-246.

11. Quoted in Arthur S. Link, *Woodrow Wilson and the Progressive Era* (New York: Harper & Brothers, 1954), p. 77.

12. See Joseph S. Clark, *Congress: The Sapless Branch* (New York: Harper & Row, 1964).

13. See Donald H. Riddle, *The Truman Committee: A Study in Congressional Responsibility* (New Brunswick, N.J.: Rutgers University Press, 1963).

14. This account relies upon *The New York Times*, October 21-November 2, 1962.

15. See Theodore C. Sorensen, *Decision-Making in the White House* (New York: Columbia University Press, 1963), pp. 32-36.

16. See Peter Woll, *American Bureaucracy* (New York: W. W. Norton & Co., Inc., 1963), pp. 120-122.

17. *The New York Times,* August 25, 1964.

18. See Henry C. Metcalf and L. Urwick, eds., *Dynamic Administration: The Collected Papers of Mary Parker Follett* (New York: Harper & Brothers, 1942), pp. 147-286.

19. See *The New York Times,* April 26, 1963.

20. Quoted in Irving Brant, *James Madison: Secretary of State, 1800–1809* (Indianapolis: The Bobbs-Merrill Co., 1953), p. 159.

21. Harold L. Ickes, *The Secret Diary of Harold L. Ickes: The Inside Struggle* (New York: Simon & Schuster, Inc., 1954), p. 339.

CHAPTER SIX
1. Frank L. Klement, *The Copperheads in the Middle West* (Chicago: University of Chicago Press, 1960).

2. See Irving Brant, *James Madison: Secretary of State, 1800–1809* (Indianapolis: The Bobbs-Merrill Co., 1953), pp. 125-134, and William P. Cresson, *James Monroe* (Chapel Hill: University of North Carolina Press, 1946), pp. 183-189.

3. Oscar Underwood, *Drifting Sands of Party Politics* (New York: The Century Co., 1928), p. 10.

4. *The New York Times,* April 15, 1945.

5. Quoted in William Hesseltine, *Ulysses S. Grant, Politician* (New York: Dodd, Mead & Co., Inc., 1935), p. 392.

6. Richard Hofstadter, *The American Political Tradition* (New York: Alfred A. Knopf, Inc., 1948), Vintage edition, p. 116.

7. Quoted in Cresson, *James Monroe,* p. 449.

8. See Philip S. Klein, *President James Buchanan* (University Park: Pennsylvania State University Press, 1962), p. 331.

9. Herbert Simon, *The Science of Management Decision* (New York: Harper & Brothers, 1960), pp. 1-2.

10. John Hope Franklin, *The Emancipation Proclamation* (Garden City, N.Y.: Doubleday & Co., Inc., 1963), pp. 21-22.

11. *The New York Times,* June 11, 1964.

12. Rexford Tugwell, *The Democratic Roosevelt* (Garden City, N.Y.: Doubleday & Co., Inc., 1957), p. 547.

13. Theodore C. Sorensen, *Decision-Making in the White House* (New York: Columbia University Press, 1963), pp. 34-35.

14. Cited in James MacGregor Burns, "The Four Kennedys of the First Year," *New York Times Magazine,* January 14, 1962, p. 72.

15. See Chapter Three, pp. 77-78.

16. See Chapter Five, pp. 131-138.

17. Bryan's climactic words were "You shall not press upon the brow of labor the crown of thorn. You shall not crucify mankind upon a cross of gold."

18. See Louis W. Koenig, ed., *The Truman Administration* (New York: New York University Press, 1956), pp. 241-247.

19. For further elaboration, see Marshall E. Dimock, Gladys O. Dimock, and Louis W. Koenig, *Public Administration*, rev. ed. (New York: Rinehart & Company, Inc., 1958), pp. 354-356.

20. See E. Pendleton Herring, *Group Representation before Congress* (Baltimore: Johns Hopkins University Press, 1929).

21. This analysis is adapted from Norton E. Long's analysis of local government and politics. See his "The Local Community as an Ecology of Games," *American Journal of Sociology*, XLIV (November 1958), 251-261, which is reprinted in Charles Press, ed., *The Polity: Norton E. Long* (Chicago: Rand McNally & Company, 1962), pp. 139-155.

22. See James M. Buchanan and Gordon Tullock, *The Calculus of Consent* (Ann Arbor: University of Michigan Press, 1962).

23. See Ralph K. Huitt, "The Outsider in the Senate: An Alternate Role," *American Political Science Review*, LV (September 1961), 566-575, and Donald R. Matthews, *U.S. Senators and Their World* (Chapel Hill: University of North Carolina Press, 1960), pp. 116ff.

24. See Peter H. Rossi, "Four Landmarks in Voting Research," in Eugene Burdick and Arthur J. Brocheck, eds., *American Voting Behavior* (New York: The Free Press of Glencoe, 1959); Angus Campbell, Philip E. Converse, Warren E. Miller, and Donald Stokes, *The American Voter* (New York: John Wiley & Sons, Inc., 1960); and Bernard B. Berelson, Paul F. Lazarsfeld, and William N. McPhee, *Voting: A Study of Opinion Formation in a Presidential Campaign* (Chicago: University of Chicago Press, 1954).

BIBLIOGRAPHICAL ESSAY

Additional sources to which the student may turn concerning the subjects treated in this book are so numerous and ever-growing that no more than a sampling can be ventured here. Those selected are arranged according to the major divisions of this study.

THE POLICY-MAKING COMMUNITY

Among the many volumes serving as an introduction to political science, several are recommended for their special usefulness as background for a study of policy-making. These include: Robert M. MacIver, *The Web of Government* (New York: The Macmillan Co., 1947); David B. Truman, *The Governmental Process* (New York: Alfred A. Knopf, 1951); Charles Hyneman, *The Study of Politics: The Present State of American Political Science* (Urbana: University of Illinois Press, 1959); and Roland Young, ed., *Approaches to the Study of Politics* (Evanston, Ill.: Northwestern University Press, 1958).

The several orders composing the policy-making community are well represented in the literature. Concerning the economic order, Adolf A. Berle, *The American Economic Republic* (New York: Harcourt, Brace & World, Inc., 1963) and Marshall E. Dimock, *The New American Economy* (New York: Harper & Row, 1962) are particularly recommended. Historical emphasis is to be found in Louis M. Hacker, *American Capitalism: Its Promise and Accomplishment* (Princeton, N.J.: D. Van Nostrand Co., Inc., 1957). The place of the corporation in the economy is viewed in Edward S. Mason, *The Corporation in Modern Society* (Cambridge, Mass.: Harvard University Press,

1960). For a thorough presentation of the interrelationships of government and the economy, see Merle Fainsod, Lincoln Gordon, and Joseph C. Palamountain, Jr., *Government and the American Economy* (New York: W. W. Norton & Co., Inc., 1959).

The social order is treated in works such as Floyd Hunter's *Community Power Structure: A Study of Decisions* (Chapel Hill: University of North Carolina Press, 1953). Frequently cited studies include two by Robert and Helen Lynd, *Middletown: A Study in Contemporary Culture* (New York: Harcourt, Brace & Co., 1929) and *Middletown in Transition: A Study in Cultural Conflict* (New York: Harcourt, Brace & Co., 1937). The role of social classes is treated in Reinhard Bendix and Seymour Martin Lipset, eds., *Class, Status and Power: A Reader in Social Stratification* (Glencoe, Ill.: The Free Press, 1954) and Bernard Barber, *Social Stratification* (New York: Harcourt, Brace & Co., 1957). The convergence of social and political power is viewed in Robert A. Dahl, *Who Governs?* (New Haven, Conn.: Yale University Press, 1961), a study of political power and social groups in New Haven. Similarly useful is Donald R. Matthews, *The Social Background of Political Decision-Makers* (Garden City, N.Y.: Doubleday & Co., Inc., 1954).

Concerning the moral and cultural orders, the following are particularly recommended: Will Herberg, *Protestant, Catholic, and Jew* (Garden City, N.Y.: Doubleday & Co., Inc., 1955), which presents the religious phases of American society; Peter H. Odegard, ed., *Religion and Politics* (New York: Oceana Publications, Inc., 1960); and John Dewey, *Human Nature and Conduct* (New York: Henry Holt & Company, 1922).

For background reading on the governmental and political orders, see Alfred H. Kelley and Winfred A. Harbison, *The American Constitution* (New York: W. W. Norton & Co., Inc., 1955), describing the development of the constitutional system, and an earlier work, Andrew C. Mc-Laughlin, *A Constitutional History of the United States* (New York: The Macmillan Co., 1935). Analyses of major elements of the Constitution are to be found in Edward S. Corwin, *The Constitution and What It Means Today*, 11th ed. (Princeton, N.J.: Princeton University Press, 1950), and Louis Hartz, *The Liberal Tradition in America* (New York: Alfred A. Knopf, Inc., 1955). The adjustments of the Constitution to change are treated in Howard L. McBain, *The Living Constitution* (New York: The Workers Education Bureau Press, 1927, 1942); and Carl B. Swisher, *American Constitutional Development* (New York: The Macmillan Co., 1954). A lively, insightful account of the American political landscape is provided by Max Lerner in *America as a Civilization* (New York: Simon and Schuster, Inc., 1957).

Major political ideas that have affected the American experience are discussed in Alpheus T. Mason, *Free Government in the Making* (New York: Oxford University Press, 1956); Alpheus T. Mason and Richard H. Leach, *In Quest of Freedom: American Political Thought and Practice* (Englewood Cliffs, N.J.: Prentice-Hall, Inc., 1959); Ralph H. Gabriel, *The Course of American Democratic Thought* (New York: The Ronald Press Company, 1940); and Merle Curti, *The Growth of American Thought* (New York: Harper & Brothers, 1943).

The role of politicians and political leaders in the development of American political thought is analyzed in Richard Hofstadter, *The American Political Tradition* (New York: Alfred A. Knopf, Inc., 1948).

CONGRESS

The classic study of Congress is Woodrow Wilson's *Congressional Government* (Boston: Houghton Mifflin Company, 1885), analyzing nineteenth-century congressional dominance over the presidency. Comprehensive contemporary studies of Congress include Stephen K. Bailey and Howard D. Samuel, *Congress at Work* (New York: Henry Holt & Company, 1952); George Galloway, *The Legislative Process in Congress* (New York: Thomas Y. Crowell Co., 1953); Ernest S. Griffith, *Congress, Its Contemporary Role*, rev. ed. (New York: New York University Press, 1956); Bertram M. Gross, *The Legislative Struggle: A Study in Social Combat* (New York: McGraw-Hill Book Co., 1953); and Floyd M. Riddick, *The United States Congress: Organization and Procedures* (Washington, D.C.: National Capitol Publishers, 1949).

Several works concentrate on particular functions or processes of Congress. Representative government is examined in Alfred de Grazia, *Public and Republic* (New York: Alfred A. Knopf, Inc., 1951); the development of a bill into law in Stephen K. Bailey, *Congress Makes a Law* (New York: Columbia University Press, 1950); legislative decision-making processes in Roland Young, *The American Congress* (New York: Harper & Row, 1958); and the exploration of congressional behavior through mathematical analysis in David Truman, *The Congressional Party* (New York: John Wiley & Sons, Inc., 1959). Julius Turner's *Party and Constituency* (Baltimore: Johns Hopkins Press, 1952) analyzes the impact of party and constituency on congressional voting; and Duncan MacRae, *Dimensions of Congressional Voting* (Berkeley: University of California Press, 1958) analyzes voting patterns in the 81st Congress.

The House of Representatives, its functions and processes, is treated analytically against a strong historical background in George Galloway, *The House of Representatives* (New York: Thomas Y. Crowell Co., 1961, 1962). A more contemporary emphasis is given in Neil MacNeil, *Forge of Democracy: The House of Representatives* (New York: David McKay Co., Inc., 1963). Charles L. Clapp, *The Congressman, His Work as He Sees It* (Washington, D.C.: The Brookings Institution, 1963) surveys the congressman's relations with the House and its processes on the basis of interviews with many legislators.

We lack a satisfactory, up-to-date, comprehensive work on the Senate. The standard account, although outdated, is George H. Haynes, *The Senate of the United States,* 2 vols. (New York: Russell and Russell, Inc., 1960). An old but arresting interpretation is Lindsay Rogers, *The American Senate* (New York: Alfred A. Knopf, Inc., 1926). A more recent account that is approving, if not adulatory, is William S. White, *Citadel: The Story of the U.S. Senate* (New York: Harper and Row, 1957). More balanced is Donald R. Matthews, *U.S. Senators and Their World* (Chapel Hill: University of North Carolina Press, 1962). Joseph P. Harris, *The Advice and Consent of the Senate* (Berkeley: University of California Press, 1953), examines the Senate's role in appointments.

A number of studies of congressional committees exist. Among these are David N. Farnsworth, *The Senate Committee on Foreign Relations* (Urbana: University of Illinois Press, 1961); Holbert N. Carroll, *The House of Representatives and Foreign Affairs* (Pittsburgh: University of Pittsburgh Press, 1958); Robert K. Carr, *The House Un-American Activities Committee* (Ithaca, N.Y.: Cornell University

Press, 1952); and Telford Taylor, *Grand Inquest* (New York: Simon and Schuster, Inc., 1955). Gilbert Y. Steiner, *The Congressional Conference Committee* (Urbana: University of Illinois Press, 1951), studies the operations of such committees from the 70th to the 80th Congress. Kenneth Kofmehl, *Professional Staffs of Congress* (West Lafayette, Ind.: Purdue University Studies, 1962), analyzes the development since 1946 of professional staffs for congressional committees.

Close-ups of the men who make the laws are sometimes provided in the biographies and memoirs of legislators. Among the more useful of such volumes are L. S. Busbey, *Uncle Joe Cannon* (New York: Henry Holt & Company, 1927); Tom Connally, *My Name Is Tom Connally* (New York: Thomas Y. Crowell Co., 1954); George Norris, *Fighting Liberal* (New York: The Macmillan Co., 1945); Joe Martin, *My First Fifty Years in Congress* (New York: Harper & Brothers, 1960); A. Robert Smith, *The Tiger in the Senate: The Biography of Senator Wayne Morse* (Garden City, N.Y.: Doubleday & Co., Inc., 1962); Oscar W. Underwood, *Drifting Sands of Party Politics* (New York: The Century Co., 1928); Arthur W. Vandenberg, Jr., *The Private Papers of Senator Vandenberg* (Boston: Houghton Mifflin Company, 1952); Burton K. Wheeler, *Yankee from the West* (Garden City, N.Y.: Doubleday & Co., Inc., 1962); and C. Dwight Dorough, *Mr. Sam* (New York: Random House, 1962).

In the 1960's, more than at any other time in its history, Congress has been dealt with critically. Illustrative of the criticism are Robert Bendiner, *Obstacle Course on Capitol Hill* (New York: McGraw-Hill Book Co., 1964); James MacGregor Burns, *The Deadlock of Democracy* (Englewood

Cliffs, N.J.: Prentice-Hall, Inc., 1963); and Joseph S. Clark, *Congress: The Sapless Branch* (New York: Harper & Row, 1964).

The student of Congress' role in public policy development will be interested in several key publications providing invaluable research material. *Congressional Quarterly*, published by Congressional Quarterly News Features (1156 19th St., N.W., Washington, D.C.) is issued weekly and summarizes congressional and presidential-congressional activity. Roll-call votes, the progress and status of bills, data on congressional elections and other aspects of Capitol Hill matters are presented. The material is compiled conveniently in an annual, single volume, *The Congressional Quarterly Almanac*.

A wealth of government publications deal with the work of Congress. The *Congressional Record* closely reports the words and actions transpiring on the floor of each house. Less used and more skimpy are the House and Senate Journals. Congressional committees are represented by their *Hearings*, which contain verbatim testimony taken in public hearings of the committees, and by their *Reports*, which convey the committees' recommendations to their respective houses. Acts of Congress, or statutes, are available as *The United States Statutes at Large*, which are bound volumes carrying, in chronological order, the texts of laws passed by each Congress. Congressional acts are also codified in the *United States Code* and the *United States Code Annotated* (the latter is published privately). The code arrangement groups under subject-matter headings laws in effect when the code is published. A statute is available, promptly after its passage, in Slip Law form, or as a pamphlet, bearing a designation such as

"Public Law 231, 87th Congress; Chapter 546-1st Session."

Biographical information concerning members of a given Congress is contained in the *Congressional Directory*, published by the Government Printing Office, Washington, D.C. Similar information about past members of Congress is found in *The Biographical Directory of the American Congress*, also published by the Government Printing Office, which covers everyone who served in Congress and predecessor national legislative bodies between 1774 and 1949.

THE PRESIDENT

Because it is such a dynamic office, there is a steady flow of books about the presidency. For brief, readable, and insightful treatments of the subject, see Clinton Rossiter, *The American Presidency*, rev. ed. (New York: Harcourt, Brace & World, Inc., 1960) and Harold Laski, *The American Presidency* (New York: Harper & Brothers, 1940). More extended treatments of the office include Wilfred Binkley, *The Man in the White House* (Baltimore: Johns Hopkins University Press, 1959); Edward S. Corwin, *The President: Office and Powers*, 4th ed. (New York: New York University Press, 1957), which is especially strong in its presentation of legal aspects; Sidney Hyman, *The American President* (New York: Harper & Brothers, 1954); Louis W. Koenig, *The Chief Executive* (New York: Harcourt, Brace & World, Inc., 1964); and Rexford G. Tugwell, *The Enlargement of the Presidency* (Garden City, N.Y.: Doubleday & Co., Inc., 1960), rich in historical fact and interpretation. An astute analysis of the "practical politics" of the presidency is Richard Neustadt's *Presidential Power* (New York: John Wiley & Sons, Inc., 1963), a book credited with influencing President Kennedy's conduct of the office.

Several Presidents have provided thoughtful interpretations of the office. William Howard Taft did so in *Our Chief Magistrate and His Powers* (New York: Columbia University Press, 1916), written following his service in the presidency. Prior to holding the office, Woodrow Wilson made perceptive observations in the course of lectures collected in his *Constitutional Government in the United States* (New York: Columbia University Press, 1908).

For studies that are critical, in a comprehensive way, one may turn to Herman Finer, *The Presidency: Crisis and Regeneration* (Chicago: University of Chicago Press, 1960), and William Y. Elliott, ed., *United States Foreign Policy* (New York: Columbia University Press, 1952).

The origins of the presidency are dealt with by James Hart, *The American Presidency in Action* (New York: The Macmillan Co., 1948), and Charles Thach, Jr., *The Creation of the Presidency* (Baltimore: Johns Hopkins University Press, 1922).

The several functions or roles of the President are well represented in political science literature. His capacity in foreign affairs is dealt with perceptively by Sidney Warren, *The President as World Leader* (Philadelphia: J. B. Lippincott Co., 1964). The executive agreement is treated historically in Wallace McClure, *International Executive Agreements* (New York: Columbia University Press, 1941), a subject that badly needs to be brought up to date. The President's military powers, particularly as they affect the private individual, are discussed in Clinton Rossiter, *The Supreme Court and the Commander-in-Chief* (Ithaca, N.Y.: Cornell University Press, 1951). For discussion of the President's growing

activity in civil rights, see Richard Longaker, *The President and Civil Liberties* (Ithaca, N.Y.: Cornell University Press, 1961). The President's concerns with the economy can be viewed in Marshall E. Dimock, *The New American Economy* (New York: Harper & Row, 1962) and Adolf A. Berle, *The American Economic Republic* (New York: Harcourt, Brace & World, Inc., 1963).

In addition to the several policy areas for which he is responsible, the President carries on functional activities inherent in the nature of his office. These, too, are well represented in the literature. For the President's concerns with Congress, see the excellent works of Wilfred Binkley, *President and Congress* (New York: Alfred A. Knopf, Inc., 1947), which is historical in its approach, and Lawrence H. Chamberlain, *The President, Congress, and Legislation* (New York: Columbia University Press, 1946), which examines the origins and development of a number of acts of Congress in terms of the influence of the presidency and Congress. The President's position as party leader is treated in James MacGregor Burns, *The Deadlock of Democracy* (New York: Prentice-Hall, Inc., 1963), and Malcolm Moos, *Politics, Presidents and Coattails* (Baltimore: Johns Hopkins University Press, 1950). His capacity as public leader is treated comprehensively in Elmer E. Cornwell, Jr., *Presidential Leadership of Public Opinion* (Bloomington: Indiana University Press, 1965). His role as administrative chief is analyzed in two official studies and reports. One is the Brownlow Committee, known more formally as The President's Committee on Administrative Management, *Report with Special Studies* (Washington, D.C.: Government Printing Office, 1937), a study having important repercussions on the composition and make-up of the President's staff. The other is the report of the first Hoover Commission, which also has a more formal and formidable name—Commission on Organization of the Executive Branch of the Government; of its several reports, that on the *General Management of the Executive Branch* (Washington, D.C.: Government Printing Office, 1949) deals most centrally with the presidency.

An overall treatment of the several kinds of personal and institutional staffs that serve the President is found in Edward H. Hobbs, *Behind the President: A Study of Executive Office Agencies* (Washington, D.C.: The Brookings Institution, 1954), and Bradley D. Nash, *Staffing the Presidency* (Washington, D.C.: National Planning Association, 1952). More specialized studies include Richard Fenno, *The President's Cabinet* (Cambridge, Mass.: Harvard University Press, 1959); Corinne Silverman, *The President's Economic Advisers* (University, Ala.: University of Alabama Press, 1959); Herman M. Somers, *Presidential Agency: OWMR* (Cambridge, Mass.: Harvard University Press, 1954); and Louis W. Koenig, *The Invisible Presidency* (New York: Rinehart & Company, Inc., 1960), a discussion of selected presidential advisers and confidants. The President's relationships with staff institutions and associates in the context of decision-making is analyzed by a leading member of the Kennedy administration, Theodore C. Sorensen, in *Decision-Making in the White House* (New York: Columbia University Press, 1963).

The selection of the President is treated in books that either view particular parts of the process or deal with it comprehensively. The latter is the approach of Theodore H. White in his popular *The Making*

of the President, 1960 (New York: Atheneum Publishers, 1961); Eugene H. Roseboom, *A History of Presidential Elections* (New York: The Macmillan Co., 1957); and Nelson W. Polsby and Aaron Wildavsky, *Presidential Elections* (New York: Charles Scribner's Sons, 1964). More specialized studies are Paul David, Malcolm Moos, and Ralph Goldman, *Presidential Nominating Politics*, 5 vols. (Baltimore: Johns Hopkins University Press, 1954), and Lucius Wilmerding, Jr., *The Electoral College* (New Brunswick, N.J.: Rutgers University Press, 1958). Questions concerning the President's tenure have been the focus of increasing interest in recent years, owing to the sudden trajectory of Vice-President Truman into the presidency upon the death of President Roosevelt, the illnesses of President Eisenhower, and the assassination of President Kennedy. Among the more useful studies are Richard Hansen, *The Year We Had No President* (Lincoln: University of Nebraska Press, 1963), which deals with instances of major presidential illness, and Ruth Silva, *Presidential Succession* (Ann Arbor: University of Michigan Press, 1951). The vice-presidency is treated historically and analytically in Edgar W. Waugh, *Second Consul* (Indianapolis: Indiana University Press, 1956), and Irving G. Williams, *The Rise of the Vice Presidency* (Washington, D.C.: Public Affairs Press, 1956).

Some of the best writing on the presidency is to be found in biographies of Presidents. Among the more useful for a study of the office are James MacGregor Burns, *John Kennedy: A Political Profile* (New York: Harcourt, Brace & World, Inc., 1960) and *Roosevelt: The Lion and the Fox* (New York: Harcourt, Brace & World, Inc., 1956); Douglas Southall Freeman, *George Washington* (New

York: Charles Scribner's Sons, 1954–1957), Vols. VI and VII; Arthur S. Link, *Wilson: The New Freedom* (Princeton, N.J.: Princeton University Press, 1956) and *Woodrow Wilson and the Progressive Era* (New York: Harper & Brothers, 1954); Allan Nevins, *Grover Cleveland: A Study in Courage* (New York: Dodd, Mead & Co., Inc., 1932); Henry S. Pringle, *Theodore Roosevelt* (New York: Harcourt, Brace & Co., 1931) and *The Life and Times of William Howard Taft* (New York: Farrar and Rinehart, 1939); Frank Freidel, *Franklin D. Roosevelt: The Triumph* (Boston: Little, Brown & Co., 1956); and Rexford G. Tugwell, *The Democratic Roosevelt* (Garden City, N.Y.: Doubleday & Co., Inc., 1957).

Presidents themselves have written memoirs and diaries that provide useful insights into the office. Among the principal ones are Charles Francis Adams, ed., *Memoirs of John Quincy Adams*, 12 vols. (Philadelphia: J. B. Lippincott Co., 1875); Dwight D. Eisenhower, *Mandate for Change, 1953–1956* (Garden City, N.Y.: Doubleday & Co., Inc., 1963); Herbert Hoover, *The Memoirs of Herbert Hoover* (New York: The Macmillan Co., 1951–1952); Allan Nevins, ed., *James K. Polk: The Diary of a President* (New York: Longmans, Green & Co., Inc., 1929); Harry S Truman, *Memoirs*, 2 vols., (Garden City, N.Y.: Doubleday & Co., Inc., 1955–1956); and Theodore Roosevelt, *Autobiography* (New York: The Macmillan Co., 1913).

THE NATIONAL ADMINISTRATION

The national administration is an enterprise that can be viewed from several bibliographic vantage points: historically; in terms of organization, personnel, and finance; and in its relation to politics.

The best historical view of the national administration is afforded by the monumental studies of the late Leonard D. White of the University of Chicago, a former member of the United States Civil Service Commission. His works include *The Federalists* (New York: The Macmillan Co., 1948); *The Jeffersonians* (New York: The Macmillan Co., 1951); *The Jacksonians* (New York: The Macmillan Co., 1954); and *The Republican Era* (New York: The Macmillan Co., 1958). White's pioneering text, *Introduction to the Study of Public Administration*, 3rd ed. (New York: The Macmillan Co., 1948), also views the subject historically.

A perspective on the national administration as a structure of organization and bureaucracy can be obtained from a substantial body of literature, much of it produced in the 1950's and 1960's. A classic statement of organizational theory is found in Luther Gulick and Lyndall Urwick, *Papers on the Science of Administration* (New York: Institute of Public Administration, 1937). For writings that employ sociological and psychological analysis for an understanding of organization, consult Herbert Simon, *Administrative Behavior*, rev. ed. (New York: The Macmillan Co., 1957), and Victor A. Thompson, *Modern Organization* (New York: Alfred A. Knopf, Inc., 1961). Robert Presthus in *The Organizational Society* (New York: Alfred A. Knopf, Inc., 1962) views modern organization as an aspect of general society, a phenomenon treated in William Whyte's popular *The Organization Man* (New York: Simon and Schuster, Inc., 1956).

The national administration can also be seen as a gigantic manifestation of bureaucracy. Writings on bureaucracy are much influenced by the German economist and sociologist Max Weber. For a useful, well-edited collection of Weber's writings, see Hans H. Gerth and C. Wright Mills, *From Max Weber: Essays in Sociology* (New York: Oxford University Press, 1946). Discussions of bureaucracy centering particularly upon the American national administration include Peter Blau, *The Dynamics of Bureaucracy* (Chicago: University of Chicago Press, 1955), and Peter Woll, *American Bureaucracy* (New York: W. W. Norton & Co., Inc., 1963).

The national administration is also well represented in the literature on personnel management. A standard comprehensive work on this subject is O. Glenn Stahl, *Public Personnel Management*, 5th ed. (New York: Harper & Row, 1962). A lively and informed analysis of federal personnel issues is found in American Assembly, *The Federal Government Service* (New York: Columbia University School of Business, 1954). For background on the experience and influences affecting the development of the federal service, see Paul P. Van Riper, *History of the United States Civil Service* (Evanston, Ill.: Row, Peterson & Co., 1958). The Brownlow Committee and the two Hoover Commissions both made important recommendations in the field of personnel. The Brownlow Committee's views are contained in its *Report with Special Studies* and the first Hoover Commission's in two publications: *Personnel Management: A Report to the Congress* (1949) and *Federal Personnel: Task Force Report* (1949). The second Hoover Commission likewise presented two publications on the subject: *Personnel and Civil Service* (1955) and Task Force Report on *Personnel and Civil Service* (1955). The publications of all three commissions were published in Washington by the Government Printing Office.

The national administration also exists in terms of several major types of administrative organization, such as the department, the independent regulatory commission, and the government corporation. Several official studies of considerable consequence deal with all of these organizations. The Brownlow Committee's 1937 *Report with Special Studies* bears upon all these forms of organization, as do the reports of the first and second Hoover Commissions (published in 1949 and 1955, respectively). Particularly useful is the report of the first Hoover Commission itself and its task force on *Departmental Management*. Theoretical issues concerning departmental organization are presented in Schuyler C. Wallace, *Federal Departmentalization* (New York: Columbia University Press, 1941). A biographical study of national departmental administrators together with an analysis of their functions is presented in Arthur W. Macmahon and John D. Millett, *Federal Administrators* (New York: Columbia University Press, 1939).

The independent regulatory commissions are treated comprehensively in Marver H. Bernstein, *Regulating Business by Independent Commission* (Princeton, N.J.: Princeton University Press, 1955); Emmette S. Redford, *Administration of National Economic Control* (New York: The Macmillan Co., 1952); and Robert E. Cushman, *The Independent Regulatory Commissions* (New York: Oxford University Press, 1941). An insightful discussion of the commissions by a former member is provided by James M. Landis, *The Administrative Process* (New Haven, Conn.: Yale University Press, 1938).

The most perceptive treatment of the government corporation in our national government is to be found in Marshall Dimock, "Government Corporations: A Focus of Policy and Administration," *American Political Science Review*, XLIII (October 1949). One of the most important corporations is reviewed in C. Herman Pritchett, *The Tennessee Valley Authority* (Chapel Hill: University of North Carolina Press, 1943). The student who wishes to compare the experience of the American corporation with the British, who make extensive use of the corporate device, can consult William A. Robson, ed., *Problems of Nationalized Industry* (London: George Allen and Unwin. Ltd., 1952).

Financial management, including budgeting and accounting, is discussed in the Brownlow Committee report and in the reports on *Budgeting and Accounting* by the first and second Hoover Commissions. For treatments of budgeting, see Jesse Burkhead, *Government Budgeting* (New York: John Wiley & Sons, Inc., 1956), and Arthur Smithies, *The Budgetary Process in the United States* (New York: McGraw-Hill Book Co., 1955). A present-day book-length study of the Comptroller General is badly needed; the latest is Harvey Mansfield, *The Comptroller General* (New Haven, Conn.: Yale University Press, 1939).

ELEMENTS OF POLICY
AND THE POLICY PRODUCT

Formal literature concerning policy-making, whether as process or product, is rather limited. A growing body of work on decision-making well serves the needs of policy-making analysis. A standard introduction to decision-making processes is Richard C. Snyder, H. W. Bruck, and Burton Sapin, *Foreign Policy Decision-Making* (New York: The Free Press, 1962). Decision-making by the American President is analyzed by Theodore

C. Sorensen, special counsel to President Kennedy, in *Decision-Making in the White House* (New York: Columbia University Press, 1963). The reader will find particularly stimulating Harold D. Lasswell's *The Decision Process: Seven Categories of Functional Analysis* (College Park: University of Maryland Press, 1956). Facets of administrative decision-making are treated in Herbert Simon, *Administrative Behavior*, rev. ed. (New York: The Macmillan Co., 1957) and *The New Science of Management Decision* (New York: Harper & Row, 1960). For insightful material on legislative decision and policy-making, see Bertram Gross, *The Legislative Struggle: A Study in Social Combat* (New York: McGraw-Hill Book Co., 1953).

Game theory is also applicable to policy-making analysis, a task that has been accomplished most successfully by Norton E. Long in "The Local Community as an Ecology of Games," *American Journal of Sociology*, XLIV (November 1958), 251-261. The techniques of group analysis are applied by Donald R. Matthews, *U.S. Senators and Their World* (Chapel Hill: University of North Carolina Press, 1960), and Ralph K. Huitt, "The Outsider in the Senate: An Alternate Role," *American Political Science Review*, LV (September 1961), 566-575.

For discussions of the techniques of voting research, also useful in policy-making analysis, see Eugene Burdick and Arthur J. Brodbeck, eds., *American Voting Behavior* (New York: The Free Press, 1959); Angus Campbell, Philip E. Converse, Warren E. Miller, and Donald Stokes, *The American Voter* (New York: John Wiley & Sons, Inc., 1960); and Bernard B. Berelson, Paul F. Lazarsfeld, and William N. McPhee, *Voting: A Study of Opinion Formation in a*

Presidential Campaign (Chicago: University of Chicago Press, 1954).

There is developing a growing body of case studies of policy-making, in both the legislative and administrative processes. Illustrative are are Daniel M. Berman, *A Bill Becomes a Law: The Civil Rights Act of 1960* (New York: The Macmillan Co., 1962), and Aaron Wildavsky, *Dixon-Yates: A Study in Power Politics* (New Haven, Conn.: Yale University Press, 1962). Collections of case studies dealing with the involvements of the legislature, the presidency, and the national administration in policy-making are to be found in Alan F. Westin, ed., *The Uses of Power* (New York: Harcourt, Brace & World, Inc., 1962) and *The Centers of Power* (New York: Harcourt, Brace & World, Inc., 1963). For cases devoted particularly to the national administration, although with some stress upon the President and the legislature, see Harold Stein, ed., *Public Administration and Policy Development* (New York: Harcourt, Brace & Co., 1952); this volume has an excellent introductory essay relating policy development to political analysis.